DØ367852

Contents

Introduction

Until recently, race was a central category in international relations. Yet most studies of twentieth-century diplomacy treat race as marginal to their subject matter. The rise of Nazi Germany and the ascendancy of apartheid in South Africa are often interpreted as exceptions to or even violations of the norms of international relations. *The Silent War* sets out to question this colour-blind interpretation of international affairs.

Unlike current times, the turn-of-the-century foreign policy elites of Britain and the United States had no inhibitions about expressing their view of the world in the language of race. Assumptions about the superiority of the white races were rarely contested in Europe or the United States. The domination of the world by the West was seen as proof of white racial superiority. At the same time, this superiority became a justification for further Western expansion. Today, when racism has been discredited, it is difficult to understand that early in the twentieth century race was a source of public pride for the Anglo-American elite. At the time, race was a central element in the composition of Western identity. It shaped the wider definition of Western culture as well as influencing individual psychology.

Since the Victorian era, both the meaning and the significance attached to race have undergone continuous modification. This book examines the evolution of the Western racial imagination and its relationship to international relations. This was driven by important changes in the world order. The greatest influence on racial thinking was the emergence of resistance to Western domination. Fears about the decline of the West were often expressed in a racial form and implicitly contested the idea of white superiority. Race, which was a positive ideal in the self-image of the West, had become a source of anxiety by the end of the First World War; by the 1920s, the Anglo-American foreign policy elites regarded racial thinking as having the potential to disrupt the world system; and by the end of the Second World

War racism was so discredited that Western diplomats were forced
to devote considerable resources to eliminating it from international affairs altogether.

The changing dynamic between Western identity and racial
thinking is most vividly expressed as a shift from racial confidence
to racial fear. The chapters that follow document how apprehensions about Western global decline helped stimulate the emergence of race relations as a discipline. From its inception this new
discipline regarded racial tension as not merely dangerous, but
specifically a threat to Western interests. This belief was based on
the proposition that racial conflict would inevitably be directed
against the status quo, that is a world dominated by Western,
white races. The problem was defined as a racial threat posed by
people of colour against the white race. As Tinker pointed out,
'the "race problem", then, was the problem of the non-white who
would not accept the leadership of the white'.[1]

Ideas about race relations evolved in an attempt to minimise
the danger of racial conflict. The impulse of pre-emption influenced the emergence of the early race relations industry. The main
policy outcome of this discussion was the need to curb open
manifestations of white racism in order to contain reactions to it.
This attitude cannot be described as anti-racist. It expressed fears
about racial conflict and demanded a pragmatism that amounted
to a kind of voluntary self-censorship. One of the important
paradoxes of this development was that precisely those who
believed that race relations constituted a major problem in
international relations also felt reluctant to tackle it openly. This
lack of openness meant that it became all too easy to overlook the
significance of race in the conduct of international affairs.

The Silent Race War Theme

From time to time theorists of race relations have acknowledged
the silent protocol that permeates such conflict. Robert Park, the
influential pioneer of American race relations theory, observed
that racial conflict has a character that is 'silent and often
unnoticed'. More recently, an American authority on the history
of race relations theory remarked that 'compared with the open

bigotry and explicit color lines of old', contemporary 'prejudice and discrimination are becoming increasingly more subtle and indirect'.[2] Adorno, in his classic *Authoritarian Personality*, noted a widespread reluctance on the part of the people interviewed to discuss the issue openly. He noted that the predominant reaction among conservative subjects was to state 'that the best approach to the "race problem" was not to "stir up anything"'. More recent studies confirm that public discussions are filtered through a mechanism of censorship. Jencks has pointed out that American white conservative beliefs about black crime are seldom published in the media.[3]

The tendency to hesitate before engaging in open discussion of racial issues has often been rationalised on the grounds that the special sensitivity of the subject means that public discussion could inflame passions and make the situation far worse. According to Adorno, it was widely believed that racial conflict was driven by uniquely destructive forces, and there was therefore a desire to evade the issue altogether:

> Indeed, it is with a sense of relief today that one is assured that a group conflict is merely a clash of economic interests – that each side is merely to 'do' the other – and not a struggle in which deep-lying emotional drives have been let loose.[4]

Presenting racial conflict as irrational, incomprehensible or intensely destructive expresses deeply rooted anxieties. Such fears were often predicated on the anticipation of racial revenge, when those hitherto oppressed will seek to even the score. Dollard's classic study, *Caste and Class in a Southern Town*, offers one of the most vivid explorations of this fear, and highlights the all-pervasive character of the white fear of black people. According to Dollard, fear, which was completely 'disproportionate to the threat from the Negro's side', was often based on 'the fear of retaliation for the gains aggressively acquired by the white caste at the expense of the Negro'.[5] This anxiety was seldom expressed openly. Racial fears were suppressed and even in the relatively racist South, many things were understood to be best left unsaid.

The sentiment that it is 'best not to talk about it' summed up the attitude of American and British diplomats to race relations during the first half of the twentieth century. Thus a 1921 British Foreign Office memorandum, *Racial Discrimination and Immigration,* bluntly stated: 'Great Britain, the Dominions and the United States are all equally interested in avoiding a discussion of this subject.' The author of the memorandum, Ashton-Gwatkin, claimed that there was 'no subject more fundamental' for the 'ultimate settlement' of tensions in the Pacific. But in his view the issue of racial discrimination was not susceptible to a solution since the 'white and the coloured races cannot and will not amalgamate'. 'One or the other must be the ruling caste', he argued.[6] Whitehall fully endorsed the memorandum. The standard response it adopted towards racial issues was not to discuss them. Such an approach continued to inform British and American foreign policy even after the principle of race equality had been accepted in the 1940s.

Many officials and public relations advisers believed that discussing racism in itself drew attention to a problem that was intrinsically irresolvable. The fundamental principle of American and British policy on race relations propaganda was one of evasion. Such manifest deception was rationalised in a variety of arguments. During the 1940s and 1950s, British officials argued that 'the emotionalism which surrounds the whole question of race and colour prejudice' made rational discussion impossible.[7] Another argument used to play down the issue of race was the proposition that an open discussion of the subject would make people of colour more conscious of their differences compared with Europeans. From the Anglo-American perspective, even the mention of the problem appeared to encourage a reaction against the West. These sentiments were based on the widely held, if rarely expressed, view that racial conflict was inevitable.

The lack of openness reflected a sense of disquiet about strongly held views that could no longer be voiced in public. This was an issue that called into question fundamental assumptions about the global and historical role of the West. The silencing of race relations was symptomatic of a defensiveness about beliefs that were central to the outlook of the Western ruling classes. Our argument is that apprehensions about the future of race relations were, at least in part, the product of tension in the Anglo-American ruling class. A sense of superiority – be it biological, moral, cultural – was central to this outlook. Racial thinking had a strong undercurrent in Anglo-American political culture. For this reason the problematisation of race called into question the positive self-image of the Anglo-American elite. What had hitherto been an affirmation of superiority and a source of cohesion now served as a reminder of dangers to come. Racial fears dictated a pre-emptive strategy towards race relations. Assumptions of superiority could no longer be expressed openly. Race had become an issue the Anglo-American elite were no longer comfortable with. How they negotiated the shift from a celebration of superiority to a formal acceptance of racial equality is one of the subjects of this book.

A Dramatic Shift in Racial Thinking

Today it is difficult to comprehend the significance of the formal acceptance of race equality. But until the late 1930s, racial thinking was an accepted part of the intellectual climate. Important characteristics were attached to racial differences and the view that some races were superior assumed the status of a self-evident truth. These sentiments permeated academic communities. They were part of the self-knowledge of the Anglo-American political elites and were strongly absorbed into what passed for common sense.

As indicated previously, race was central to the identity of the Western political elites. It was inextricably linked to the Western notion of 'civilisation', which on the ideological level at least informed international relations. Studies suggest that the sentiment of a 'civilising mission' inspired the actions of Western diplomats. According to one account, this mission 'remained a moral crusade, with all the self-confidence and zeal that many thought the Christian reformers were losing in the face of secular science's challenge'.[8] The principle of Western racial superiority guided the informal and formal actions of white diplomats and politicians. This principle was enshrined in the conventions of the international order until at least the late 1930s. According to Hedley Bull, by the time the First World War broke out, 'with the important partial exception of Japan, those racially and culturally non-European states that enjoyed formal independence laboured under the stigma of inferior status: unequal treaties, extraterritorial jurisdiction, denial of racial equality'. Bull adds that this situation continued more or less intact until after Second World War.[9]

That race had become a source of embarrassment is a fact that many conservative thinkers find difficult to accept. The British historian Michael Howard expresses a degree of ambivalence about it:

> Even the most traditionally-minded of imperial historians are reluctant to endorse the belief that was not only universally held in nineteenth-century Europe but was for a time accepted among most of the other societies subjugated by the Europeans; that European societies asserted dominion over non-Europeans because they were *superior*.[10]

That views which were once universally held were now unacceptable was bound to engender unease amongst those brought up with the certainties of racial thinking.

For the British Prime Minister Harold Macmillan the changing relationship between white and non-white people was disturbing. In a letter written to the Australian Prime Minister Robert Menzies in 1962, he noted they were both 'born into a very different world'. This world was one where European domination was unquestioned and 'where the civilised world meant really Europe and its extensions overseas'. But according to Macmillan, European domination had been undermined by the upheavals of the twentieth century. The consequence of this process is 'the end of the white man's accepted predominance'.[11] For those who had been brought up in a world where white superiority was accepted as self-evident, the new climate of egalitarianism was difficult to accept. Macmillan's term 'different world' was apposite in pointing to the shift between the pre- and post-Second World War climate of opinion.

What is striking is how little racist thinking was questioned before the Second World War. Even radical critics of imperialism were reluctant to criticise the racist justification for national expansion. According to Hofstader, anti-imperialist critics in America at the beginning of the twentieth century, 'preferred to ignore the broad theme of racial destiny'. In Britain many of the prominent critics of imperial policy in the interwar period remained strongly influenced by racist theorising. And even those who rejected racist theory nevertheless embraced many of its assumptions. Julian Huxley, who attacked scientific racism before it was fashionable to do so and who was appointed first Director of UNESCO, still took it upon himself to defend Britain's imperial record as late as 1944. He implored his readers not to forget that 'Africa remained for the most part in an early stage of barbarism'. According to Huxley, what was needed was co-operation to help the 'development of backward areas and backward peoples'.[12]

It is worth noting that Huxley was in the vanguard on the question of race, and played a central role in combating the pretensions of scientific racism in the 1930s when the Western intelligentsia was still influenced by racial thinking. Nancy Stepan has drawn attention to its impact on the sciences. She observes how 'one is struck by the extraordinary durability of racial ideas in biology and biometry' and adds that 'only in the 1920s and 1930s did old racial typology begin to get worn away at the edges through a series of scientific, social and political changes'.[13] The same could be said for the social sciences. Even in anthropology and sociology, critics of racism were very much in a minority in the 1930s.

The climate of opinion before the Second World War regarding race relations is illustrated by the terminology used to describe it and related matters. The term 'racism' as a negative phenomenon acquired currency in the 1930s. At this time racism was often defined as an ism, an ideology of Nazi race hatred. Barkan asserts that the 'use of "racism" as a derogatory neologism was first recorded in English in the 1930s' and concludes that this suggests that the 'debunking of race theories and their crude political analogies began sometime earlier'.[14] However, in the 1930s the term racism was far from current and the intellectual community was ambivalent about using it. In popular usage the term did not yet have an unambiguously negative connotation.

It is interesting to note that in the Anglo-American media, academic publications and within official circles words such as 'racialist' and 'racialism' were used to describe those who reacted to their oppression. So, for example, during the course of anti-colonial agitation and labour disputes in British Guiana during the late

1930s, British officials routinely described the action of the protesters as having a 'racial character' or 'racial feeling'. The Governor blamed the 'disturbing influence of racial antagonisms and prejudice'.[15] What motivated the Governor to use these terms was the conviction that, in the context of the rejection of white rule, racial antagonism and prejudice became a disturbing influence. Tinker's study of race conflict confirms that this was a widespread reaction among the Anglo-American elite. Tinker argues that when the 'terms "racialist" and "racialism" entered the English language between the two world wars, they were applied to those who sought to overturn white dominance, whether in the domestic politics of the American South or in the context of Western colonialism'.[16] The terms racist, racialist or racialism were often used to describe the rejection of white leadership.

Even in academic circles there was little consensus on the legitimacy of the term racist. Many writers implied that it was too controversial to have a role in everyday scientific discourse. A book review of Ruth Benedict's *Race: Science and Politics* in *The American Journal of Sociology*, published in January 1941, illustrates the ambivalence that surrounded the subject. The review by the well-known Chicago sociologist and authority on race relations, E.B. Reuter, is clearly dismissive of the term. Reuter uses quotation marks when he uses this term to signify his disapproval. He also self-consciously defined the term – thus implying that the readers of the *Journal* would be unfamiliar with it. It is also worth noting that Reuter defined racism not only to inform his readership but also because he wished to affirm the view that racism had no theoretical content.

> 'Racism' is used throughout the book as a descriptive epithet designating beliefs, dogmas, doctrines, theories, etc., that advance biological and racial facts in explanation of cultural realities.[17]

By defining racism as an epithet, Reuter calls into question the objectivity of those such as Ruth Benedict who used the concept.

Linking negative traits with racist attitudes and practices is thus a recent phenomenon. That the legitimacy of the term racist could be contested in academic circles even in the early 1940s is a testimony to the durability of racial thinking.

That durability should come as no surprise when one considers the weakness of anti-racist intellectual currents. A survey of the literature critical of scientific racism suggests that it was often ineffective and defensive in tone. Gossett's study in the United States highlights how even liberals could be seduced by it. He argues that 'part of the reason why racism flourished so mightily in this period is that it had no really effective opposition where one might have accepted it, since it also flourished among the liberals'.[18] All shades of intellectual opinion in early twentieth-century America were influenced by some variant of racial thought. In Britain, it was much the same. Rich argues that in the 1930s there was considerable confusion in liberal and missionary circles about the significance of race and race differences. He points to the failure of British anthropologists to combat the rise of racist politics in the late 1930s. Indeed, it can be argued that the use of racial typology by British physical anthropologists survived into the 1940s.[19]

Barkan's path-breaking study *The Retreat of Scientific Racism* demonstrates the reluctance of the scientific community to confront Nazi race theory and politics. Barkan argues that it was not until 1938 that there was a concentrated attempt by Anglo-American academics to refute Nazi race theories.[20] Moreover, these belated attempts often lacked an egalitarian perspective.

The criticisms of racial thinking in the 1930s were narrowly focused on Nazi propaganda. The condemnations of Nazi racial theories represented attacks on the tendentious use of science or on the legitimacy of their scientific claims. The object was to question the employment of racial theories in the spheres of politics and culture rather than to put the case for social equality. One of the few consistently anti-racist intellectuals in the 1930s, Lancelot Hogben, criticised British intellectuals who attacked Nazi racism but were indifferent to comparable practices in the Empire and South Africa.[21] But Hogben was very much a lone voice; the principle of racial equality had few intellectual defenders in the 1930s. It is all the more surprising then that a few years later the principle of race equality would become an accepted part of Western political culture and would be endorsed as a fundamental principle of international affairs. The main catalyst for this development was, without doubt, the experience of the Second World War.

Throughout the war race relations were continually under discussion by government officials, publicists and post-war planners in Britain and in the United States. It was accepted that relations between the races could not return to the pre-war status quo. Racial discrimination was widely practised and assumptions of racial superiority were still widely held. But there was considerable unease about the inconsistency of waging a war against racist Nazi doctrines while tolerating discrimination in the British Empire, South Africa and the United States.

The need to reorient race relations was not merely driven by intellectual concerns or troubled consciences. Among the Western political elite the issue of race was identified as a practical problem. It was now characterised as a potentially destabilising element in the international order. Alongside the discussion on post-war economic reconstruction and the deliberations on the future world order, it was concluded that the acceptance of the principle of racial equality could no longer be avoided. Race relations had become a problem of international relations, and Western leaders feared that the war would intensify the demand for racial equality and push African and Asian people in an anti-white direction. This fear was widely expressed by politicians and experts across the political spectrum.

The most influential and widely quoted contribution to the discussion on race relations was Gunnar Myrdal's *An American Dilemma*. Although this massive tome, written in 1942 and published in 1944, has as its subject the 'Negro Problem' in America, it can also be read as a call to eliminate racial oppression internationally.

Like many officials in the State Department, Myrdal regarded racism as the Achilles' heel of American diplomacy. He shared the fear that racial conflict in the United States would undermine its ability to influence world affairs. The US's claim to embody a superior polity was put into question by its poor record on race relations. At a time when non-white nations were becoming an important factor in the international political calculus, America's race record was bound to have important diplomatic repercussions. Myrdal was convinced that America had to 'take world leadership' but feared that 'few white Americans fully realize all the obvious implications'.

America then will have the major responsibility for the manner in which humanity approaches the long era during which the white peoples will have to adjust to shrinkage while the colored are bound to expand in numbers, in level of industrial civilization and in political power. For perhaps several decades, the whites will still hold the lead, and America will be the most powerful white nation.[22]

Myrdal's defensive tone was characteristic of the age. It was based on the recognition that white nations were morally in an indefensible position and that unless something was done the issue of race would explode in a new cycle of confrontation.

Japan's rapid military advance through Asia in the early 1940s and its ability to mobilise significant regional support for its anti-Western propaganda were interpreted as a indications of the dangers to come. British policy-makers were bitterly humiliated at the speed with which their Asian colonies collapsed in face of the Japanese advance. The loss of Malaya became at once the symbol of imperial decline and the confirmation of deeply held racial fears. It placed the racist practices of the Empire on the agenda of policy-makers in Whitehall. Those involved in public relations complained that racial discrimination was the one issue for which they had no plausible answers.

British imperial anxieties following the fall of Malaya are well captured in a memorandum written by a PR specialist in December 1941. According to its author, Edmett, the question of colour was the most important issue facing the Empire. He warned:

The stark and obvious fact which the British Empire has to face is that four-fifths of it is not British, and as long as the majority believes the Empire is run on a set of values which puts the interests of the European minority above those of the alien majority, there will be disunity, unhappiness and demoralisation. By the liberation of slaves Britain amassed a great deal of goodwill amongst the coloured races which it has steadily squandered by the application of the colour bar.

Edmett argued that what was needed in the colonies was the 'active abandonment of racial priorities and the creation of a public relations organisation to expand and solidify equal relations between peoples of all races, colours and creeds'. On an ominous note he concluded that if the Empire did not solve this problem it would be 'broken by it'.[23]

From 1942 onwards, officials in the US Department of State held weekly meetings to prepare a draft international bill of human rights, and in early 1943 a special project group of the Department of State was actively drafting anti-discriminatory provisions for the future United Nations. British diplomats who were aware of these developments recommended that London follow suit and accept the new anti-racist consensus. Sir Alexander Cadogan, head of the British delegation at the Dumbarton Oaks negotiations, telegraphed to Whitehall that Britain had no choice but to accept the new consensus. Cadogan referred to this initiative as a 'sphere of great delicacy', which highlighted the difficulties posed by the issue of race relations. The gap between egalitarian rhetoric and discriminatory practice was one which Britain did not want exposed to international scrutiny.[24]

Race relations continued to be regarded as a sensitive issue in London and Washington throughout the 1940s. Support in principle for equality was not enough: a change of image was also required. It is interesting to note that by early 1949 both Britain and the United States were actively considering the implications of employing black diplomats in order to strengthen their anti-racist credentials. In January 1949, Arthur Creech Jones, the Secretary of State for the Colonies, informed his officials about the 'need to appoint a person of colour to a Colonial Governorship'. Although this discussion carried on inconclusively for another two years and had no direct outcome, it nevertheless revealed Whitehall's concern. A few months after Creech Jones raised this problem with his officials, a State Department memorandum discussed the viability of dispatching an 'outstanding Negro' to an 'appropriate country' as an American ambassador.[25]

It was not only diplomats who were reconsidering the issue of race relations. It was also on the agenda of the Conference of Allied Ministers of Education. The discussion at these conferences showed a preoccupation not only with Nazi racial doctrines but also with the necessity of not offending non-Westerners in the post-war world. A memorandum entitled 'Education and Racial Tolerance', written by Alf Sommerfelt of Norway, argued for a programme of anti-racist education. Sommerfelt emphasised his apprehension of the danger posed by Japan's anti-Western propaganda:

> The instruction envisaged in this memorandum will be of importance not only in combating fascist and nazi ideas but also in furthering a more tolerant and comprehending attitude towards people of non-European civilisation. With the growing industrialization of Asiatic and African countries and the Poisonous effects of Japanese propaganda it is of the utmost importance to exterminate racial prejudice.[26]

These sentiments were broadly shared by others and in March 1945, the Conference passed a draft resolution in support of an enquiry into the theory of race. On behalf of the Science Commission of the Conference, C.D. Darlington, J.B.S. Haldane and J.S. Huxley drafted a statement 'refuting Nazi claim of a hierarchy of racial merit'.[27]

The outcome of the discussions at the Conference of Allied Ministers of Education was the establishment of the United Nations Educational, Scientific and Cultural Organisation (UNESCO) in 1946. In later years this organisation was to be in the forefront of developing a new agenda on race.

The co-operation of the international intellectual community against racism under the aegis of UNESCO stood in sharp contrast to its inaction in the period before the Second World War. Both the League of Nations and the International Institute of Intellectual Co-operation had failed to take a stand on this issue. In the 1930s, a number of scientists and intellectuals had intended to challenge the premise of the Nuremberg race laws but could not convince the International Institute of Intellectual Co-operation to back them.[28] The period from 1935 to 1945 saw a dramatic change in the intellectual climate as far as this was concerned.

To place in perspective the shift in attitudes and policy it is worth comparing the post-war negotiations on the emerging international system in 1945 with the Paris Peace Conference in 1919. By the time the United Nations Charter was drawn up in 1945, the principle of racial equality was accepted by the key governments. As one former League of Nations Official put it, 'there is something like official unanimity of opposition to this species of primitive prejudice'.[29] This attitude was strikingly different from that which prevailed before the Second World War. In Paris in 1919, many of the representatives had been bitterly opposed to the principle of racial equality.

The UN Charter was the embodiment of a dramatic shift in attitude towards race relations. The issue was now placed at the centre of a most prestigious international forum. As Lauren suggests, 'the subject of racial prejudice and human rights quickly became inextricably intertwined with many of the post-war world's most critical and controversial problems'.[30] And as Vincent confirms, in contrast to the League of Nations Covenant, the Charter of the United Nations was a 'declaration for racial equality and self-government'.[31]

The corollary of the acceptance of the principle of race equality was the widespread condemnation of racial discrimination. Both racism as a theory and discrimination as a practice acquired negative connotations. Unlike at the Paris Conference of 1919, in the post-Second World War era it was difficult to find any credible public figure who would defend racist theory or the practice of discrimination. An extraordinary shift in attitude and perception had taken place. The reason why is far from self-evident. In the following sections of this chapter the nature of this revolution in attitude and its causes will be outlined.

The speed with which the principle of racial equality was accepted was truly astounding. As late as March 1941, the Foreign Office had come out unambiguously against the proposal for publicly supporting the principle of racial equality. In March 1941, R.A. Butler had proposed issuing a statement that made 'it clear that the white races and the dark races are not unequal'. He justified this on the grounds that it could minimise the danger of conflict with Japan. Butler himself was of the view that it was 'impossible for discrimination to be allowed to exist in the world as it stands today'. Others agreed. 'An improvement in the matter of racial discrimination is certainly one of the items which should form part of a new Anglo-American world order', was the view of Ashley-Clarke. Nevertheless Ashley-Clarke, like his colleagues, felt that such a declaration would create problems for the United States and the Dominions. Sir Horace Seymour argued that if the declaration implied the equal treatment of the Japanese, the Australians would never accept it. Seymour added that the 'Americans also are far from any real belief in racial equality'.

There is little doubt that the references to the Dominions and the United States were designed to avoid confronting Britain's own unease with the issue. Butler was forced to conclude that these responses 'blow up the possibility of a racial discrimination declaration'.[32]

Although the Foreign Office opposed issuing a declaration on race equality in 1941, most of the participants were aware that it was simply a matter of time before such concessions had to be made. Within a year, the sentiment in favour of accepting the principle of equality had gathered strength. By 1944 it had become unofficial policy.

It is easy to underestimate the speed with which public attitudes towards racism changed. Certainly many post-war writers accept as self-evident what was in fact a minority point of view in the 1930s. Consequently, the volte-face is often overlooked. Some writers in the 1960s assumed a lengthy anti-racist tradition and asked why there had been such a delay in implementing these principles in terms of civil rights. So Kenneth B. Clark, one of the editors of an influential American survey of race relations in the 1960s, asked why America had 'moved toward the goal which seemed so obvious in terms of its own ideals but which was so long in coming'.[33] However, what was obvious in the 1960s was fiercely contested in the 1930s. The shift in attitude was so swift and apparently so widely endorsed that the previous longevity of anti-egalitarian and racist sentiments can and was easily lost sight of. It is now pertinent to ask why this shift occurred.

The Pressures Towards the New Consensus

According to most serious accounts of the history of racial thinking, the shift towards a new anti-racist consensus was part of a reaction to the devastating consequences of Nazism. The association of racial politics with Nazi Germany had the effect of compromising racial science and ideology. After the Second World War many anti-Hitler conservatives and eugenicists were forced on the defensive. This is evident in the writings of the British eugenicist, C.P. Blacker. His sense of frustration is palpable when he noted the 'unpopularity today of the word race which to many has a fascist ring'. For Blacker the problem was not racial thinking as such but the 'behaviour of the Nazis' and 'their conduct in the last war'.[34]

The retreat of racial thinkers was paralleled by the reaction against Nazism. Having experienced the consequences of racist politics many were now prepared to attack the ideas on which they were based. According to Rich, 'the outbreak of war in 1939 acted as a shock wave on many British anthropologists, who began to ask why no greater stand has been made in the 1930s against the use of anthropology in racist and nazi ideologies'.[35] Barkan suggests that the 'uniqueness of Nazism underscored the immanent wickedness of racism'.[36] There can be little doubt that Nazism played a major role in the revision of attitudes at the theoretical level.

It is, however, unlikely that the reaction to Nazism alone explains the post-war convergence of opinion around egalitarian principles. The rejection of Nazi racial science and politics did not necessarily point to egalitarian conclusions. Indeed, the reaction was often to the particular brand of racism represented by the Nazi regime. As Greta Jones suggests, although 'anti-Semitism had become disreputable' other races 'remained vulnerable to prejudice'.[37] Many Anglo-American thinkers saw no inconsistency between their condemnation of Nazism and their acceptance of the racial status quo in the colonies or in the United States. Revulsion at the Holocaust did not lead to the transformation of white attitudes towards, say, blacks in America or South Africa, or towards Asians.

An argument presented by Vincent, in his discussion of the change in approach towards race by the United Nations, exemplifies this:

> What stood behind this change was not a recognition on the part of the white world that they had been racialist long enough in their relations with the non-white world, but the abhorrence felt at the working out of a noxious doctrine of racial superiority within the Western world. The non-white world benefited, according to this view, from a Western lesson learnt, but it was the Nazis and not the non-white world that taught it.[38]

The reaction to Nazism no doubt had the effect of undermining racial certainties. In this new climate, colonial nationalists had no problem in exposing the inconsistency between anti-Nazi rhetoric and imperialist practice. However, other experiences were at play. Some of these are outlined next.

The Crisis of the West

At the intellectual and cultural level racial certainties were being questioned some time before the Nazis seized power. The Second World War served to confirm already existing anxieties regarding Western civilisation. As Gong suggests, 'the horrors perpetuated in Europe itself during the two world wars did much to discredit Western claims of cultural superiority'.[39] However, war acted as the *confirmation* rather than the cause of this crisis of confidence. Fears regarding the dominance of the West were in evidence at the beginning of the twentieth century.

Symptomatic of deep anxieties concerning racial superiority was the overreaction in the West to Japan's defeat of Russia in 1905. Discussion in Europe at the time and in subsequent decades almost invariably hints at some sinister force at work which would lead to decline of the white race. Oswald Spengler's *Decline of the West* is symptomatic of this *Zeitgeist*. In Europe this sense of decline was part of a general crisis of confidence in the future of Western civilisation. And one product of this experience was the erosion of racial certainties. In political circles it was an open secret that the global line of colour could no longer be held. The real question was how to reform race relations with the minimum of conflict.

Bad Faith and the Fear of Revenge

Intellectual doubts about the claims of Western superiority were closely linked to the sentiment that recognised racial discrimination as inconsistent with the norms of democracy. An examination of the literature during the first half of the twentieth century indicates that with the passing of time, those who sought to defend the racial status quo carried less and less conviction and appeared more defensive. Increasingly, the literature implied that there was something wrong, shameful or even self-serving about Western attitudes to race.

Gong suggests that it may have been the 'experience with self-confident nationalists in the peripheries' which 'underscored the moral inconsistencies of standards based on differences of race, colour, or creed'.[40] No doubt such experiences, as well as the encounter with an increasingly strident Japan, helped undermine the cult of superiority. However, the growing awareness of bad faith regarding racial matters was above all the product of anxieties concerning the future reaction of those subject to white arrogance. To put it bluntly, the fear of racial revenge helped concentrate the mind.

In the popular and specialist literature on international relations of the period 1910–40, there are repeated allusions to the coming war between races. This was not merely the preoccupation of the unapologetic promoters of race politics. Centrist, liberal and left-wing writers were also involved. Many counselled Western statesmen to be more sensitive so as not to provoke the 'coloured races' to rise up against the West. Missionaries, liberals and socialists throughout the West called for the exercise of tact and sensitivity in racial matters.

The relationship between a sense of bad faith and the fear of revenge is inexact. The fear of revenge may well have been the consequence of the belief that the exercise of Western racial domination was morally wrong or intellectually indefensible. In some cases it may have been the product of guilt provoking an exaggerated fear of retribution. As I shall argue in chapter 3, these fears had little foundation in the power equations of the interwar era. But whatever the cause of these fears, there was a growing consensus that *the conflicts of the future would be racial in character*.

Concerns regarding the impending racial conflict appeared to be confirmed by the outbreak of the Second World War. It is important to note that despite the anti-Nazi rhetoric, the problem of race was primarily perceived amongst the Anglo-American political elite in terms of the unpredictable reaction of people of colour. And, anti-Nazi propaganda notwithstanding, Britain and the United States tended to regard the war against Japan in racial terms. The Japanese advance in Asia seemed to confirm fears of racial revenge.

Most recent studies suggest that Britain and the United States fought Japan in part as a racial crusade. Tinker states that it was 'openly a race war' and that the allies 'retaliated with an outburst of hatred which consigned the Japanese to the category of sub-humans'. Dower's well-documented study of American reactions to the Japanese during this war confirms Tinker's thesis.[41] From the evidence it appears that Anglo-American fears were not restricted to Japan's military threat. Concern was expressed that the Japanese challenge to the West would encourage other non-white people to revolt against the racial status quo.

Thorne's pioneering study 'Racial Aspects of the Far Eastern War of 1941–1945' argues that there were fears in Washington that 'given a chance, America's blacks, too, would side with Japan'. Although fears such as these had little foundation, American blacks came to regard the war as an opportunity to demand equal rights. In 1942, the Congress of Racial Equality (CORE) organised its first campaign for civil rights in the United States. CORE's leader, Walter White, wrote to President Roosevelt, 'should this war end with the continuation of white overlordship over brown, yellow, and black peoples of the world, there will inevitably be another war and continued misery for the colored peoples of the United States, the West Indies, South America, Africa, and the Pacific'.[42] Reactions such as this were long anticipated by those who had warned of racial revenge in the previous decade.

The old fear of racial revenge now seemed on the verge of realisation. The Japanese challenge and the general weakening of Western dominion created a situation in which the demand for racial equality was increasingly difficult to refuse. And moral unease and fear of revenge disposed the Anglo-American elite to accommodate new realities. This disposition preceded and to some extent survived independently of the revulsion against the horrors of Nazi politics. Nevertheless the two interacted and helped shape the emerging climate of opinion.

The Challenge from the Colonies

So far we have emphasised pressures that were largely internal to the crisis of Western identity. By the early 1940s this malaise was confronted by the challenge from the colonies. After the Second World War the colonial world could not survive intact. It was inevitable that the movement against colonialism would reject the racial assumptions of the imperial powers.

The weakening of the Western grip on the colonies, Japan's humiliation of the European powers in Asia and a war conducted in the name of democracy and freedom all coalesced to strengthen anti-imperialist and anti-racist aspirations. According to Lauren:

> The principles enunciated in the Atlantic Charter and declaration of the United Nations, and the declared struggle against Nazi racial doctrine, accentuated this development even further. In the Far East, the Indian subcontinent, and the Pacific, the war generated extensive discussions about race ... The war similarly gave great stimulus to the Pan-African movement.[43]

It was the very assertion of power by the non-white world that forced attitudes to race relations in international relations to change.

The movement against colonial domination was not primarily motivated by the desire to redefine relations between the races. This was a challenge against the existing relations of global power. However, since the object of their struggle was the transformation of an international system run by white states it was inevitable that the demand for racial equality would be on the new diplomatic agenda. Many would interpret this process as a revolt against the white world. For Bull, the principal feature was the unprecedented 'solidarity of non-whites against whites'. He saw the emergence of the Third World as part of a revolution in race relations.[44]

The colonial revolt and the subsequent emergence of the Third World forced a major reappraisal in Washington and London. The US State Department in particular was sensitive to the demands for racial equality. To consolidate its position in Africa, Asia and the Middle East, it needed to distance itself from the record of the European imperialist powers. At the same time it needed to reform race relations at home. It feared that its history of racial oppression would undermine its credibility in the non-white world. Myrdal underlined these apprehensions:

> the treatment of the Negro is America's greatest and most conspicuous scandal. It is tremendously publicized, and democratic America will continue to publicize it itself. For the colored peoples all over the

world, whose rising influence is axiomatic, this scandal is salt in their wounds.[45]

Pragmatically, Myrdal linked his call for reforming race relations with the need to acknowledge the rising influence of non-white people. Conscious of the urgency to establish close links with the non-European world, the State Department's conclusions were similar to Myrdal's. In part at least, the concessions on civil rights that followed were driven by international diplomatic considerations.

The Pressure of the Soviet Alternative

One of the reasons why American diplomats were keen to promote civil rights legislation was to pre-empt the growth of Soviet influence in the non-Western world. Throughout the period under discussion the Soviet Union had a reputation for eschewing racist practices. Many Western observers feared that as a result, the Soviet Union would win the sympathy of the non-white world and thus establish a fertile terrain for the growth of communism.

The anti-racist reputation of the Soviet Union – whether deserved or not – was already a significant factor in the 1930s. Hans Kohn, in his discussion in the *Encyclopedia of the Social Sciences*, noted that the Soviet Union was the 'only large area inhabited by many races, free, as far as governmental agencies are concerned, of any form of race prejudice'. He added that these 'egalitarian and humanitarian policies' have contributed to 'the awakening of underprivileged races'.[46] Written in the early 1930s, this would have provoked little controversy in the West; it was generally accepted in the 1930s and 1940s that the Soviet Union was colour-blind.

Foreign relations experts in London and Washington regarded race as a liability in the context of the ideological struggle with the Soviet Union. It was felt that in this respect at least the Soviet Union occupied the moral high ground. Many of the calls for the reform of race relations were motivated or justified by the need to deprive Moscow of this moral advantage. The absence of racial discrimination in Russia is 'well known and advertised', Myrdal warned.[47]

Myrdal's warning did not go unheeded. Western rivalry with

the Soviet Union helped encourage a new climate of race relations. The pressure of an apparently colour-blind Soviet alternative was evident in the 1960s. In a major debate, Kenneth Clark argued that Cold War rivalry might have been the 'ingredient' behind the civil rights revolution of the post-war period:

> Perhaps ... America may have been caught with its ideals exposed by a new type of challenge in the world at large, by the emergence of an adversary, which offered effective ideological, psychological, and military competition.[48]

While it is difficult to assess the impact of Soviet ideological competition on race relations, there can be little doubt that it forced Western diplomats to make concessions towards egalitarian demands from the non-white world.

Western, and in particular American, diplomacy sought to prevent the linking of the aspiration for racial equality with an identification with the Soviet cause. In the Anglo-American literature of the early Cold War period, the fear of the Soviet appeal and of the anti-Western reaction of the 'coloured races' was often expressed as part of the same problem. One British authority noted:

> if Communism succeeded in enlisting most of the discontented or the non-European races on its side, so that the frontier between democracy and its enemies was a racial as well as an ideological and political frontier – then the danger would be greatly multiplied, and the chance of our eventually coming out on top would be so much the poorer.[49]

Not surprisingly Western diplomats were concerned that the Soviet Union should not be able to claim that it alone championed the cause of race equality. Thus, paradoxically, the Cold War created a political climate which favoured improved race relations.

The Weak Point of the Anglo-American Political Culture

Although at the beginning of the twentieth century race served to inspire confidence in what was portrayed as a unique and superior Western civilisation, by the 1940s it had become an ideological burden, and indeed a liability in international relations. It was also becoming an embarrassment to those who promoted the ideology of the Western way of life. Racism was now experienced as the weak point of Anglo-American political culture. There was always an inconsistency between the principle of formal equality, which liberal democracy upheld, and the reality of discrimination. With the discrediting of scientific racism and Social Darwinism, the logical flaw of racial practices could no longer be ignored. A growing awareness emerged of the gap between the public commitment to egalitarian principles and practices which directly contradicted official doctrine.

For many observers, racism was the weak point in the liberal-democrat ideological armoury. It undermined the ability of the West to compete with the Soviet Union in the non-Western world. It also weakened the coherence of the liberal worldview. A clear awareness of these problems could be discerned. The Anglo-American discussion of racism, at virtually every level, was strongly defensive in tone in the 1940s. Writing in 1950, one American sociologist recalled:

> On the entry of the United States ... into the second world war it became evident to all progressive minded people that we could not tolerate the evil old American custom of discrimination of employment on account of race, religion, color, and national origin. We could not afford so shocking a flaw in our democratic pretensions.[50]

Sensitivity to this 'shocking' flaw was particularly acute in liberal intellectual circles. But hard-headed diplomats were also drawing the conclusion that something had to be done. Despatches from American diplomats abroad confirmed an awareness that discriminatory practices weakened America's global position.

Towards a New Race Etiquette

Many of the influences that worked towards the erosion of racial thinking preceded and were separate from the reaction to the Nazi experience. Even during the course of the Second World War, the experience of a racialised conflict in Asia placed greater pressure on racial etiquette than the horrors of Nazi Germany. The Nazi experience served to discredit racist politics and helped focus international opinion. But in the 1940s, and especially during the war, other factors appeared to be more directly relevant. Issues such as anti-colonial nationalism or the challenge posed by Japan's triumphs in Asia weighed far more heavily on policy-makers.

Let us take as an example the Committee on Africa and Peace Aims. This was a body established during the war to draft policy proposals for the post-war era. Most specialists in the field in the American interwar race relations industry were consulted. The committee's report, *The Atlantic Charter and Africa from an American Standpoint*, published in 1942, provided a number of compelling arguments for reforming race relations. The authors noted that after Japan's success in Asia, 'the white races, and especially Great Britain, can no longer control the world in the imperial way'. They also observed that racial discrimination in the United States undermined the Americans' moral influence abroad. And they warned that 'racial and color solidarity have a tremendous emotional appeal and that it is dangerous to permit it to have any justification for falling under the influences of communistic or other radical agitators'.[51]These arguments had a pragmatic and pre-emptive character. Their emphasis was not so much on the acceptance of racial equality as on the need to prevent a conflict that would be damaging to everyone's interests.

A new race etiquette had emerged, one that was driven by pragmatic considerations. But as chapters 7 and 8 indicate, the racial etiquette that emerged in the 1940s stopped short of advocating a policy of equality. The fact that race relations emerged before a thoroughgoing critique of racism was undertaken allowed for evasive strategies to be practised both domestically and internationally. It is for this reason that so much confusion still haunts contemporary discussions of race.

1   The Troubled White Consensus

In recent decades the major emphasis of race relations literature
has been oriented towards explaining the representation of the
Other and the racialisation of social situations. Most specialists are
concerned with the power relations that are experienced and
affirmed through race, and with the causes and dynamics of racist
ideology.[1] Today we recognise that these are crucial issues and,
clearly, the subject of power is inseparable from the discussion of
racial oppression. However, this touches on only one side of the
problem. Racial thinking is not merely an expression of the
impulse to dominate and oppress. At times it expresses a *defensive*
response; a manifestation of the fear of losing power. It is worth
noting that some of the most extreme expressions of racial
thinking emerge when assumptions of white superiority are
contested. The apartheid system in South Africa, of course, was a
post-Second World War development. This formalisation of
segregation and the extension of new forms of discrimination can
be interpreted as a response to the realisation that one is losing
control. The 1940s, a period when agitation for Afro-American
civil rights was gaining momentum, also saw the expansion of
segregation in the United States: in 1940, Atlanta segregated its
taxis; in 1944, Virginia segregated its airports.

The theme of racial fears recurs time and again in discussions of
race relations. That is why it is difficult to find any serious contribution on this subject which does link the concept of race to a problem.
One of the important paradoxes of our time is that although racial
thinking has become an important part of the political culture of the
West, the ruling elites have rarely felt comfortable with it: certainly
not during the twentieth century. Historically, race has been central
to the self-affirmation of the Western elites. At the same time, these
elites have often interpreted the weakening of their power and authority as a manifestation of racial decline. Through racial ideology
both an aggressive and a defensive consciousness can be articulated.
As this chapter argues, the conceptualisation of race relations has

often been informed by a defensive consciousness. Consequently, the many efforts to hold the racial line can be interpreted as a defensive affirmation of status, identity and power. This defensive consciousness was most forcefully expressed in debates about racial fitness, competitive fertility and panics about the decline of the West. Measures such as the introduction of immigration control in the United States in the 1920s and the institutionalisation of segregation in South Africa were influenced by racial uncertainties in the 1920s. As the next chapter argues, disillusionment with the West ran parallel with the expansion of racial fears in the interwar period.

Despite their prevalence during the first three decades of the twentieth century, racial fears have rarely been the subject of serious social analysis. One reason for this important gap in the literature may be that the strident and extreme form of racism has obscured the anxieties that inspired the fear. The aggressive discourse of racial thinking can mask the profound anxieties that underpin it. Indeed, the very development of racial thinking reflected a conservative commitment to preserve the power relations. The language of race served to naturalise social differences and inequalities. By articulating the social order as natural, racial thinking contributed to its defence. Racial thinking, and in particular the attempt to explain social through biological concepts, invariably expressed a desire to preserve the status quo. Through biology, notions of superiority and inferiority were rendered natural and reconciled with the prevailing relations of power.[2] Thus, in the widest sense, racial thinking can be seen as a warning against change.

One reason why the problematic of racial fears is so seldom engaged may be because an explicit biological discourse on international relations coincided with unparalleled Western expansion. As Langer observed in his study *The Diplomacy of Imperialism*, 'the phrases *struggle for existence and survival of the fittest* carried everything before them' in the last decade of the nineteenth century. As Langer contends, the biological conception of international relations was most prevalent in the Anglo-American setting.[3] Although this perspective soon declined, the underlying shift was not evident to many observers. The Social Darwinist rhetoric taken at its face value gave an impression of a bold and aggressive racial thinking, and students of the history of racial thinking have often projected this wave of racial confidence forward into the twentieth century. Yet a sense of defensiveness is palpable in early twentieth-century literature on race, revealing anxieties about the future. These apprehensions were expressed in a variety of forms – concern with racial fitness, with comparative fertility rates, the problem of decadence and moral decline. What gave a peculiar edge to these anxieties was the emergence of perceptions of racial threats in international relations. Race and racial conflict were always perceived as problems since they threatened the balance of power. That is why long before the West faced any systematic challenge to its hegemony, fears about the threat to the white race were widely voiced, whether in warnings about the 'Yellow Peril' or predictions of the imminent decline of the West, even if, typically, these warnings were vague about the object of their fear.

Imperialist expansion helped establish a world where power, privilege and race coincided. This was a world where the balance of power was readily conceptualised in racial terms. The very success of the West had contributed to the racialisation of international relations. As the British historian Arnold Toynbee remarked, 'the triumph of the English-speaking peoples has imposed on mankind a "race question"'.[4] From an Anglo-American perspective, maintaining the balance of power was closely associated with the global management of race relations. In intellectual terms, the issue was transformed into a generic problem of white versus the rest. The political classes of the West regarded their experience of race worldwide as involving essentially a similar if not the same dynamic. According to the American historian Jack Temple Kirby:

> The years of South African accommodation, American colonial expansion and the southern racial settlement witnessed increased communications and a heightened sense of comradeship among whites on three continents. English men, Boers, English South Africans and Americans paid close attention to developments on either side of the Atlantic, read and reviewed each other's books and took comfort in comparing each other's racial problems and solutions.[5]

Another manifestation of white solidarity was the tendency to interpret the racial problems faced by one group as a potential threat to the white race as a whole. Often their deliberations on race relations amounted to little more than a warning of greater dangers to come.

The importance of these warnings should not be assessed from the standpoint of practical outcomes. The various exchanges were essentially conversations within an elite audience. Racial calculations were part of the received wisdom of the prevailing political culture.[6] They shaped attitudes, or to be more precise, made more tangible the already existing anxieties about the future. Warnings about racial conflict were seldom elaborated or self-consciously justified. They did not need to be. Since most officials and experts shared the same outlook, there was no need to dwell on the danger. Thus, when the British imperial publicist, Lionel Curtis, informed the American Institute of Politics in 1922 that 'all policies in the last analysis now turn on the mutual relations of the white races of Europe, America, and Australia to those of Asia and Africa', his audience would have readily understood the argument;[7] it did not require further elaboration.

A Troubled Consensus

The role of racial calculations in twentieth-century international relations is hard to determine. It remains an unexplored subject, one that is rarely discussed as a problem in its own right. One of the rare contributions pointed to the difficulty in ascertaining 'the relative weight of racial considerations' in decision-making in world affairs 'since it is quite likely that these will be relatively obscured by decision makers through rationalisation for public consumption'.[8] The hidden character of racial calculations was the result of the recognition that Western racism had become a dangerous and destabilising force – one that could galvanise people of colour. It is worth noting that racial calculations never became a dominant theme in international affairs because the energies of Western diplomats were above all absorbed in dealing with the rivalries among white powers and later with the conduct of the Cold War. Nevertheless, the racial perspective on global affairs informed the management of a world where a relatively small number of Western powers dominated the world of colour and, as this chapter argues, a consciousness of white solidarity informed diplomatic affairs. Otherwise bitter rivals were aware that being white made a difference in international affairs. White solidarity was more of an ideal than a guide to action, but it did influence the conduct of international affairs.

The Anglo-American elite's sense of race strongly influenced perceptions of developments in international relations; one of the most visible manifestations of this outlook was the racial interpretation of events as they involved Western powers and societies in Africa and Asia. So, for example, external relations with Asia tended to be understood in racial terms. Acts by non-white interests were assessed not merely in terms of how they affected the particular European power concerned, but also from the wider perspective of an international racial balance. Thus during the Egyptian crisis of 1882, *The Times* insisted on the importance of saving 'European', rather than British or French, 'prestige'. It opposed the intervention of Turkish troops on the grounds that it would undermine this objective. One of its correspondents argued that 'it is European prestige that has suffered and, if Egypt is to become again habitable to Europeans, it is European prestige which must be restored'.[9] Although competition with other Western powers dominated British strategic thinking on Egypt, the theme of European prestige was still a matter for serious consideration. This was also the perspective that many American and British observers took in response to the defeat of Italy by Ethiopia in the battle of Adowa: 'The defeat of the Italians by the Abyssinians in 1896 may indeed be noted as the first decisive victory gained by troops that may be reckoned as oriental over a European army in the open field, for at least three centuries', commented Sir Alfred C. Lyall.[10] It was evident to Lyall that this incident did not have implications for Italy only, but also for Europe as a whole.

The reaction of American and British diplomats to the victory of Japan over Russia in 1905 is interesting in this respect. Geopolitically, Britain and the United States were closer to Japan than to Russia. Yet their reaction to Japan's victory was clearly informed by racial calculations. The strong awareness of race in the Western imagination led to the conclusion that this was not simply a conflict between two nations. As Vincent argued, 'the victory of the Japanese over the Russians in 1905 was widely presented not as a local triumph of one nation over another, but as a victory with global implications, of the Mongolian people over the European'.[11] Consequently, Japan's victory was understood to have implications not only for the vanquished nation but for the entire race, of which the Russians were a part. Such an interpretation was driven by the view that any clash between whites and people of colour had far-reaching consequences. Had the Japanese defeated Thailand rather than Russia the outcome would have been represented in an entirely different vocabulary.

Throughout the following decades, whenever Western powers were challenged, someone would point to the Japanese–Russian war as the beginning of a new era in international affairs. Even distant events, such as the emergence of African nationalist protest, would be linked to it. A British missionary in a lecture on World Movements given to his colleagues in Northern Rhodesia in 1931 remarked that the myth of white invincibility was exposed by the Japanese victory. 'Indeed it marked a new era in the attitude of Coloured peoples to the White race', he noted.[12] Lord Hailey wrote in the same vein when he noted that 'historians have seen in the Russo–Japanese War one of the earliest causes for the change of attitude of the Asiatic peoples, particularly those of India towards European rule'.[13] The underlying premise was the assumption that a setback to any section of the white race inflicted by people of colour would weaken the existing balance of racial power. In the interwar period, Western diplomats were not prepared to integrate Japan into their club on equal terms. As one British Foreign Office document conceded, 'Japan in the only non-white first class Power', but 'however powerful Japan may eventually become, the white races will never be able to admit her equality'.[14]

The perspective of race informed the Anglo-American discourse on Asia throughout the period under consideration. The American imperialist naval strategist Admiral Alfred Thayer Mahan saw Asia as a threat to the West:

> Our Pacific slope, and the Pacific colonies of Great Britain, with an instinctive shudder have felt the threat, which able Europeans have seen in the teeming multitudes of central and northern Asia; while their overflow into the Pacific Islands shows that not only westward by land, but also eastward by sea, the flood may sweep.[15]

The solution favoured by the American establishment was sea power, combined with the exclusion of Orientals through immigration control; the latter would keep the alien race at bay. Controlling the movement of Orientals was based on the supposition that relations between races necessarily implied the domination of one by the other. As Ashton-Gwatkin of the Foreign Office reported in a discussion on discrimination, white nations 'with a sure instinct for self-preservation' will 'never open their doors to the influx of a coloured race'.[16] The reference to the instinct for self-preservation suggested that race involved survival itself.

It is not surprising then that a racial threat was perceived to be more dangerous than conflict between white nations. Paradoxically, this outlook was already prevalent at a time when the balance of power was overwhelmingly in favour of the West. This was the motif that excited the imagination of the British Fabian Beatrice Webb as rumours of war circulated after the assassination of Archduke Franz Ferdinand in 1914. Webb saw the 'impending catastrophe' in terms of a racial invasion of 'outcasts from Southern Europe, migrants from Algeria, and from coolies from China'. 'This', she wrote, 'seems to me a bigger tragedy than any hypothetical defeat by an army of Germans'.[17] If Germany could appear less threatening than impoverished Chinese to this influential British Establishment figure, it is a testimony to the deep passions roused by race.

Webb's reaction to the involvement of non-white people in the impending conflict was fully shared in Germany. According to Snyder, 'prejudice against Negroes transcended inter-white rivalries'. So, at the outset of the First World War, the German High Command proposed to the Allied powers that the neutrality of the African colonies be maintained 'on the ground that it was important for all white men to maintain their hold over inferior black races'.[18] In practice, the European powers had no hesitation in employing large numbers of non-white soldiers in their colonies, but there was an unwritten rule that these soldiers would not be deployed against white armies.

This tacit agreement had its origins in the resurgence of imperialist expansion in the latter part of the nineteenth century. At the outbreak of the Anglo–Boer war it was understood that blacks should not be armed. A statement issued by the Natal government indicated that the 'employment of Natives' would 'be in opposition to the general acknowledged trend of Colonial opinion and would ultimately lead to the lessening of the prestige of the white man and the Natives' respect for the power of the British government'.[19] Nevertheless this understanding was repeatedly broken. The British, in particular, took a pragmatic attitude towards arming black Africans. Lord Kitchener confessed in private that he had used large numbers of armed Africans. According to one study, 'blacks served as armed scouts for mobile columns, and they were the main source of intelligence and advance work'.[20] In the Boer War as in the First World War the tacit understanding about not arming people of colour was outweighed by the demands of military survival.

White racial solidarity was never a fully worked out doctrine. Nevertheless the international system was dominated by white powers at the beginning of the twentieth century. Most of Africa and Asia was colonised and therefore affairs in those two continents were regulated by practices that were markedly different from those applied to the West. This was a global framework where double standards were institutionalised and ideas and diplomatic practices reflected the differential treatment of races. A world system run by the whites could not eliminate inter-Western conflict, but it helped foster a climate in which a unity could be forged in relation to matters that affected a racially different people.

White solidarity had more the character of an informal convention than a formal principle. Nevertheless a considerable degree of unity was displayed in Western states' dealings with Africa and Asia. The relatively orderly 'Scramble for Africa' exemplified how European powers could regulate their relations at Africa's expense. For example, the head of the British military expedition to Kumasi sought to avoid embarrassing the French in front of Africans. Brigadier-General Sir James Willcocks recalled that 'it is always judicious in Africa never to give the black man an idea that you seek his assistance against other white men'. He added:

Even with our ... [black] ... soldiers, although we gave them to understand that we would fight if the French attempted to molest us in any way, we always spoke as if all they would have to do would be to fight the other black soldiers and avoided reference to their white commanders; and that the men thoroughly understood the position I am convinced. First must come the white, to whatever race he may belong; and I never regretted our methods.[21]

The belief that 'first must come the white' did not prevent conflict between European nations, but it did help forge an informal alliance between colonial powers in Africa. This white consensus – what Kiernan aptly called 'European solidarity' – led to extensive co-operation in the subjugation of the colonial world. According to Kiernan, to the 'non-white world it might well seem that all Europeans were as thick as thieves'. And from a different perspective Bull wrote:

> In their attitudes to other peoples, moreover, the Western powers displayed a measure of unity, of which a striking expression in 1900 was the intervention in China to suppress the Boxer Rising. The leading states of the old, European-dominated international order sank their differences and sent an international army that inflicted humiliation upon the greatest of non-Western societies.[22]

Joint military action in China probably represented the high point of white solidarity. Soon great power rivalries would weaken this solidarity against the non-white world.

The Anglo–Japanese Alliance of 1902, the German alliance with Turkey prior to the First World War and the use of non-white soldiers by European powers in the war indicated that white solidarity was prepared to give way to national interest. The anticipation of a breakdown of white solidarity was a theme that stirred the emotion of many Western writers concerned with the future of race relations. Nevertheless, the white consensus which embodied a differential attitude to Western and non-Western interests in international relations survived the trauma of the First World War.

Racial assumptions continued to inform the work of the League of Nations. As Roger Louis argued, the Mandate System classified groups of 'backward races' into different categories of civilisation.[23] The attitude of diplomats to non-Western societies was largely shaped by elementary racial assumptions. The German Ambassador to Tokyo wrote in July 1927 that the 'coloured peoples of the whole world have been seized by a powerful impulse for independence'. His response was to evolve a system of co-operation in respect to the

colonial possessions of the Western powers. While diplomatic collaboration was difficult to achieve, it was possible to engage in joint
ventures in the sphere of 'science'. A memorandum regarding the
future work of the International African Institute observed that the
'continent of Africa is in a sense a laboratory and experimenting
ground for research in the social sciences, for all the nations who
administer the colonies there'.[24] Edwin Embree, President of the
Julian Rosenwald Fund, and a key American race relations lobbyist
in the interwar period, argued for the setting up of an Institute of
Race Relations because:

> Half a dozen industrial powers rule or control hundreds of millions of
> very divergent native peoples. The new order has grown up without
> deliberate planning, and the terrific stresses and strains of conflicting
> cultures are only beginning to be realized ... The rulers are finding that
> an understanding of the native peoples is essential to effective
> government, and that without co-operation revenues fail, discontent
> even insurrection arise, continued domination is increasingly difficult
> if not actually impossible.[25]

The collaboration of American, British, French, German and
South African specialists indicated that here at least the white
consensus prevailed.

Consensus also survived as far as immigration controls were concerned. The years following the First World War saw increasing
pressure for a more comprehensive system of control over the movement of Asiatics. This agitation culminated in the United States in
the anti-immigration law of 1924. Controlling 'Oriental immigration' was accepted as a necessity by politicians and publicists on both
sides of the Atlantic. An article entitled 'The Empire and Asiatic
Immigration', published in London by Vance Palmer in the *Fortnightly Review*, described this issue as critical to the future of the
Dominions. Palmer sought to minimise the racist dynamic and
present immigration as a threat to Anglo-Saxon culture and institutions. He is worth quoting at length since he provides a summary of
the mainstream consensus on Asian immigration:

> It is not a fact that in Canada or Australia there is any contempt for the
> coloured races as such. The two countries are faced with the problem

of keeping their civilisations intact and their blood pure while huge migratory populations are knocking at their doors. Their political systems are democratic, giving the same right to every citizen, and they have made no allowances for the incorporation of an alien labouring class such as is to be found in South Africa. If immigration were to be allowed without restriction they would be submerged entirely in a few years by the mobile proletariat of Asia, people who have no intimate acquaintance with political institutions in their own countries, and who have a marked tendency to coagulate in large masses that disturb the social balance. And inevitably there would be the racial feuds, embitterments, and exasperations which destroy all the felicities of life wherever the races live freely side by side.[26]

The presupposition of the argument was that racial feuds are inevitable and therefore the different races are best kept apart. Moreover an egalitarian framework would lead to the submergence of the white race. Therefore, if the different races had to live in close proximity, the South African model was to be preferred. Segregation was the corollary of immigration controls. 'The segregation of the three races is desirable', was the conclusion drawn by the conservative American race thinker Professor J.W. Gregory. From a relatively liberal American missionary perspective, W.C. Willoughby justified the colour bar in Africa on the grounds that race contact led to the moral degeneration of the native.[27]

The white consensus remained reasonably solid in relation to the colonial world. It is important to recall that in the 1930s the term 'Colonial Question' did not mean the problem of how to respond to the grievances of the people of the colonies; it related to the demands of Germany, Italy and Japan for a share of colonial possessions. At the League of Nations there were few objections to the morality of Germany claiming colonial possessions. Instead, the argument mounted against Germany was that the possession of colonies would not help overcome Germany's economic difficulties.[28] The right to possess colonies and exercise 'trusteeship' over backward races was inherent in the principles of League of Nations diplomacy.

The British government under Neville Chamberlain was prepared to accommodate German demands for colonies. Discussions in 1937 in the Foreign Policy Committee indicated that colonial appeasement had become acceptable. Crozier's research suggests that there was a measure of sympathy for the Nazi programme of colonial redistribution. 'Imperialists themselves the British understood this to be a natural aspiration', he wrote.[29]

What is most striking about the discussion that surrounded the 'Colonial Question' was that virtually no one questioned the legitimacy of the colonial enterprise. Those who attacked colonial appeasement as a betrayal of the 'interests of the natives' did so on the ground that Britain had a moral duty to exercise its trusteeship. More typical was the reaction of *The Times*:

> The colonial problem will be the next great question to be faced in Europe. It lies at the bottom of the Italian adventure, and it may be found at the head of the next list of German demands. Here in England there are thoughtful people who think that revision of the distribution of colonies is inevitable sooner or later, and that the sooner the fact is frankly faced the easier and less costly revision will be.[30]

A wide range of opinion, including that of the Prince of Wales and the Archbishop of York, accepted that Britain's diplomatic difficulties should be resolved at the expense of the people in the colonies; they were prepared to allow Germany to lay claim to possessions in Africa. The right of Western powers to dispose of colonies as they saw fit was also accepted by the Trades Union Congress and the Labour Party, both of whom passed the following resolution at their 1935 conferences:

> We call upon the British Government to urge the League of Nations to summon a World Economic Conference and to place upon its agenda the international control of the sources of supply of raw materials, with the application of the principle of equality of opportunity to all nations in the undeveloped regions of the earth.[31]

Despite the reference to equality of opportunity, the call for the international control of resources was an attempt to respond to the demands of the so-called have-not European powers.

The response of the American elite to colonial issues had as its fundamental premise the assumption of white superiority. Quincy Wright, Professor at the University of Minnesota, a specialist on the

League of Nations Mandate System and future consultant to UNESCO, complimented British officers for training the Iraqi army and saw it as an example of the 'tutelage of adolescent peoples'. According to Wright this was a pleasant exception to the 'general slovenliness of the East'.[32] The white consensus on colonialism in America was particularly striking in relation to Italy's invasion of Ethiopia in 1936. Public criticism of Italy in Britain and the United States was motivated by diplomatic considerations rather than genuine sympathy for the Ethiopian people.

Arthur Steiner, Professor of Political Science at UCLA and future adviser to the State Department on South East Asia, portrayed the Italian invasion as the latest episode in the enactment of the White Man's Burden:

> great amount of genuinely constructive work was accomplished in the first two months of the Italian occupation ... With the administration of native justice, the Italians have had an abundance of experience, in most instances satisfactory ... Italians, with wide experience, have shown commendable willingness to study scientifically the institutions of native and particularly Moslem, law.[33]

Steiner's verdict suggested a studied indifference to the fate of a hitherto independent nation. They were natives who required the white man to show the way. Steiner's empathy for Italian rule in the Horn of Africa was but an expression of the legacy of the white consensus in international affairs.

The Breakdown of White Solidarity

Throughout the twentieth century, whenever great power interests contradicted the principle of white solidarity, the latter became expendable. White solidarity was primarily an intellectual and ideological response to events rather then a practical principle. For all that, is was not unimportant in shaping attitudes towards the conduct of international relations. It is possible to detect an implicit assumption of differential treatment of members of different races by Western powers in their approach towards international affairs.

After the turn of the century Europe could no longer close ranks against non-Western powers. White racial solidarity was fundamentally undermined by the Anglo–Japanese alliance of 1902. Rivalries amongst Western powers during the First World War led to pragmatic manoeuvres which further eroded the existing racial lines. Britain encouraged an Arab nationalist revolt against the Ottoman Empire, while Germany worked closely with Turkey. In Africa, Britain sought to undermine Germany by organising a propaganda campaign which accused the latter of atrocities against the inhabitants of its colonies.[34] During the war, European powers employed non-white troops, thereby eroding the informal convention to which Western nations hitherto paid lip-service.

Apprehensions of the breakdown of white solidarity featured prominently in the racist literature of the interwar era. For many contributors this development represented a betrayal of the race. One of the first British alarmist works, Putnam Weale's *The Conflict of Colour*, was inspired by the desire to disown Britain's alliance with Japan. Weale was convinced that a 'struggle has begun between the white man and all the other men of the world'. His fear was that Britain's alliance with an Asian nation had undermined the dominant position of the West. He argued that 'the present balance could be maintained if Europe was not divided' and that it was 'evident that if an absolute agreement among the White Powers to preserve the *status quo*, could be really arrived at, no great breach could occur'.[35]

The importance of the racial perspective on international relations is illustrated by representations of the First World War as a 'civil war' between white nations. In the minds of contemporary observers this was the death blow to the notion of white solidarity. The practice of decoding this experience in terms of exposing white weakness, discussed earlier in this chapter, was linked to the perception of the demise of racial solidarity. Those who perceived the war in these terms decried not only the fact that white armies were slaughtering each other, but that African and Asian troops were employed on the battlefields. As Vincent wrote: 'not only were the whites laying to rest the notion of their instinctive comity by butchering each other in such unprecedented numbers, but they were also showing their neglect of race in favour of nation in using non-white troops to advance the slaughter'.[36] This interpretation of events has continued to inform the discussion. A recent American study recalled that 'Europe's prestige was ruined by the First World War, a suicidal war of an intensity and scale never before seen, into which the European powers drafted Indian regiments, Senegalese and Moroccan infantry and cavalry, and Indochinese and Chinese auxiliaries, while implicating – to its fatal misfortune – Ottoman Turkey. The notion of the moral superiority of the West was finished in Asia after that.'[37]

At the time many Western observers believed that the First World War had helped accelerate a future race war. The deployment of non-white troops by European powers was seen as the symbol of racial decline. Criticism was particularly directed against the French, who used African troops during the occupation of the Ruhr in 1920. Fryer has documented how even British left-wing and liberal periodicals attacked France for 'thrusting her black savages' into the 'heart of Germany'.[38] Mainstream voices in Britain and the United States were even more agitated by the use of black soldiers to police a white population.

Racial fears after the First World War led to the emergence of a new genre of alarmist literature on the subject of racial decline. Sir Leo Chiozza Money's *The Peril of the White*, published in 1925, is representative. Sir Leo was driven by a desire to counteract the process whereby 'whites in Europe and elsewhere are set upon race suicide and internecine war'. His invective was especially directed against the French:

> And then we are compelled to pass from the picture of France as a civiliser to the spectacle of France looking to Africa for troops with which to support her military power in Europe ... The French Budget provides for an establishment of over 160,000 native troops. The provisioning and training of this great force is an ill-service to European civilisation for which not only France but all the White Man's World, will have to pay bitterly ... Europeans cannot expect to teach Africans to use modern arms and to employ them against other Europeans, without creating a weapon against themselves and their posterity ... What a mournful problem it is, this of France believing herself forced to frame a great black army in anticipation of the failure of her white manhood.[39]

In reality the French had no monopoly over the employment of

black troops. Leo Amery, Under-Secretary at the Colonial Office,
may have been dismissive of the French for wanting 'nigger
conscripts' to 'hold down Arabs & Germans', but at the same time
the War Office had no inhibition about looking to Africa for
conscripts.[40] Pragmatism coexisted with a sense of anxiety and
unease about the consequences of deploying colonial troops.

The link between the erosion of white solidarity and the
employment of colonial troops was made time and again by those
concerned with upholding the 'prestige' of the white race. Those
inspired by racialist doctrine such as the Nazi Party often
condemned other powers for breaking racial solidarity. Nazi
propaganda criticised Western colonial powers for undermining
'white supremacy' by failing to take a decisive stand on the racial
question,[41] but it was not just the Nazis who were preoccupied by
this issue. It is useful to recall that it was only in the final months
of the Second World War that the American military allowed
black and white enlisted men to fight in the same units.[42]

The association of the Great War with the breakdown of white
solidarity became part of the self-knowledge of the Anglo-
American elite. More than 40 years after the end of the First
World War, the British Prime Minister Harold Macmillan was
still preoccupied by the loss of white prestige. He recalled:

> what the two wars did was to destroy the prestige of the white people.
> For not only did the yellows and blacks watch them tear each other
> apart, committing the most frightful crimes and acts of barbarism
> against each other, but they actually saw them enlisting each their own
> yellows and blacks to fight other Europeans, other whites. It was bad
> enough for the white men to fight each other, but it was worse when
> they brought in their dependants.[43]

Macmillan saw a clear link between the experience of war and the
revolt of the 'yellow and blacks'. Despite such setbacks Macmillan
still hoped to rescue the white race from defeat. Emotionally he
was drawn to the challenge of preserving a degree of white
consensus. He confessed to his correspondent that the 'reason that
I have tried so hard to bring about at least some kind of détente'
was to minimise the possibility of the Afro–Asian bloc taking
advantage of Cold War rivalries.

It seems that Macmillan even went as far as considering that racial matters outweighed ideological differences with the Soviet Union. Did Macmillan really believe that 'some day, a generation or two on, we may able to persuade the Russians that they are Europeans and not Asiatics'?[44] That he attached some importance to his observations on the future of the white race is testified by the fact that instructions were given to send a copy of this letter to Her Majesty, the Queen. For Macmillan at least the need for a white consensus was an elementary article of faith.

But we are jumping ahead. The breakdown of white collaboration appeared to many as confirmation of their fears about the conflict of race. Consequently there was widespread concern about the prestige of the white race. The erosion of white solidarity at once made racial concerns more credible and created a defensiveness towards related subjects. It was feared that the erosion of the white consensus would encourage people of colour to contest the prevailing world order. In this situation race had become a troublesome issue in international affairs. This outcome contained more then a hint of irony. Having racialised world affairs in the nineteenth century, Western powers soon began to fear that the reaction to the existing arrangement would assume a racial form. The 'theme of Europe racializing the world, and suffering now from the effects of a colour consciousness', according to Vincent, has become increasingly prominent.[45] The more that racial matters were seen to work against those who were originally inspired by it, the more it became an embarrassing subject to be avoided in public discussions.

The Final Stand

During the interwar period, the Anglo-American elite still retained a vision of an international system dominated by a small group of white powers. However, the ascendancy of Japan to the status of a major power created the need for accommodating an Asian society as a partner in international affairs. Western powers were prepared to make diplomatic adjustments, but they were clearly not prepared to accept the principle that all people, regardless of their race, would be treated equally. Western opposition to racial equality was evident at the Paris Peace Conference of 1919. In what would prove to be the final public stand against racial equality, Japan's attempt to secure this principle in diplomatic relations was rejected.

At the 1919 Conference, Japan proposed that the clause in the League of Nations' Covenant providing for religious equality should be extended to include the equality of races. The Japanese expected that for reasons of international diplomacy their request could not be rejected. To their surprise, the Anglo-Saxon nations – in particular Australia, Britain and the United States – took strong exception to the Japanese amendment.

The dominant personality at the Paris Conference, the American President Woodrow Wilson, had no doubts about where he stood on this question. Previously, he had argued against Asian immigration on the ground that 'we [Americans] cannot make a homogeneous population out of a people who do not blend with the Caucasian race'. His views on racial segregation in the American South were similar. When a group of black representatives protested to him about segregation, Wilson informed them: 'segregation is not humiliating but a benefit, and ought to be so regarded by you'.[46] However, during the negotiations, Wilson kept his views to himself. Others, such as William Hughes the Prime Minister of Australia, had no such inhibitions. Hughes denounced the principle of racial equality as dangerous nonsense. According to one account, Hughes threatened to mobilise the 'yellow press' in Britain and the United States against the Japanese amendment, if there was a chance of its acceptance.[47]

The Japanese amendment to the freedom of religion provision of Article 21 of the draft League of Nations Covenant stated:

> Equality of nations being a basic principle of the League of Nations, the High Contracting Parties agree to accord as soon as possible to all alien nationals of State members of the League, equal and just treatment in every respect, making no distinction, either in law or in fact, on account of their race or nationality.

Diplomatic niceties and the desire not to offend Japan gave way to racial calculations. American diplomats were concerned about the consequences that this policy could have for white–black relations at home, while Hughes was preoccupied with preserving the 'White Australian policy'. The British representative at the negotiations, Lord Robert Cecil, saw the amendment as a challenge to the management of the Empire. Harold Nicolson, a member of the British delegation, regarded the Japanese proposal as a 'painful amendment'. He dreaded the idea of a Covenant that 'implied the equality of the yellow man with the white man' and worse still 'might imply the terrific theory of the equality of the white man with the black'.[48]

More broadly, many Western diplomats in Paris, and their governments at home, perceived the Japanese amendment as a threat. Its nature was seldom expressed clearly, but what was at stake were the widely accepted assumptions of Western superiority. According to Griswold, the Japanese amendment was 'palpably a challenge to the theory of the superiority of the white race on which rested so many of Great Britain's imperial pretensions'.[49] A similar characterisation could be made of the challenge that the amendment represented to the policies of Australia, Canada and the United States. What was at issue was not superiority of the white race as such. The Anglo-American elites showed little inclination to advertise their sense of superiority. Rather, they feared that if equality was accepted, the system of discrimination which underpinned the prevailing global order would become discredited and eventually undermined.

Western diplomats were aware of the inconsistency between their rhetoric about the right of nations to self-determination and of democracy and their rejection of the Japanese amendment. It was also clear to many that the failure to make even a mild diplomatic gesture towards the Japanese initiative contained the seeds of future conflict. That they would rather live with the possibility of this conflict than accept the amendment indicates just how reluctant they were to make concessions to the principle of racial equality in 1919. The Western response to this debate was to act as if it never happened. A British diplomatic report on Japan in 1919 complained that in the press the issue of racial discrimination was 'indeed discussed ad nauseam' and 'frequently with a bitterness and acrimony which seemed somewhat out of proportion to the practical value of the issues at stake'.[50] This was certainly not an accusation that could have been made of the Western press's minimalist treatment of the subject.

Despite the attempt to marginalise the debate on the Japanese amendment, the issue of race as a problem for international relations could not be wished out of existence. Throughout the interwar period, race relations were perceived as a major source of international instability. The Japanese had placed the issue of race equality on the international diplomatic agenda and after 1919 the issue would not go away. A discussion of 'Race Conflict' in the *Encyclopaedia of the Social Sciences* in the 1930s articulated the contemporary concerns. It noted that 'the suppressed races and classes have pointed to the philosophy of equal rights in protest against the theory of permanent race inequality' and warned that 'racial relations, today present more dangerous features in the field of interhuman relations than any other point of conflict'.[51]

For its part, Japan had scored a propaganda coup. By appearing to champion the principle of racial equality it won enthusiastic support from the Afro–Asian world. Even the Chinese, who opposed Japan on other matters, expressed firm support for the initiative. In the eyes of many Asian nationalists, Japan emerged as the potential leader of anti-imperialist resistance.[52] By the 1930s, many anti-imperialist thinkers regarded Japan as a rare source of inspiration. The Afro-American intellectual DuBois wrote in October 1935: 'Japan is regarded by all coloured peoples as their logical leader, as the one non-white nation which has escaped for ever the dominance and exploitation of the white world.'[53]

The debate on race equality in 1919 was systematically played down in the West – to this day it is rarely discussed in the historical literature. Public embarrassment coexisted with private fears. In the diplomatic exchanges of the time it is evident that American and British officials expected Japan or China or some other party to raise the issue again. Consequently, even during the early stages of the Second World War there was intense behind the scenes discussion about how to come to terms with the issues raised in 1919.

In the United States, the Commission to Study the Organisation of Peace, a body consisting of distinguished academics, pointedly referred to the 1919 debate in its report *International Safeguard of Human Rights*, published in 1944. The report warned: 'we may be chastened by Wilson's rejection at Paris of the principle of racial equality – a rejection which embittered the

Oriental world'.[54] Others too recalled the 1919 debate. In February 1942, the US Embassy in London sent a State Department paper to the Foreign Office. Its title was 'Japan and the Issue of Racial Equality at Paris, 1919'. Although the paper sought to fudge the issues, it conceded that race relations fundamentally affected international relations. It observed that the 'racial equality issue was not isolated but closely connected with the whole settlement of the Pacific'.[55] By inference it argued that the future settlement of international conflict required a more positive approach towards the question of racial equality.

The rejection of the Japanese amendment in 1919 indicated that a degree of white solidarity still prevailed in international relations, but this was a troubled white consensus. Western diplomats clearly felt uncomfortable; it was a decision that they would have rather not taken. They sensed that an unambiguous and public rejection of the principle of racial equality was likely to rebound against the Western powers. Their response was to avoid any major public discussion on this subject. Since racist practices could no longer be defended openly, it was felt best to silence any discussion on this subject altogether. As the following chapters indicate a similar approach characterised the domestic deliberations on this subject.

2 Early Warnings – Presentiment of Racial Conflict

Racial fears about white solidarity reflected apprehensions about the dominant global status of the West. One symptom of these anxieties was the overreaction in the West to Japan's defeat of Russia in 1905. Such reactions were most pervasive amongst conservative and restorationist European figures, and were most coherently articulated by those who were scandalised by the mass radicalisation and the upheavals of the post-First World War era. Reflections on these and other racial experiences during the first three decades of the twentieth century often hinted at some ominous force inexorably leading to the decline of the white race. Oswald Spengler's *Decline of the West* was symptomatic of this *Zeitgeist*. In Europe it was part of a general crisis of confidence in the prevailing institutions and values. When the philosopher Karl Jaspers wrote 'people are coming to believe that everything is breaking down: there is nothing that can't be questioned: nothing that is real stands the test', he summed up the mood of the time.[1]

Interwar pessimism was not simply a cultural matter. Some experienced it as *racial decline*. Many Westerners in the East reported on their perception of the decline of white prestige. This sensitivity reflected strong doubts about Western superiority. Nothing expresses this sentiment more poignantly than George Orwell's description of the time when, as a minor colonial official in Burma, he was called on to kill a rampaging elephant:

> And it was at this moment, as I stood there with the rifle in my hands, that I first grasped the hollowness, the futility of the white man's domination in the East. Here was I, the white man with his gun, standing in front of the unarmed crowd – seemingly the leading actor of the piece; but in reality I was only an absurd puppet punched to and fro by the will of the yellow faces behind. I perceived in this moment that when white man turns tyrant, it is his own freedom that he destroys.[2]

Others drew conclusions less lucid and radical than Orwell's, but were no less uncertain about the 'white man's burden'.

This crisis of confidence may have directly influenced a relatively small section of society. But through the reactions of these opinion-makers, artists and the intelligentsia wider sections of society were seized by the cultural and racial pessimism of the time. These sentiments did not lead directly to more enlightened thinking or to support for the principle of racial equality. Rather their effect was to undermine belief in the superiority of the white race. The result was the growth of relativism, particularly the cultural relativism of American anthropology and the weakening of the imperial tradition in Europe. But whatever the response, those educated in the assumptions of Western superiority were filled with doubt. Even the upholders of the culture of imperialism were becoming apprehensive about the future.

It seems that sentiments regarding racial superiority disintegrated some time before the principle of racial equality became integrated into Western political culture. It is this evolution of a highly alarmist representation of racial conflict before the existence of any serious current of anti-racism that is one of the most interesting features of twentieth-century racial thought. The confident racial moment had passed before the case for equality was seriously considered. Race had become problematised and most people saw it as the producer of destructive and irrational forces.

In both popular and specialist literature on international relations for the period 1910–40, there are repeated allusions to the imminent war between races. Nor was this the preoccupation of the unapologetic promoters of race politics. Centrist, liberal and left-wing writers also responded. Many of these authors counselled Western statesmen to be more sensitive so as not to provoke the 'coloured races' to rise up against the West. Missionaries, liberals and socialists alike called for the exercise of tact and sensitivity in racial matters.

The American periodical *Journal of Race Development*, established in 1910, was almost entirely devoted to minimising or pre-empting the coming conflict between races. Although far from advocating race equality, it argued for sensitivity in the handling of race relations. Philip Means called for the cultivation of 'race appreciation'. Writing towards the end of the First World War, he

predicted that in the future the 'vast majority of the problems will
be racial and cultural not only purely so, but also by implication
and association'.[3] In subsequent decades, predictions such as this
would become more and more routine. What prompted this
reaction and why there was a presentiment of danger before any
obvious threat of a race war are the immediate questions raised by
the reading of this material. An examination of early twentieth-
century racial fears and their significance for later developments
constitute the subject of this chapter.

The Presentiment of Danger

During the interwar period future international conflicts were
under continuous discussion in the media and among intellectuals. A new global war was widely anticipated and many argued
that the conflict could be racial in character. The aggressive stance
of Nazi Germany underlined the importance of racialist politics.
But the issue of race was perceived in a wider sense as a
confrontation between colours. Alarmist accounts argued that in a
future conflict the protagonists would be the white and non-white
races. These interwar contributions were characteristically incoherent and unfocused. Allusions to racial competition and unspecified hints about growing resentment against the white race
were the usual fare. Racial fears were seldom engaged openly and
the object of anxieties was usually vague. This lack of specificity
was based in part on the relative dearth of experience to
substantiate such pessimism. These were unsubstantiated fears,
which said more about those who suffered from them than about
any clearly defined dangers.

Without any specific experience of a 'clash of colour' it is
striking just how extensive these fears were. In the aftermath of
the First World War, apprehensions about racial revolts against
white rule were widely expressed. In the Southern states of the
United States, for example, anxiety among whites was acute.
According to Mark Ellis, 'whites were on the verge of uncontrollable and violent panic across the South during the first months of
the war'.[4] Despite the absence of any tangible threat to the existing
racial order, otherwise impartial observers invested their reputa-

tion in alarmist accounts of racial unrest. They invariably communicated an intense sense of urgency. This was a defensive response that revealed a sense of dread about the possible outcome of racial conflict. The obsessive and even panic-like character of the white response was acknowledged by some observers at the time. Indeed, it was the fear that these panics would lead to a white backlash that led to the establishment of some of the early race relations institutions. The Commission of Interracial Co-operation, founded in April 1919, sought to defuse the effects of outbursts of white racial fears during this period.

A report outlining the work of the Commission of Interracial Co-operation noted:

> Then, it will be remembered, the country was seething with interracial distrust and hostility, which had taken deep hold upon both races. White people were obsessed with fear of what the returning Negro soldiers might do or demand, as a result of their training in arms and their experience abroad. Hence, the Negro veterans, who had gone away acclaimed as heroes, were met on their return with averted looks, suspicion, or open hostility. Their surprise and disappointment were tragic.[5]

The establishment of institutions such as the Commission led to the development of what would eventually become the new field of race relations. The literature produced by those concerned about the 'state of race relations' decried manifestations of racial violence. It argued that white 'over-reaction' would only make the situation worse. Paradoxically, its appeals for moderation and common sense were conveyed in a distinctly alarmist tone.

The newly emerging race relations field was not oriented towards domestic matters only. The international dimension was also of profound interest. Discussions of the time emphasised the possibility of a conflict in which the West would have to face the resentment of those excluded from the management of international affairs. The problem of race was depicted as a challenge to white domination in different settings, but since these were depicted as essentially similar in character, they invited similar solutions. So, for example, the Commission of Interracial Co-operation provided the model for the establishment of a parallel initiative in South Africa. The literature of the interwar period continually focused on the global dimension of the problem. As an editorial in the *Journal of Applied Sociology* put it:

> The Europeanization of the world has lost its momentum. The World War augmented the spirit of nationalism in nearly all countries with the result that India, Turkey, Egypt, the Philippines, the South American republics, as well as China and Japan, are asking, if not demanding, autonomy regarding changes in their cultures and traditions.[6]

Such a general diagnosis provided a vague and incoherent outline of just what constituted the problem of race relations. 'Racial antipathies are rising' warned a statement issued by the newly established Institute of Pacific Relations (IPR), in 1925, but typically it provided little empirical evidence of the growth of new hatreds.[7] Warnings about the future of race relations were fundamentally defensive and insecure. The underlying premise was that all these developments had the potential of threatening a white-dominated world order. The urgency of preventing such dangers expressed the principal motif in the field of race relations of the interwar period.

Louis Snyder's *Race: A History of Modern Ethnic Theories* is symptomatic of this response. This widely cited attack on racist politics was published in 1939 and was very much part of the first wave of race relations literature of the interwar period. Yet at the same time it can be read as representing raising the alarm of racial fears. 'To-day, the danger of war between the so-called races becomes more and more intense', warned Snyder in the introductory chapter.[8] His critique of supremacist politics was in part justified on the ground that such an outlook would actually encourage hatred and breed a violent reaction against the West.

Unlike most other contributions of this period, Snyder attempted to elaborate the character of his fears. But in the act of engaging the problem, his lack of clarity about what the danger was became evident. And he made no attempt to cover up the speculative character of his discussion.

> Alarmists claim that the next challenge to the white man may be expected from the yellow race under the energetic leadership of recently awakened Japan. Others believe that in this gigantic 'war of the races', the blacks will one day enter their own bid for power.

Although by implication Snyder distanced himself from accusations of alarmism, he shared all the assumptions. He was uncertain how and in what form the danger would emerge, but he was convinced that it would: 'It is as yet too early to know the form in which pan-Africanism will become consolidated.' However, it was not too early to identify the risks at stake. 'It appears certain', he wrote, that the 'movement will one day progress beyond its present stage'; the 'union of all the black peoples, may one day become a force with which the white man will have to reckon'.

According to Snyder an unspecified threat from Asia was also imminent:

> Pan-Asianism has not yet crystallized into an active and competing force. Still somewhat vague and intangible in concept, there is no doubt that it will one day be grounded solidly in the mass mind of Asiatics through propagandistic methods learned from the West.[9]

It is curious that Snyder had no 'doubts' that something that was still intangible would become a formidable force in the future. Snyder's conviction is all the more striking since the author was aware that Western reactions to developments in the East were often panic-like. In this connection he mentioned the reaction of the Western media to the First Pan Asiatic Congress held in Nagasaki in 1926. This informal gathering of a handful of individuals was greeted by the press as confirmation of its previous racial fears. Stories of the new 'Oriental menace' and the 'Yellow Peril' were widely circulated. Snyder observed that this 'incident was significant because it indicated the concern with which a really effective pan-Asiatic movement would be greeted by the Western powers'.[10] In other words, it was the Western reaction rather than the event that was noteworthy. Yet the ability to grasp this point did not prevent Snyder from exhibiting some of the same apprehensions about different circumstances.

Western expectations about an impending clash of colour were the product of an imagination that was pessimistic and insecure. Interwar pessimism did not require any evidence of race conflict. Nor did the absence of any agreement about what actually constituted the danger ahead weaken the sense of dread attached to deliberations of race relations. Like Snyder, observers could at once be both unspecific and offer a variety of hypotheses about where the threat lay. Kohn's discussion on the geographical flashpoints of racial conflict left little to chance:

> The major contemporary arenas of race conflict are now the Pacific regions where the white and yellow races are struggling for supremacy, the United States with its Negro problem; and the Indies and Africa.

Unlike most writers on the subject, Kohn saw the threat mainly in terms of the reaction of blacks to white racism. In a rather bizarre aside he noted that 'as the Negro race is the most numerous of all the backward races, the result of its struggle for emancipation will determine to a large extent the future nature of race conflict and race prejudice all over the earth'.[11] Just what formed the basis of this conclusion was left to the reader's imagination.

As with Snyder and Kohn, the warnings contained in the literature were unfocused about the source of their racial fears. In one breath Sir Reginald Coupland, Beit Professor of Colonial History at Oxford, could state: the 'Colour Problem is most urgent and most critical in Asia', only to add: 'it is more difficult and morally most dangerous in Africa'.[12] Terms such as 'urgent', 'dangerous' and 'critical' were deployed without any attempt to justify their usage. The absence of any contemporary questioning of these warnings suggests the belief that these terms did not require elaboration. The pessimistic intellectual climate of the time was hospitable to speculation about the deterioration of race relations. The founding statement of the Institute of Pacific Relations that 'racial antipathies are rising' also pointed to the 'period of disillusionment' that prevailed.[13] In this time of disillusionment, the public mood was receptive to alarmist accounts about the future.

Apprehensions regarding future racial conflict were seldom linked to a specific incident. However, the one event that authors pinpointed as the decisive influence on the state of race relations was the experience of the First World War. This conflict loomed large in many of the contributions on the topic of race relations. In the 1920s and 1930s, the Great War was often portrayed as a symbol of Western weakness and decline. Many reviews of international politics treated this experience as an historic blow against white moral authority. In the eyes of many observers, the war had discredited assumptions of racial and moral superiority. Sections of the Anglo-American political classes believed that the experience of this purposeless global carnage gave the game away: the hypocrisy of the white man was there for everyone to see. Many observers concluded that the horrors of the war dealt 'white prestige' a blow from which it could not recover.

The experience of the First World War had a particularly important impact on the worldview of Anglo-American Christian missionaries. It led to an important change in missionary thinking about the contact of culture between the West and the East. A sense of disillusionment, if not despair, regarding the claims of Western civilisation characterised the outlook of many leading missionaries. Stanley has represented this reaction as a 'gradual disintegration of Christian confidence in Western cultural values'. Consequently, for many missionaries in Africa, 'aspects of tribal society began to appear less "dark" and indeed preferable to the secular modernity of the West'.[14] This disillusionment with Western civilisation made missionaries sensitive to the racial grievances of African and Asian people. Defensiveness about the record of colonial powers coincided with concern that racial grievances would lead to a rejection of Christianity because of its association with the West.

Missionary societies, concerned with evangelising, were acutely aware of the resentment that Western domination provoked. This was reinforced by the fear that the carnage of the First World War had done irreparable damage to what they called European prestige. The loss of white prestige was the underlying theme at a conference of the Institute of Pacific Affairs held in Honolulu in 1925. This conference, which was primarily devoted to a discussion of race relations, had a significant missionary bias. Speakers continually emphasised their pessimism about the future and their apprehension regarding the conflict of races. Arthur Dean, the President of the University of Hawaii, articulated the widely held view that the civilisation of the West 'often deteriorates into mere materialism and restlessness'. Some of the Asian delegates in attendance drew the correct conclusion that Western concern with race relations was connected to the trauma of the First World War. T.Z. Koo, a Chinese delegate, reminded the audience that the *fact* of Western prestige in the East has disappeared ever since the war in Europe but the paraphernalia of bolstering up this fancied prestige is still there'.[15]

The spiritual collapse of the white man was the subject of a wide body of missionary literature. The link between this and the problem of race was the main theme of Mathew's *The Clash of Colour*. This text, written from a liberal missionary point of view, was concerned with how the authority of the European was 'crushed in moral ruin in the war of 1914–1918'. Mathew observed that 'the authority of the white man in the sense of its automatic acceptance by the other races as inevitable and enduring has ended'.[16] Mathew and his colleagues were profoundly concerned with the impact of Western 'materialism' on the spiritual climate in the colonial world.

Many missionaries feared that anti-colonial passions would severely damage their work. At missionary conferences the danger presented by independent, indigenous or separatist churches was a regular subject of discussion. The response of leading missionaries was to try to distance Christianity from its Western associations. This point was strongly promoted at the 1928 Jerusalem Conference of the International Missionary Council (IMC). William Patton, the IMC's secretary, reported that a strong Christian message was needed so that 'in the face of nationalist feeling the Christian claim for Christ' could not 'so easily be made to appear as a mere piece of white imperialism masquerading in spiritual dress'.[17]

Because of their vocation and their peculiar sensitivity to the potentially explosive rejection of the West, missionaries came to play a pioneering role in the emerging field of race relations. Their sensitivity towards the problem was reflected in their literature and their organisational initiatives. It was their influence that led to an important study of race relations in the United States in 1923 and to the establishment of the Institute of Pacific Relations and the International Africa Institute. These institutions were in close collaboration with many of the leading American foundations and British research institutions. Research on race relations during the interwar period was informally co-ordinated by a small number of individuals affiliated to the Carnegie Corporation, the Phelps-Stokes Fund, the IMC and specialists from the British Colonial Office. Their research agenda was strongly influenced by the apprehensions of the missionary lobby.

In exposing Western pretensions, the First World War was seen to have had a profound impact on perceptions of the world-wide racial balance. This perception informed many of the contributors to a conference of American academics on 'Public Opinion and World Peace' in December 1921. Typically, their fear was that the war had 'laid bare the skeleton in the closet of western civilization', in the words of one contributor, who added: even 'the most backward of these countries is now alive to the spirit of renewed nationalism that is sweeping the world'.[18] This view of the impact of the Great War on race relations informed most of the interpretations of the succeeding decades.

Indeed, the correlation between the First World War and the Western perception of white racial decline is difficult to sustain. It was not the experience of the First World War that initiated the anxieties and obsessions that informed the discourse of the problem of racial conflict. Alarmist reactions pre-date the war by at least two or three decades. In the United States panics about the Yellow Peril were in evidence in the 1880s. The racial fears expressed in these panics were captured in the 'vision of the vast multitudes of Asia uniting and advancing on Europe and the Western Hemisphere like the reborn hordes of Genghis Khan'.[19] By the turn of the century alarmist accounts of race conflicts to come were widespread and fascinated many thinkers. Max Weber, as a 16-year-old student, organised his essay on world history around the 'age-old conflict between Orient and Occident'. The deep 'antipathies between the Indo-European and the Semitic races' were central to his theme.[20] Such concerns were shared by most sections of the European intelligentsia. The French Socialist leader Jean Jaurès warned two years before the outbreak of the First World War that the races 'who have seemed inert' and 'sunk deep in eternal sleep ... are now awakening, demanding their rights, and flexing their muscles'.[21]

Indeed, alarmist accounts of a racial challenge to the white race tended to surface whenever a Western power experienced a setback or was confronted with a revolt in the colonial world. As we saw in the last chapter, the defeat of General Gordon and Italy's humiliation in the battle of Adowa provoked media speculation about the implications of these events for the white race. These speculations acquired momentum in the aftermath of Japan's victory over Russia in 1905. This event more than any other helped give shape to fears about the durability of a Western-dominated world order. The reaction of Alfred Zimmern – then a young lecturer at Oxford, and later an eloquent defender of the British Empire and one of the central figures in the establishment of UNESCO – to Japan's victory well illustrates the response. He informed his class that he was cancelling the subject of his lecture that morning:

> Because, I said, I feel I must speak to you about the most important historical event which has happened, or is likely to happen, in our lifetime; the victory of a non-white people over a white people.[22]

A reading of the literature of the period indicates that Zimmern's response was not particularly eccentric. In the case of this war between two powers, the usual geopolitical calculations were qualified by racial consideration. At the time this racial interpretation of the Japanese–Russian conflict characterised the commentary of the Western media. That Zimmern and others responded in this way hints at a defensiveness regarding Western civilisation.

The presentiment of racial danger that preceded the First World War was clearly demonstrated during the proceedings of the first Universal Races Congress held in London in July 1911. This unofficial congress attended by delegates from both East and West had as its starting point the assumption that the future relation between white and non-white was fraught with danger. Indeed, this was the rationale for holding the conference. Lord Weardale's introduction to the Congress proceedings assumed that his view that 'nearer and nearer we see approaching the day when vast populations of the East will assert their claim to meet on terms of equality the nations of the West' was not controversial.[23] Other delegates were no less certain that the time of racial reckoning was approaching.

The existence of a substantial body of discussion on the threat – actual or potential – to the white race some time before the First World War does not mean that this event was unimportant. The years following the war saw an upsurge of anti-colonial activity. In the United States there was a perceptible rise in black militancy. One American sociologist argued that black assertiveness had put white racists on the defensive. 'Negroes are less patient in their endurance of discriminatory treatment', he wrote.[24] Clearly, the moral authority of the West and the claims of superiority of the white man were becoming open to question. But again the reaction of many Anglo-American observers was a disproportionate one. It was a reaction that was also shaped by developments that were not directly linked to racial issues. Interwar pessimism reflected anxieties about the problem of order and the future of Western civilisation.

As far as race relations were concerned, the importance of the Great War was to *consolidate* the already existing doubts about Western superiority. This event helped to establish a climate of intellectual malaise – one where, for example, Spengler's *Decline of the West* could appear as a plausible interpretation of the world.[25] One consequence was a heightened sense of danger from without. Lack of confidence in the West disposed some towards an exaggerated assessment of the threat from the East. An important manifestation of this response was the upsurge of racist politics in the United States, which culminated in the immigration laws of the early 1920s. Another symptom was the outburst of a panic-stricken racist literature. Myrdal captures well the scope of this reaction when he noted how in the 'years around the First War' there was a 'cascade of scientific and popular writings with a strong racialistic bias'.[26] The title of Lothorp Stoddard's widely quoted *The Rising Tide of Color Against White World Supremacy* clearly highlights the focus of this genre of literature.[27] In this literature, the different dimensions of interwar pessimism were interpreted through the prism of race. The general concern about the future acquired a tangible form in the racial fears of the political classes. The overreaction to racial threats was an expression of wider doubts that the elites had about their way of life.

That the primary stimulus to the alarmist discussion of racial conflict was the crisis of confidence in the West is shown by the volatile and unstable character of these fears. The shift of impending peril from one group to another indicated that concern with the problem existed in separation and before any actual conflict. The threat was very much an imagined one. It had the character of expectations. Sometimes empirical evidence was ignored in favour of the presentiment of racial danger. So in an exchange of views in the British periodical *Sociological Review*,

Professor Caldecott took as axiomatic that the 'national and ethnic affinities of the Japanese and the Chinese ... are likely to keep them in a quasi-unity in respect to all the white races'. This view, which he referred to as a 'commonplace of world-politics', assumed a unity between well-known rivals without even a pretence of any substantiation.[28] Views such as Caldecott's continued to be held even after the outbreak of a bitter Sino–Japanese conflict. Some Western observers continued to fear that some transcendental Asian consciousness would be forged in the battle against the white man. Akira Iriye has noted that in Britain and the United States, 'the fear of a pan-Asian combination against the West was vastly exaggerated'. Iriye has interpreted this over-reaction as a reflection of the 'West's insecurity about its position in Asia'.[29]

The corollary of the presentiment of racial conflict was the belief that there was a spontaneous anti-white force at work that would result in the unity of coloured people. Consequently, every Western setback was interpreted as a direct boost to anti-white consciousness. Writing of the Turkish victory over the Greeks in 1923, Matthews observed that this outcome was 'discussed in every bazaar in India ... and in student debates from Cairo to Delhi, Peking and Tokyo'.[30] It probably was not. For such a sophisticated level of unity was more the product of Matthews' imagination than of reality. Other writers too were convinced that something was astir. According to Professor Coupland, even 'that swarming fecund Negro race, the most backward among the great races of mankind' was 'stirring now under the impact of new ideas'.[31] The scenario that emerges from this literature is that of non-white races reaching out for each other to unite against the West.

Many of the leading individuals associated with the newly established institutions devoted to the management of race relations were haunted by the prospect of an anti-white revolt by people of colour. Probably the most influential British figure in the emerging race relations lobby in the interwar era was the missionary intellectual, J.H. Oldham. Oldham continually stressed the danger of an impending racial conflict in his discussions with American and British funding bodies. In his brief to the Rockefeller Foundation, he claimed that the problems facing Africa could not be reduced to the relationship between black and white. 'Asia stands in the background', stated Oldham, before warning that 'Islam is penetrating the continent'. He added that the question of race relations in Africa could no longer be separated from that of the United States. It had become 'one element in a world problem of the relations between the white and the black races'. Oldham's close collaborator, the leading anthropologist Bronislaw Malinowski, echoed this theme. Malinowski argued that world events had conspired to unite the 'world of coloured peoples against Western influence and above all against Great Britain and the United States'.[32] The prominence given to these dangers was no doubt partly motivated by the hope of prodding donors into action, but there can be little doubt that Oldham and Malinowski were genuinely concerned about the potential for race war. The impact of this vision of anti-white unity on institutions such as the New York-based Phelps Stokes Fund and the Carnegie Corporation was a decisive one. Key documents of the period point to the possibility of racial grievances in one part of the world deepening the 'bitterness in the minds and souls of the American Negro'.[33]

The vision of racial conflict that prevailed imagined that, because of the universality of white racism, the world of colour would somehow respond in kind and unite against the common enemy. This imagination was rarely elaborated consciously. It had the air of an educated speculation, whose wisdom would be confirmed by each instance of anti-colonial protest, no matter how unconnected they were to each other. The academic literature of the period clearly expressed this vision of racial conflict. An influential article in the *American Journal of Sociology* in 1908 pointed out that one of the 'best indices to the possibilities of increased racial friction is the negro's own recognition of the universality of the white man's racial antipathy towards him'.[34] The underlying premise of this analysis was that the intensity of white racial fears would provoke an equally strong reaction from people of colour.

It was the semi-conscious awareness of the potency of white racial sentiments that informed the writing of American social scientists. As a result, racial conflict was endowed with intrinsic explosive qualities. From this perspective, the very contact between races contained the potential for conflict. Park and

Burgess, in what was probably the most influential American textbook on the subject in the 1920s, argued that 'nowhere do social contacts so readily provoke conflicts when racial differences are re-enforced, not merely by differences of culture, but of color'. The unique quality of the conflict of colour was presented as so beyond the norm that it was difficult to fathom. Park and Burgess remarked that it was 'difficult to analyse and define'. They added that 'no one has succeeded in making it wholly intelligible'.[35] Along with most academic specialists in this period, Park and Burgess warned of the dangers ahead.

Interwar accounts of racial conflict continually insisted on its unique combustible properties. Their warnings expressed the conviction that racial tensions unleashed destructive passions that were beyond the usual forms of human restraint. According to this thesis racial motives could never be susceptible to rational considerations. The dominant view was that, once out of control, they unleash destructive forces on a scale hitherto unimaginable. The American social scientist Jerome Dowd posited a model of conflict that was not susceptible to resolution. He suggested that whenever two races came together there was 'always a racial conflict', which would lead to 'political and social disorder, and sometimes to wars of extermination'. 'From Palaeolithic times to the present, the greatest wars of the world have been due to the presence of some race outside of its geographic unit', observed Dowd.[36]

It was the belief that race conflict possessed a peculiarly dangerous property that informed the thinking of Anson Phelps Stokes, the head of the Phelps Stokes Fund, one of the leading American foundations devoted to the funding of work in this area during the interwar era. Phelps Stokes feared that racial conflict could cause a 'world conflagration', and that the kind of explosion that detonated in Sarajevo in 1914 could be repeated through a 'flare up' in South Africa or Kenya.[37] Others applied this analysis to different racial trouble-spots.

According to William Crocker, the widely published Australian imperial publicist, those who warned of racial conflict in the Pacific carried a presumption of an unavoidable struggle. Crocker pointed out that 'explicit reasons for the opinion are seldom given, but behind it may generally be detected the feeling that some predestined force of historical *entwicklung* is unwinding itself.'[38] Coupland's warnings were expressly motivated by such dangers. As Crocker suggested, in line with prevailing literature, no explicit reasons were offered to support the argument. Coupland regarded the association of race relations with the shedding of blood as a matter of common sense. For Coupland a 'conflict of colour' was 'more terribly primitive in its impulses, more inexorable, more destructive than any of its predecessors, the authentic Armageddon, stamping out in blood and ruin the last hope of civilization'. To those who thought such remarks as unnecessarily alarmist Coupland retorted:

> I am not trying to make anyone's flesh creep – there is nothing, indeed, so hateful as thoughtless scare mongering on this theme – but unthinkable as such a conflict may seem, it is idle to suppose it could not happen.[39]

Coupland felt no need to go beyond this throwaway remark to justify his thesis. Nor did he attempt to explain why the 'conflict of colour' should be any more destructive than other types of struggle. The special quality of race conflict did not require empirical validation – it could be asserted because he could justifiably assume that his readers shared his assessment. When Hans Kohn concluded that 'race relations today present more dangerous features in the field of interhuman relations than any other point of conflict', he too could suppose that his audience would readily understand the point.[40]

Even those isolated observers who disagreed with the thesis of the unique character of racial conflict had little doubt about the significance of this conflict in international relations. The American sociologist Frederick Detweiler argued that the very belief in the special character of racial conflict had made it a powerful factor in international affairs:

> We have no proof that actual differences between races extend any farther than certain matters of bodily form, structure, color and dimensions. Yet in the world in which we live there is now a powerful belief that race is a hidden and decisive force lurking, tigerlike, in the essential makeup of the man above, the man below, or the man outside. Unfounded as these apprehensions may be, they are active forces in national and international politics.[41]

Detweiler's emphasis was on the perception of a 'hidden and decisive force', rather than on its material reality. But for all that it appears as no less powerful than in the more sensationalist mainstream accounts.

Sentiments about the peculiarly destructive capacity of race conflict were based on perceptions of nature-given struggles for survival. It presupposed the annihilation of one and the survival of the other side of the conflict. Snyder was one of the few interwar writers who attempted to expound this subject:

> For the last century there has been growing in the popular mind the belief that race is a hidden and all-powerful force essential and decisive for the human animal in his evolutionary process. It is held to embrace an extraordinary range, being responsible for cultural clashes between nations, for economic rivalries, for the necessary enslavement of inferior races, for revolts against authority, for migration and wars.[42]

Assumptions about this 'hidden all-powerful force' were expressed in coded metaphors. It was almost as if writers felt that it was better not to be too public about such apprehensions in case it invited a racial response. Race conflict was depicted in a zero-sum way. Success for one race was presented as the inevitable prelude to the subjection, if not the destruction, of the other.

There were undoubtedly important forces at work in Africa and Asia. The anti-imperialist temper of the times was unmistakable. As Gong has argued, it may have been the 'experience with self-confident nationalists in the peripheries' that underscored the moral inconsistencies of standards based on differences of race, colour or creed'.[43] And no doubt such experiences combined with an increasingly strident Japan helped undermine the culture of superiority. But the perceptions of racial revenge were not simply an exaggerated response to events. They expressed a tendency to interpret responses to Western domination in racial terms. In this way reactions to social or economic grievances could be understood as essentially racially motivated. The presentiment of a clash of colour discussed above developed more as a product of Western racial thinking than by the intensity of anti-white sentiment. A crisis of confidence about the status quo disposed the Anglo-American elites to develop strong racial fears.

The Sense of Race

The emergence of early twentieth-century anxieties about race was rooted in the system of ideas that influenced elite thinking at the time. The *sense of race* was deeply embedded in the worldview of the Anglo-American elites. Turn of the century social theories had a strong biological foundation on both sides of the Atlantic and the fear of change was often experienced as the problem of racial decline. A re-reading of the literature suggests a strong fascination for naturalistic explanations. Inequalities and differential social status were invariably explained as at least in part the consequence of superior/inferior individual capacities.

There were certainly no fixed boundaries between biological and social theories. Freeden convincingly argues that sociology in Britain was an 'extension of nineteenth-century biological thought'. Even a liberal thinker such as Hobhouse, who reacted against the biological explanations of social phenomena, was not entirely free from this perspective. Thus Hobhouse conceded that 'we are bound to regard biology and all the physical sciences as one of the roots of sociology'.[44] In Hobhouse's case, this outlook was subordinated to a broader sociological one. However, mainstream sociology at least until 1920 tended in a Social Darwinist direction.

Racial categorisation and conceptualisation were prevalent in nineteenth-century sociology. In the United States the first books to bear the title 'sociology' were pro-slavery tracts such as George Fitzburgh's *Sociology for the South or the Failure of Free Society*, published in 1854.[45] American sociology was strongly influenced by the Social Darwinism of Spencer, with race as one of its central categories.[46] Racial categorisation was no less important in Britain. As Jones points out, the typologies of race and class were virtually interchangeable in the discussion of social inferiority. The discussion of social hierarchy was generally presumed to have a natural causation. Those occupying the bottom rung of the social ladder were deemed to be different morally and biologically. According Gertrude Himmelfarb, the poor were represented as 'not so much a distinctive class' but as a 'distinctive "race" as Mayhew put it'.[47]

The racial component of nineteenth-century social theory was always susceptible to politicisation. The importance attached to race suggested that some groups, classes, nations and cultures were more worthy than others. According to Jones, this perspective was often linked to a vision of a 'special British destiny'.[48] Most imperial publicists believed that the unique quality of British destiny was connected to the superiority of its ruling class, rather then its people as a whole. In racial thinking the revulsion against the 'inferior' European classes and non-European races were inseparable from one another. Thus Alfred Marshall's consideration of differential birth rates targeted both the domestic poor and the 'inferior' races:

> There can be no doubt that this extension of the English race has been a benefit to the world. A check to the growth of the population would do great harm if it affected only the more intelligent races and particularly the more intelligent classes of these races. There does indeed appear some danger of this evil. For instance, if the lower classes of Englishmen multiply more rapidly than those which are morally and physically superior, not only will the population of England deteriorate, but also that part of the population of America and Australia that descends from Englishmen will be less intelligent than it otherwise would be. Again if Englishmen multiply less rapidly than the Chinese, this spiritless race will overrun portions of the earth that otherwise would have been peopled by English vigour.[49]

Marshall's celebration of English racial superiority was qualified by his revulsion at the fertile lower orders and his affirmation of English superiority was tempered by the fear of racial decline. The cause of this danger came from the lower classes. It was difficult for Marshall and his fellow thinkers to be confident of the future as long as the fitness of the English race was under question. At this time, as Malik noted, 'for many, the degeneration within European nations was a far greater problem than the racial inferiority of non-European peoples'.[50]

Those who shared Marshall's concern were not restricted to those who formally adhered to Social Darwinism or to those who later supported eugenic principles. Concern with racial fitness was integral to the Anglo-American elite culture. It was through race that the sense of superiority was affirmed. At the same time, often it was through race that the ruling class's fear of the masses was experienced. Elitist theories of society often expressed a concern with the threat from below with warnings about the uncontrolled passions of the multitudes.[51] By the turn of the century the tone of elitist literature had become increasingly defensive. Attempts to project a positive assertion of superiority often appear contrived. This literature conveyed a far greater enthusiasm in its display of contempt for the elite's inferiors. Masterman's account of the 'multitude' in London well illustrates this trend:

> And there is London: a population, a nation in itself; breeding, as it seems, a special race of men: which is also produced, and that in less intensive cultivation, in the few other larger cities – Glasgow, Manchester, Liverpool – where the conditions of coagulation offer some parallels to this monster clot of humanity.[52]

Masterman's contempt for the urban poor barely concealed his apprehension regarding the future. Concern with this 'special race of men' indicated that elite thinkers often saw the working classes through the prism of race. This thinking consisted of a mixture of fear and loathing. In virtually every Western society debates about national fitness expressed a dread of the inferior masses.[53] Racial fitness was the metaphor of the elitist vision of a healthy society. The Fabian socialist Sidney Webb feared that Britain was 'gradually falling to the Irish and the Jews' and warned of 'race deterioration, if not race suicide'.[54]

The elitist thinkers of the nineteenth century often drew self-conscious analogies between the predicament of the poor in their society and the situation in the colonies. So when William Booth, the founder of the Salvation Army, wrote of the poor as the 'Darkest England' his readers would not have missed the analogy with 'Darkest Africa'. Walter Bagehot explicitly linked the morality of the English poor with 'savages'.[55] Gustave Le Bon, whose theory of the crowds influenced the intelligentsia on both sides of the Atlantic, saw both the masses in the West and the people of East as a combined threat to the elites. According to Nye's authoritative account, the 'revolt of the "barbarian" hordes of Asia and the "crowds" of the European homeland against their rulers' constituted the core problem in Le Bon's vision of the future.[56] Ideas about the inferiority of the African or the Asian were shaped by a pre-existing vision of the European masses. The Western sense of race was as much about the preservation of order at home as it was about the threat from alien people. Concern with the racially unfit lower orders informed the discussion about the future of the white race internationally.

The convergence of racial fears around concern with the fitness of the white race influenced the deliberations of the emerging Anglo-American race relations industry. It is worth noting that the first major research project in South Africa funded by Carnegie was the study of the so-called poor white problem. Throughout the 1920s, associates of Carnegie continually referred to this problem. Poor whites were represented as a threat to the existing racial balance since their very existence undermined the assumption of superiority. According to one memorandum sent to Carnegie, there was 'little doubt that if the natives were given full economic opportunity, the more competent among them would soon outstrip the less competent whites'. Frederick Keppel, the President of Carnegie, reported back from his tour of South Africa, that the poor white problem was of the 'utmost gravity, which neither sociology, nor economics, nor public health, nor psychology and education can deal with alone'. Keppel suggested that to avoid 'possible complication, an invitation to the Corporation from some non-political body to support the study is essential'.[57]

Keppel's enthusiasm for the poor white study was motivated by his concern with the maintenance of existing racial boundaries. The Carnegie Commission's *The Poor White Problem in South Africa* gave voice to the prevailing racial fears. The premise of the report was that segregation was a 'wise policy' since the 'consequence of social intercourse with non-Europeans' led to the 'lowering of the European standard of living to one approximating to the standard of the native'. The report was relieved to find that the 'great majority of poor whites are still imbued with the conviction of their superiority over the non-Europeans' and that this 'feeling has played an important part in preventing miscegenation'. However, it feared that unless something was done to help them, this state of affairs could not endure for long and some form of racial deterioration would be the outcome. The unspoken objective of the report was the maintenance of the prevailing line of race in South Africa.

The report pointed to 'indisputable signs that social intercourse on an equal footing between white and coloured races is on the increase'. It noted that owing to the growth of class distinctions amongst Europeans, poor whites have become isolated from their employers. It reported:

> Thus the poor white in time comes to associate with non-Europeans. The result is that the respect of the coloured man for the European fellow-workers disappears, and from social intercourse to miscegenation is but a step.

The report feared the loss of white racial pride and in particular pointed to the danger that the poor white would not be able to resist the process of Africanisation. Its lack of confidence in holding the racial line was illustrated by references to the influence that African servants had on the lifestyles of poor white families. 'Uncivilised native habits often affect the white family and break down the work of the church, the school, and the home', reported the Commission.[58]

The preoccupation of the Carnegie Corporation with the so-called poor white problem in South Africa was at least partly the outcome of similar misgivings about the state of poor whites in the American South. In both situations, the integrity of the white race appeared to be put at risk by the fitness of the lower classes. Such fears would recur in the subsequent deliberations on the emerging agenda of race relations.

An inspection of the discussions of the 1920s and 1930s indicates that there was a close connection between the anxieties expressed in the elitist literature regarding the masses and the intensification of a sense of race. An insecure elite fearing for its future experienced its difficulties in terms of being overwhelmed by the sheer weight of numbers of the multitudes. The ideas with which it sought to make sense of this reality were strongly influenced by naturalistic conceptions of social hierarchy and categories of race. New problems seemed to strengthen its sense of race. But whereas in the nineteenth century the sense of race endowed elite life with a dynamic of a positive sense of superiority, by the interwar period it served only to highlight its weakness. The sense of race now expressed isolation and a mood of powerlessness. The racial fears discussed in the previous section are but one expression of this response.

In some cases, for example that of Spengler, the concerns were articulated through a call for a revitalised, aggressive Western civilisation. Spengler's hero was Cecil Rhodes, whom he called the 'first man of a new age'. For Spengler, Rhodes' phrase 'expansion is everything' was the key to the perpetuation of civilisation.[59] Some of these ideas resurfaced in Nazi racial ideology. However, this aggressive expansionist response was not typical of the intellectual climate – certainly not in Britain and the United States. More typically the sense of race expressed itself through defensive reactions that expressed the loss of faith in the Western way of life. In particular it stimulated a response that aimed to avoid, minimise or postpone race conflict. Despondent in tone, at least on an unconscious level, the warnings of conflicts to come represented a hidden agenda calling for the careful management of race relations.

The Numbers Game

Anxieties about racial fitness and decline were not just about the quality of people but also about quantity. The vitality of a race was most clearly manifested through its fertility. The corollary of the problem of racial decline was the growth of numbers of competing races. Racial fears – spoken and unspoken – were fuelled by perceptions that the white race was under pressure from more fertile others. 'The factor of numbers embraces, indeed, the very crux of the problems arising from contact between races', argued Park and Burgess. They concluded that white racial fears were a response to demographic trends. They noted that a 'primary cause of race friction is the vague, rather intangible, but wholly real, feeling of "pressure" which comes to a white man almost instinctively in the presence of a mass of people of a different race'.[60]

The view that population pressure was in some sense linked to racial tension was rarely contested in the first three decades of the twentieth century. Most accounts of racial fears touched on the issue of numbers. Raymond Buell, probably the leading American academic expert on Africa in the interwar period, stressed this factor. 'When a white community finds itself surrounded by another race of inferior civilization and standards of living, it unconsciously feels itself in danger.'[61] There is little doubt about the validity of Buell's observation. The intensification of white panics was often associated with competitive fertility.

In South Africa, the publication of census figures was usually followed by alarmist warnings about the perils facing white people. In the aftermath of the 1918 census, white politicians and newspaper commentators became agitated by the relative decline of their race. The editor of the *Rand Daily Mail* informed his readers that there was 'grave reason to fear that if present-day tendencies continue' the future 'will be decided against the whites'. He argued that the principal question was 'whether the white race is going to maintain its place at all'.[62] Six years later, when the final report on the 1921 census was published, a minor panic erupted. One commentator concluded that the 'struggle is today going against the white race'. *The Times* of London echoed this concern. It reported that 'the black man in the Union and its borders is increasing with terrific momentum, while the white population increases slowly and is subject to periodic setbacks'.[63]

At the time, many commentators observed that it was the reaction to the publication of the 1921 census report in September 1924 that led to a new Colour Bar Bill and the extension of segregation. Even a moderate figure like the leading missionary intellectual J.H. Oldham attached considerable significance to this event. He believed that there could be 'no doubt whatever about the fundamental importance of the population question in South Africa' since 'on it depends the continued existence of a white civilization in the sub-continent'.[64] Time and again, with each census, the same sentiments were repeated. Tremendous significance was attached to the relative decline of the white population. 'The inescapable lesson presented by the census is that the white race in the sub-continent is fighting a losing battle', argued one newspaper editor in response to the 1946 census.[65]

It was not only in South Africa that the issue of population became linked with racial tension. Demography itself became a medium through which racial fears were articulated. Indeed, a significant trend in demography was the development of an alarmist literature, which regarded the high rates of population in the South as a threat to the North. This Western demographic consciousness combined the problematic of racial decline with a dread of the fecund other.

Western demographic consciousness was strongly shaped by the consideration of strategic demography. The central focus of strategic demography, in the past as it is today, is the contrast between falling birth rates in the North and rising birth rates in the South. Either implicitly or explicitly, studies of global demographic trends have assumed that population has a considerable influence on power relations. Consequently, the relative increase in the demographic weight of the South was experienced as a symptom of the decreasing global influence of the West. Since population was seen to be so directly linked to power, it became an obvious subject of comparison: demographic trends in one area were compared to those of another. It is the changing, relative population sizes that have dominated demographic debates. Concern about the relative change in population sizes between North and South stemmed from the belief that differences in the rate of fertility have important implications for the distribution of power. That is why the study of *differential fertility* has been an important part of demographic research. It is widely believed that numbers are important in settling competing claims on resources.

It is clear from the calculus that can be applied to this balance of power, that any change in population ratios must have important implications for the outcome of global competition. Consequently, the relative increase of the population of the South has long been perceived as a potential source of geopolitical upheaval. A 1949 issue of the UNESCO's *International Social Science Journal*, specially devoted to the topic of 'International Tensions', pointed to differential rates of population growth as a major cause for concern:

> The differential rate of growth, through varying degrees of control over the fertility and mortality of different continents, peoples, nations and communities, has, in a word, created the present world population problems which lead in some regions to starvation and disease, tension and wars. Whether population growth has now reached the demographic danger spot of ultimate world explosion is a question which deserves to be examined.[66]

The conceptual link between differential population growth and war which was accepted at this time has continued to inform deliberations to this day.[67]

Since concern with differential fertility expresses fundamental conflicts of interests, the issues at stake are rarely expressed openly. There is a reluctance publicly to disclose fears regarding the outcome of demographic trends. The issue of racial survival, which underpins the study of differential fertility, is far too sensitive to become the subject of an entirely open debate.

The Power of Numbers

The role of population in the determination of power is far from clear. Even military experts and strategists find it hard to establish a balance between numbers and security requirements.[68] Nevertheless, in the past, the size of population was certainly an important factor. In military conflicts, the numbers of soldiers in war were frequently decisive. National power turned on population size. For example, many experts believed that the Franco–German rivalries of the nineteenth and twentieth centuries would be decided in the sphere of demography. Sections of the French elite argued that France's declining fertility was an evil that sapped the vitality of the nation. The attempt to implement strong pro-natalist policies by successive French governments reflected their fears for national survival. But France was not alone. Teitelbaum and Winter convincingly argue that, throughout Europe, the issue of national military defence was 'often expressed' in a 'demographic form'. They suggest, too, that European apprehensions of political and demographic decadence and decline were widespread between 1870 and 1945.[69]

Between the two world wars demography remained a fundamental component of international relations theory. It was acknowledged that European empires needed to confront the challenge of rising numbers of Asians. Western hegemony was often directly linked to the outcome of differential demographic patterns. A study commissioned by the Royal Institute of International Affairs, and written by Carr-Saunders, one of the world's leading demographers, was concerned with the question of how a relatively small number of people of European origin could continue to control most of the world. In America, Warren Thompson, one of the most influential demographers of the interwar period, was preoccupied with the same issue.[70]

Western demographers were conscious of an anomaly whereby a relatively small number of Europeans monopolised most of the earth's land and resources. Pointing to the colonial empires, Carr-Saunders noted that Europeans were 'spread thinly'. He feared that the differential population growth in Europe and in the East would undermine the prevailing global distribution of power. 'This relatively light occupation of these overseas estates by their new master is one of the most important facts in the present state of world population', he argued.[71] That demographic patterns would prove decisive for the survival of the European empires was a view that the expert demographers effectively left unchallenged.

Dudley Kirk spoke for American demography when he observed, in 1944, that differential population growth could alter the existing balance of power between the West and the East.[72] But the high rate of population growth in Asia was not just an American anxiety. In Britain, in 1946, a Royal Commission on Population pointed out that the decline of population in the West in relation to Asia 'might be decisive in its effects on the prestige and influence of the West'. It added: 'the question is not merely one of military strength and security: it merges into more fundamental issues of the maintenance and extension of Western views and culture'.[73]

In the literature of the time, the Pacific was often portrayed as the area where differential patterns of population growth could erupt in violent conflict. The 'empty spaces' of Australia were often contrasted with the overpopulated regions of Asia. One demographer speculated:

> if Australia's population should cease to increase appreciably in the next ten years and if the population of Japan, China and India, and South-east Asia generally, should continue to grow as they have grown in the past half-century, the lack of balance between area and natural resources on the one hand and the population numbers on the other will lead sooner or later to some effort, violent or non-violent, to change the *status quo* in the Pacific and perhaps in the Americas.[74]

That there was a conflict of interest between thinly populated

European dominions and densely inhabited regions of Asia was not in doubt. The question posed was how this conflict would be resolved in the period ahead.

Differential population growth in the context of North–South relations acquired a practical impact in the sphere of migration. It might be argued that, through migration of Southerners to Northern regions, the world's population problems could be redistributed. However, many Western commentators interpreted the migration of people from the South as a violation of an already delicate balance of power. The titles of articles on the subject evoked powerful sentiments. Terms like 'danger' and 'peril' were typical. A 1923 paper by a leading American sociologist, entitled 'The Menace of Migrating Peoples', expressed the mainstream sentiment.[75] Migration, leading to a change in the distribution of the world's population, was seen as a further symptom of Western decline. Whereas European expansion of the previous era was seen as a symptom of dynamism and vitality, the falling rate of fertility of Western societies was represented as a testimony to impotence and decline.

The question of migration brought and continues to bring Northern fears about Southern population growth to the surface. Most Western commentators have demanded controls on Southern migration. Such controls on the movement of people were justified because immigrants are culturally or racially different from people of European origin. Behind the debate about numbers lurk other motifs. In the course of discussing global migration, demographers and other specialists reveal that their concern is not population as such but the growth of certain types of population! All the literature suggests that problems are seen not as quantitative, but as *qualitative*. Contributions on the quality of population stress intelligence, health and other biological characteristics. Discussions of 'Australia's Population Problem' self-consciously emphasised that 'coloured' migration was not the answer to this country's need for a larger population.[76] Thus, immigration controls are advocated in order to keep out the wrong kind of people.

Carr-Saunders himself wanted restricted migration because certain people could not easily be assimilated by a host society.

The exclusion of non-Europeans from European countries overseas is probably wise because the very different traditions of non-Europeans possibly expressing genetic temperamental differences, are likely to be very persistent owing to physical differentiation which makes it unlikely that the process of assimilation can be satisfactorily accomplished.[77]

Other demographers expressed similar reservations on the quality of the population of Africa and Asia.

The policies of immigration controls had respectable intellectual backing in the interwar period. Virtually no one questioned the exclusion of Asians from the white countries of the Pacific. Books on international affairs routinely took such exclusions as a prudent course of action.[78] In America highly influential academics argued the case for immigration controls in public forums. The leading American sociologist, Edward A. Ross, warned against what he called 'race suicide' – an open door policy towards immigration. Such a policy would mean that the United States 'would automatically become the home of a great variety of people of every color, of different languages, religion, and creeds and with the most discordant moral and economic ideals'. He warned that you 'would have coolies in breech-cloth as you find in the Far East, jostling the descendants of the Puritans'. Ross suggested that the 'brighter races' would be overwhelmed by the 'stupider races' whose 'animal-like multiplication' would lead to a fundamental shift in the balance of population of the United States.[79]

It is important to recall that Ross was situated in the mainstream of American sociology. Articles in the *American Journal of Sociology* in the 1920s and 1930s demonstrated a widespread concern with population and migration issues. The prominent specialist on the subject was Corrado Gini. His views on the relation between race and international relations help elaborate the consensus behind immigration controls.

Meanwhile the white races find themselves in some parts of the world closely pressed by some of those populations that should have disappeared in the face of their invasion. Even leaving aside the advance of the yellow races, which are very hard to keep from pouring over the European settlements of Indonesia and Oceania, it is the Bantus that in South Africa endanger the supremacy of the whites; it is the Mexican population in America that is gradually creeping in greater measure into the United States.

And:

> The world will probably be the field of a struggle between the young white and yellow races (if not also black, Malayan, and Indian half-breeds) which will in the future fight for supremacy. In fact, we may say that we have already started the game.[80]

Gini, one of the most prominent demographer of the interwar era, exercised considerable influence in the United States through his lectures and writings.

Silent Alarm

Studies of differential fertility, which are fundamentally about perceptions of power, and which also touch upon issues of race and culture, were often guarded in the presentation of their agenda. This point was clearly grasped by the renowned Swedish social scientist Gunnar Myrdal. In a lecture at Harvard University in 1938, he reminded his audience that in the United States, there were 'many elements' which helped to 'complicate, confuse, and emotionally disturb a general discussion of population'. He added, 'one such element is, naturally, the racial and cultural cleavages within this composite nation'.[81] Myrdal was aware of the sensitive dimension of this discourse. Views about population in the United States directly touched on racial concerns and were therefore presented in a hesitant and circumspect way.

One of the recurrent themes of American demography was the differential rate of growth of its black and white populations. Although such monographs were presented in a neutral and technical form, they could not but reveal the underlying concern with the prevailing racial balance. The literature clearly associated power and domestic influence with numerical weight. A variety of factors influencing the rate of population growth were assessed from the standpoint of the outcome of a biological competition. Thus a paper entitled 'Fertility of the Negro' observed that diseases which reduce the rate of fertility were 'definitely to the disadvantage of the coloured population'.[82] For Dudley Kirk, the author of this study, low levels of fertility implied disadvantage, not because of the health issues but because of the direct link between numbers and power. 'The Negro's importance in American civilization has been closely related to the size and distribution of the Negro population', he argued.[83] What this further implied was that a rise in the 'importance' of one section of the population could only take place at the expense of another.

Those concerned with the maintenance of white superiority were particularly sensitive to demographic trends. But even more detached observers believed that differential rates of fertility had important domestic consequences. Contributions in prestigious publications such as *Social Forces* and *The American Journal of Sociology* often presented the differential rate of fertility as an expression of an 'interracial struggle'. So a discussion on 'The Increasing Growth-rate of the Negro Population' concluded that because of this trend 'the Negro problem, instead of decreasing in relative importance, may become serious in the years to come'.[84] There was no need to explain what this 'problem' was.

The fear that a changing racial balance would create major domestic and international problems motivated some to carry out research in the sphere of demography. Frederick Osborn, in his capacity as adviser to the Carnegie Foundation on demographic research, supported an application for the funding of a project on population problems in the British Empire. He reminded the President of the Foundation: 'if Mr Carnegie was interested in the British Dominions it was presumably because he believed in the value of the English people who inhabit them, and he therefore would have been concerned at their approaching decline in numbers'.[85] Another Carnegie adviser, Newton D. Baker, proposed a major study, which would culminate with the publication of Myrdal's *An American Dilemma: The Negro Problem and Modern Democracy* (1944), because of the 'extraordinary circumstances that led to our having so large a Negro population'.[86] Differential fertility clearly influenced the Carnegie research agenda on both demography and race relations. Population control was routinely advocated for a problem that was perceived at once to be demographic and racial.

Clearly, regardless of individual motives, advocates of population control in the United States were aware that their proposals had important consequences for the domestic racial balance.

Gunnar Myrdal's magisterial study of American race relations, *The American Dilemma*, forcefully argued that population policies were linked to the relation between black and white. His research suggested that both blacks and whites were keen to increase their relative share of the population. Myrdal's writing on this subject is particularly valuable because it openly confronted uncomfortable views, which were rarely expressed in public.

Myrdal was insistent that the *'overwhelming majority of white Americans desire that there be as few Negroes as possible in America'*. He added that the corollary of this attitude was that an 'increase of the proportion of Negroes is commonly looked upon as undesirable'. Myrdal also observed that 'almost every Negro' wanted the black population to be 'as large as possible'.[87] He emphasised that these opinions were 'seldom expressed openly', but as 'general valuations' they were 'nearly always present'. According to Myrdal, it was this paradox of public silence and private preoccupation that helped explain the strength of the birth control movement in America. Pointing to the American South, where birth control was a taboo subject, Myrdal argued that it was the 'presence of the Negroes' which explained the lack of opposition to it in practice.[88] In the South racial concerns overrode moral principles about regulating fertility. The association of numbers with the so-called Negro Problem influenced demographic consciousness well into the 1950s, if not later. At a Rockefeller Foundation-sponsored conference on Population Problems in June 1952, one of the leading participants reported to a delighted audience that in many urban areas the reproductive role of the Afro-American was far below replacement level. He added that if this trend continued, 'the Negro problem is solved in a way that I am not sure the problem should be solved in'.[89]

The salience of race for demographic discourse was no less important in the international domain. In international relations before the war, shifts in the balance of population were often interpreted through a racial vocabulary. At the level of global relations, demographic patterns suggested that Western domination faced major long-term obstacles. Many writers argued that a racial confrontation could only be avoided if the West redistributed some of its resources to benefit the East.[90] Myrdal himself warned that time was running out. Pointing to the likely hegemony of the United States in the coming post-Second World War international order, he wrote: 'white peoples will have to adjust to shrinkage while the colored are bound to expand in numbers'. For 'perhaps several decades' whites would 'still hold the lead', and America would be the 'most powerful white nation'; but in the end there would be change.[91] After the Second World War, Myrdal's call for some sort of adjustment to demographic realities was widely accepted. For others, however, population control appeared as a viable policy for minimising the disruptive effects of international demographic trends. It was in this context that the benefits of population policies for the non-industrial world were first discussed.

In the interwar period racial fears were articulated through the consciousness of demography. Fears about racial decline were often expressed in the technical jargon of demography. Falling birth rates expressed a kind of 'race suicide'. They also implied a loss of power. And high rates of fertility in Africa and Asia were interpreted as a potential threat to the existing world order. According to the demographer Dudley Kirk, there was a stark choice facing people of European descent. Either 'we must be prepared to meet the emerging nations halfway' or 'we must be prepared to maintain white supremacy by force of arms'.[92] Typically, Kirk feared a racial confrontation because of its potential for destroying Western civilisation.

Early warnings of impending racial conflicts expressed a highly defensive consciousness about the future of Western civilisation. It was this consciousness that shaped the discourse of race and demgraphy during the interwar era. This presentiment of conflicts to come indicated that racial thinking had ceased to boost the confidence of Western elites. The existing order seemed precariously unstable and the manifestation of racial consciousness was now seen as a direct challenge to the international status quo.

3   The New Racial Pragmatism

The race agenda that emerged in the interwar period was strongly influenced by apprehensions concerning differential fertility, racial deterioration and race war. These anxieties were based on the premise that any impending conflicts would be at the expense of the prevailing balance of power. From the perspective of the mainstream Anglo-American thinking, racial matters were potentially destabilising and public displays of racism were to be avoided. Those concerned invariably came to the conclusion that public displays of white racial superiority had become dangerous since they invited an explosion of racial resentment. Racial politics in all its manifestations was now deemed to be not only provocative but also a threat to world order. This new racial pragmatism did not fundamentally question the assumption of superiority as such. Indeed it was even critical of those who promoted the radical idea of race equality. Such egalitarianism was characterised as extreme and inflammatory to those who feared any change in race relations. This was an approach that self-consciously ignored the fundamental question of racial oppression and focused its concern on the etiquette of race relations.

The new racial pragmatism characteristically counselled discretion over the open discussion of racial matters. Its effective censorship of widely held apprehensions about race was motivated by the intuition that publicity only invited a response that made matters worse. In other words, the outcome of racial conflict would be prejudicial to Western interests and any assertion by non-white people would have direct and negative implications for the existing balance of power. Most observers therefore came to the conclusion that overt and aggressive white racism would invite a clash of colour, the consequences of which could only be destructive.

This new racial pragmatism bridged the ideological divide between conservatives and liberals: virtually all race relations experts were critical of open manifestations of supremacism. They were also dismissive of the 1920s genre of alarmist racist literature, which speculated about impending race wars. The new racial pragmatism was particularly hostile to racially offensive behaviour and regarded it as discourteous and potentially destabilising. The more liberal, especially missionary, manifestation of racial pragmatism was also critical of discriminatory laws and measures implemented to exclude coloured immigrants from different parts of the world. It regarded such measures as provocative and likely to intensify bitterness against white domination. The missionary lobby advocated an informal, pragmatic arrangement for the regulation of racial affairs.

The elimination of displays of racial arrogance was consistently promoted by the racial pragmatists. Indeed this was the hallmark of what was considered to be enlightened opinion in the interwar period. Racial arrogance was accused of inciting many of the revolts against white domination. Sir Harry Johnston, a leading British colonial administrator, believed that the good work of the Empire was continually undermined by thoughtless displays of white arrogance. Johnston was a staunch believer in white racial superiority, but believed that it should not be publicly displayed. He warned of the dangers of racial insults in the following terms:

> The refusal of your hand in greeting to the Coloured man in West Africa has become an unpardonable insult unless you and he agree that the practice of grasping hands in the tropic should be given up as unsanitary and unnecessary. The magnificent results of the White man's engineering in Egypt are overcast by the bad manners of the English officer, sometimes of the English soldier, often of the British tourist towards the Egyptian. That must cease. So must, similar rudeness and racial arrogance in India.[1]

This was an explicit call for European behaviour towards individuals from the subject races to change. Yet Johnston's request for good manners expressed a degree of naiveté regarding racial affairs: individual decency and good behaviour were unlikely to make a significant impact on the realities of racial domination.

The dominant theme of the new racial pragmatism was the necessity for Western people to be sensitive to the grievances of non-white people. Even those who held reasonably strong racist assumptions nevertheless warned against being too public or aggressive in manifesting their supposed superiority. It was argued that too overt a display of superiority only helped to intensify conflict and accelerate the coming of a racial war. This was the argument that Valentine Chirol, the Asian correspondent of *The Times*, pressed on his audience in Chicago in 1924. The subject of his lecture was the 'Revolt of the Orient' against the 'claim of Occidental civilization to inherent and indefensible superiority over the civilizations of the Orient'. This development, Chirol claimed, threatened 'to raise a still more dangerous issue of racial conflict between the white man and the colored peoples who constitute the vast majority of mankind'. Chirol himself had no doubts about the superiority of the West: 'If one seeks to define what the Orient chiefly lacks, and has always lacked, it is the practice of freedom with the sense of responsibility, or, in one word, character.' However, Chirol was concerned that an aggressive display of this superiority had created a situation where the 'clash of color' threatened to explode into a revolt against the West.

Chirol blamed some of this problem on the arrival of a more vulgar type of European in the Orient. These new arrivals are 'more prone than those of better breeding and education to boast of their racial superiority and to impress their sense of it somewhat roughly upon the Indians or other Orientals with whom they rub shoulders'. Chirol's solution was diplomacy and tact. His advice was to live up to the ideals of Christianity.

> the more firmly we ourselves believe in the superiority of a civilization which, so far, it has been the privilege of the white man to build up in his occidental homelands, the more we are bound by its principles and the principles of the common Christianity which are its one sure foundation to do all in our power to temper the bitterness of a racial discord which, if it spreads and deepens, may threaten the future of the whole human race.[2]

Chirol – one of the most energetic exponents of Orientalism – was widely quoted on both sides of the Atlantic.[3] His intervention was situated within the conservative mainstream consensus of the Anglo-American elite. This consensus combined a private affirmation of racial superiority with a pragmatic strategy towards the problem of conflict. The scenario which this pragmatism sought to avoid was an alliance of the multitudes of Africa and Asia against the West. Tact, diplomacy, even accommodation were projected as solutions to the problem.

This pragmatic approach had it origins in the period around the turn of the century. The American philosopher Josiah Royce, for example, proposed in 1908 that expressions of racial superiority should not be taken to an extreme. He commended the supposed restraint of English officials who did not advertise that they were 'actually superior'.

> The trouble comes when you tell the other man, too stridently, that you are his superior. Be my superior, quietly, simply showing your superiority in your deeds, and very likely I shall love you for the very fact of your superiority. For we all love our leaders. But tell me I am your inferior, and then perhaps I may grow boyish and may throw stones. Well, it is so with races. Grant then that yours is the superior race. Then you can afford to say little about the subject in your public dealings with the backward race. Superiority is best shown by good deed and by few boasts.[4]

This advice would become the standard approach of Anglo-American writers on race in the interwar period, with the exception of the alarmist racist literature of supremacist writers.[5]

The need to change language and behaviour towards Africans and Asians is a theme that provides a sense of unity to the different strands of interwar literature on race. George Young, an American academic expert on race contact, offered a liberal variation of Chirol's argument. Young was strongly critical of the 'sanctimonious Anglo-Saxon attitude' during Britain's new imperialism phase. He argued that its 'assumption of a moral superiority and mental superiority' had 'already raised Asia in revolt' and would 'some day raise Africa'. The alternative that Young preferred was the paternalism of British indirect rule policies in Nigeria and Sudan, which, he argued, had a 'vitality and a virtue'.[6] But Young's preference for Lugard over Kipling suggested that his concern was conflict resolution rather then the affirmation of racial equality.

Anglo-American diplomacy also adopted a pragmatic approach towards race relations. The informal guideline adopted in London and Washington was to avoid public discussion on this issue and, whenever possible, to change the subject. A Foreign Office memorandum entitled 'Racial Discrimination and Immigration' as background to the 1921 Washington Conference provides a clear illustration of the diplomatic approach. According to its author, Ashton-Gwatkin, 'Great Britain, the Dominions and the United States are all equally interested in avoiding a discussion of this subject.' The reason for this reluctance was that the Western protagonist firmly believed in the exclusion of Oriental immigrants but felt uncomfortable about explicitly defending this policy.

One reason why the Foreign Office was keen to avoid discussion was because it feared that if it expressed its real views, the Japanese would be insulted. As the author of the memorandum explained:

> We must realise too, that, although in polite talk with the Japanese it is customary to say that the reasons for exclusion of Japanese are purely economic, yet as a matter of fact, there is a racial and a political antagonism to the Japanese in the countries concerned, which is stronger even than the economic antagonism. It is for racial reasons that the Japanese are not wanted.

The memorandum took as self-evident the autonomy of the racial dynamic. It observed that in America the 'racial antagonism to the Japanese appears to be a corollary to the negro question'. This reaction was a 'manifestation of the American's instinctive hatred of "colour" in any shade'.[7] The implication was that in so far as such instinctive hatreds were inevitable, the best course of action was to keep quiet.

Many liberals and religious leaders rejected the Foreign Office's cautious approach, and adopted a more reformist approach. Like their conservative counterparts, liberal writers counselled restraint, but in their literature there is an underlying sentiment that something positive should be done to demonstrate the good faith of the West. Mathews' *The Clash of Colour*, published in 1926, warned of the loss of the West's moral authority and of the need to accommodate the grievances of Africa and Asia. It was far more pessimistic about the claims of the West than someone like Chirol and expressed a far greater sense of urgency for ameliorative action.[8]

J.H. Oldham's *Christianity and the Race Problem*, published in 1924, provided a coherent statement from an enlightened missionary point of view. His objective was to counter the damaging consequences of racist politics. Oldham was motivated in this enterprise by the belief that racist politics was bound to provoke a counter-reaction from those who are oppressed. Oldham argued that 'nothing can be more certain' than that racist 'doctrines will evoke intense bitterness and hostility in the minds of other races'. He added:

> A claim to permanent domination exclusively on the ground of race is bound to be resisted by other peoples with all their force. A thoroughgoing racialism cannot be advocated on one side without provoking an equally intense racial consciousness on the other.[9]

Oldham's intervention was inspired by his perception of growing 'racial consciousness' in Africa and Asia. He feared that the spread of racism would unleash a cycle of reaction and counter-reaction leading to the 'self-destruction' of humanity. From this perspective, the conclusion drawn was that the promotion of racist theory rather than supporting, undermined the West. It was the same perspective that motivated Coupland ten years later to denounce racial theorists: 'It might well happen if the peoples of the West allowed themselves to be convinced by dogmatic biologists that the ultimate relations between white and coloured races can only be a fight to the death for the survival of the fittest.'[10] Coupland, like Oldham, was primarily concerned with the destabilising consequences of racist politics. They both regarded the practice of racism as a provocation which would eventually explode in the face of its practitioners. Put simply, their argument was that racism helped encourage the emergence of a colour consciousness which in turn served to undermine white domination. By summoning such a powerful anti-white consciousness, racists were sowing the seeds of the destruction of Western civilisation. This argument would gain increasing force in the succeeding decades.

Probably the most active campaigners for a pragmatic approach to race relations in Britain and the United States were the missionaries. Many missionaries were acutely sensitive to the resentment generated by racist practices. By the interwar period there were many examples of African and Asian converts revolting against European authority. Indeed, the growth of separatist churches emerged as the one key area of concern in the Anglo-American missionary literature on Africa. In Asia, many missionaries were worried that their work was compromised by association with Western domination. Missionary periodicals interpreted the racial resentment of colonial people as damaging to their enterprise. The *International Review of Missions* cited comments allegedly made by Africans to the effect that 'Christianity is the White Man's religion and must be uprooted', and concluded that such views 'deserve to be deeply pondered in relation to the whole situation in the world today'.[11] This point was echoed by several speakers at the 1928 Jerusalem conference of the IMC. One authoritative report observed that a strong Christian message was needed so that in the face of nationalist feeling the Christian claim for Christ could not so easily be made to appear as a mere piece of white imperialism masquerading in spiritual dress.[12]

American missionaries sought to establish regular forums for discussing and resolving racial conflict in the Pacific. They feared the effects of anti-Oriental immigration agitation in the United States, Canada and Australia in the years following the First World War. The public manifestation of such intense xenophobia, culminating in the anti-Oriental immigration practices of the United States in the early 1920s, had become an impediment to missionary work. Missionaries, particularly those based in China, sought to dissociate their work from the anti-Oriental sentiments that prevailed in the United States at the time.

The growth of radical anti-imperialist forces in China, Indonesia and India helped create a climate where Asian aspirations could not be ignored. In this situation the pursuit of racial arrogance could only polarise the situation and isolate the missionary movement. A 'Memorandum on Missions', written by Henry Hodgkin, Secretary of the National Christian Council of China in 1927, exemplified the new responsiveness of his movement to racial grievances. Hodgkin's memorandum dwelt on this new situation:

In recent years the sensitiveness of the non-Christian peoples in their contacts with Western nations undoubtedly increased, and this has led to a feeling among the more educated and sensitive peoples of the East

that the missionary movement in essence was an expression of racial
superiority. That missionaries have in a number of cases fallen into
this false and unchristian attitude can hardly be denied.

Hodgkin was intensely conscious of the charge that Christianity
was racist. This charge he rejected, though he conceded that until
recently missionaries adhered to the assumption of Western
superiority because it gave them prestige.

Hodgkin advocated the distancing of Christianity from the
outlook of Western civilisation on essentially pragmatic grounds.
He argued that assumptions of superiority no longer offered the
missionary any advantage. Such assumptions had lent prestige
until 'they began to be challenged and educated men from the east
began to doubt the value of many aspects of western civilization as
it was revealed through closer acquaintanceship, especially during
the Great War'. He added: 'it may be said that the missionary
movement no longer seeks to claim the whole of Western
civilization as an evidence of the value of the Christian faith and
that what was an asset has in certain respects become a liability'.[13]
It was crucial for this reasoning that doubts about the values of
Western civilisation should not be allowed to reflect on Christianity. The separation of Christianity from its explicit Western form
sought to deracialise it.

Hodgkin's memorandum was written for the Institute of Pacific
Relations. This institute was established on the initiative of a
group of Americans close to missionary circles who were concerned about the possibility of racial conflict in the Pacific. At the
1919 meeting of The Young Man's Christian Association (YMCA)
a proposal was floated for the calling of a Pan Pacific YMCA
Conference. This proposal won the backing of leading Ivy League
academics and, at a meeting of the Yale Club in February 1925,
the institute was established and officers were elected.[14] The main
initiative of the Institute was to bring together at its conferences
representatives from the different countries of the Pacific, and the
principal theme of its deliberations during the 1920s was race
relations. As one early account of the history of the Institute of
Pacific Relations recorded, its 'prime objective was to prevent a
possible Oriental–Occidental war arising in the future out of an
increasing bitterness over racial, religious, economic and political

differences'.[15] Speakers included Asian and Western representatives. At such gatherings, Western speakers tended to explain away racist practices apologetically, while those from Asia demanded action not words. The IPR, along with the various church and missionary societies, was in the forefront of promoting research into race relations. Many missionary intellectuals recognised that racial grievances against white domination undermined their quest for converts. As one American missionary residing in Hawaii stated, 'we are becoming aware of the increasing race consciousness of various people with whom we work, and it will doubtless be of great importance to us all to study the situation and analyse it without prejudice and with the highest type of scientific method of which we are capable'.[16]

Hodgkin's conviction that a previously prized asset had become a liability reflected a wider shift in the attitude of Anglo-American opinion-makers. However, for missionaries, the urgency of ridding themselves of this liability was a particularly urgent one. That is why missionaries came to play such a prominent role in the elaboration of the new racial pragmatism.

American Christian organisations were behind most of the early initiatives designed to establish racial harmony. The Commission of Inter-Racial Co-operation, founded in 1919 in Atlanta, Georgia, and the American Interracial Peace Council set up in 1926 in Philadelphia, both had a strong church input. Their objective was to promote racial co-operation. Co-operation was interpreted pragmatically and often meant restraining rather than challenging racist assumptions. Nevertheless, these organisations were often in the forefront of questioning racial discrimination. For example, the Conference of the International Missionary Council in Jerusalem declared in 1928 that 'any discrimination against human beings on the ground of race or colour, any selfish exploitation and any oppression of man by man is a denial of the teaching of Jesus'.[17] Resolutions such as this were ahead of the times and certainly ahead of practice. They represented a sensitiveness to a problem that could not be resolved by words alone.

Missionary and church bodies were soon joined by other non-official institutions in their quest for racial harmony. In America the Carnegie Foundation was actively involved in race-related projects. Academics and experts also joined in and soon the Institute of Pacific Relations was transformed into what today would be called a think-tank. The outcome of these initiatives was that the terms in which race relations were discussed changed. While diplomats sought to avoid public discussion on race-related issues, these unofficial bodies prompted exchanges on this subject. However, in reality these two approaches were not in conflict: both avoided a consideration of the substance of the issue. The framework of discussion favoured by liberal and Christian bodies was one where only the superficial aspects of the problem were touched on. The emphasis was on tact and diplomatic behaviour – the buzz word of the times was 'racial co-operation' – rather than a direct confrontation with racism. So, for example, Western speakers at the conferences of the Institute of Pacific Affairs tried to avoid confronting the practical question of immigration by suggesting that the exclusion of Orientals was motivated by concerns other than racial.

All sections of the Anglo-American elites could agree that race relations now constituted a major problem. Some preferred not to give any public expression to their apprehensions; others adopted a more activist approach and became public advocates of racial co-operation. Whatever the specific response, the dominant concern was to prevent an explosion of racial grievances in Africa and Asia, which was now expected. Western racism was perceived as a dangerous and destabilising force, which would galvanise non-white people into action. This was the point of departure of the emerging agenda on race relations. The question which preoccupied this agenda the most was: how to prevent the development of racial consciousness of people of colour. 'The increasing self-consciousness of those who regard themselves as oppressed is developing a unity of appeal and demand which civilization and Christianity cannot disregard', concluded a memorandum by the Phelps-Stokes Fund in April 1927.[18] Prevention was the objective of the newly established race relations institutions in Britain and the United States.

At a Distance

The racial pragmatism of the interwar period self-consciously avoided tackling the questions of discrimination and equality. At the time, most thinkers believed that whenever different races came into contact with one another, some form of conflict was inevitable. From this assumption they often concluded that the problem was as much racial contact as its conflictual outcome. To realise their aim of avoiding conflict, racial pragmatists sought to minimise racial contact. Many of the interwar contributors were dubious about the consequences of European expansion and were often critical of the process of westernisation itself. They believed that westernisation unsettled colonial people and, by bringing white and coloured races into close proximity, threatened to unleash conflict. Such an approach informed the work of the new institutions devoted to the management of race relations. The Phelps-Stokes Fund took the view that 'history clearly proves the danger of too complete control of colored people by white people'. It pointed to the 'increasing self-consciousness of those who regard themselves as oppressed' and predicted a 'disaster' unless more enlightened policies were adopted.[19] The aim of these more 'indirect' policies was to avoid disrupting colonial societies so that racial resentment would be suppressed.

The belief that westernisation should be reined in influenced sections of the British elite for some time. Robinson and Gallagher's study of the Victorian 'official mind' indicated that there was a discernible hesitation about the 'possibility of westernising the Oriental'. Westernisation and the 'disturbing effect of one culture upon another' were seen as destructive influences, which could unleash 'racial fanaticism' and revolt.[20] This argument was systematically pursued by the French crowd psychologist, Gustave Le Bon. Le Bon's invective was directed at those who sought to educate colonial subjects. He condemned the policy of educating the colonial elites and concluded that the British in India 'were planting the seeds of revolt'. Le Bon remarked that such education had destroyed India's racial heritage and that this would provoke an intense reaction to white rule.[21] These early criticisms anticipated the more developed arguments of twentieth-century racial pragmatists.

Many missionary thinkers involved in the field of race relations perceived westernisation and the changes it brought as essentially destructive. Their views about educated or westernised colonial people often echoed those of Le Bon. They were seen as the bearers of anti-white racial grievances. Indeed by the end of the 1930s missionary societies in Africa were seriously concerned about the hostility to their enterprise which was 'developing among educated non-Europeans of all races'.[22]

One of the most respected critics of westernisation was the anthropologist Bronislaw Malinowski. His 'Memorandum on Colonial Research', written in December 1927, had as its premise the belief that the 'conflict of race and culture' was 'rapidly becoming the burning problem of world politics'. Malinowski was concerned about the instability that the capitalist market was creating in the colonial world. He was especially apprehensive about the effects of racial contact between Europeans and people of colour. Such contact, he believed, tended to erode the existing racial line and uprooted individuals, who were particularly resentful of white rule. According to Malinowski, westernised natives were the biggest problem of all since their hostility was peculiarly bitter:

> When big masses of white and coloured are in contact, bastardisation
> must occur, and if, as is inevitable you draw the line of colour at the
> top end, you immediately introduce a pariah caste, discontented,
> rebellious and essentially subversive. The more white and civilised the
> U.S.A. Negroes become, the more irksome and unjust will they feel
> their present treatment by whites.

Malinowski believed that it was the cultural penetration of westernisation which stimulated anti-western revolts. It raised and then thwarted the aspirations of those it subjected. This process led inexorably to conflict. 'Is the whole rather virulent question of independence of India at present not largely due to a too sudden westernisation of the Hindu, and to his "detribalisation"?', he asked.[23]

In the 1920s and 1930s, Malinowski became one of the most influential advocates of indirect rule. He had direct access to many of the leading race relations institutions and to organisations such as the Rockefeller Foundation. He was a close collaborator of Oldham and his views were regularly solicited by the British Colonial Office. His analysis directly influenced the work of organisations such as the IAI and the IMC. All these organisations were committed to indirect colonial domination since they

believed that rapid change would accelerate conflict. They postu-
lated that it was better to preserve natives in their natural state
and avoid having to deal with the racial grievances of educated
colonials. Lord Lugard, the man most prominently associated
with the British policy of indirect rule, also collaborated with
Malinowski. Lugard advocated the slowing down of economic
development to allow the preservation of indigenous institutions.
He took the view that conflict-avoidance rested on the regulation
of racial contact. Malinowski, Oldham and Lugard offered an
analysis and a policy that appealed to racial pragmatism on both
sides of the Atlantic. Indirect rule, which relied on traditional
leaders and institutions, was invariably described as 'progressive'
by missionary thinkers. The emphasis on conserving tradition
also found a sympathetic hearing from the American foundations.

The racial attitude of proponents of indirect rule accorded
people of colour respect as long as they remained in their natural
state. Those who were uprooted, or who were educated, were
treated with contempt and suspicion. James Bertram, the Secretary, and Frederick Kepple, President of the Carnegie Corporation
illustrate this standpoint. In 1927 they visited Africa, and during
their visit to the Transkei, Bertram wrote in his diary: 'we were all
impressed with the beauty of the scenery, the stretches of
greenfield, the enclosed fields for cultivation and the neat huts of
the people'. In the middle of this idyllic setting, 'Kepple cried out
loud: "why can't we keep them like this"?'[24] Kepple's aside is a
testimony to the desire to turn back the clock on the whole
process of Western expansion. However, since the situation had
gone too far, the preferred policy was to minimise the effects of
this process.

One way that the new racial pragmatism sought to curb conflict
was through its advocacy of separate racial development. Most
proponents of racial pragmatism advocated some form of segregation – either formal or informal – although this policy was not
justified on the grounds that one race was superior to another.
There were usually two important arguments advanced in favour
of separate racial development. First, it was argued that this
approach allowed all races to develop according to their own needs
and in line with their potential. Secondly, it was suggested that
racial separation had the effect of avoiding direct competition and

thereby reduced conflict. These arguments were routinely aired to justify immigration control in White Australia and segregation in the American South. Critics of discrimination often admitted that at least on the social level some form of distance had to be kept, and even the more enlightened Christian lobby accepted the need for social distance. The IMC's sub-committee on The Church and Race Relations avoided taking a stand on segregation in education. It also sought to avoid taking a stand on inter-racial marriage by arguing that although the church could not forbid it, such unions were unlikely to work and therefore should be discouraged.[25]

The emphasis on distance indicated that this was a standpoint which sought to hold a racial line. It was prepared to renegotiate where the line would be held, but not eliminate it altogether. The main premise of its policies was the salience of racial difference and it self-consciously distanced itself from the demand for equality. Instead it proposed a change in racial etiquette and ignored the more fundamental question of power.

Advocacy of Difference

The new racial pragmatism advocated the view that all races were entitled to equality of opportunity, and it sought to reconcile this principle with what it considered to be the reality of racial difference. A coherent exposition of this synthesis was provided by Lord Lugard, who offered the 'true conception of the interrelation of Colour' in the following proposition:

> complete uniformity of ideals, absolute equality in the paths of knowledge and culture, equal opportunity for those who strive, equal admiration for those who achieve; in matters social and racial a separate path each pursuing his own inherited traditions, preserving his own race purity and race pride; equality in things spiritual; agreed divergence in the physical and material.[26]

Lugard's synthesis of separate development with equality of opportunity was cited by James Bertram as the perspective which should guide his organisation's work in Africa.[27] It was an approach that all main players in the interwar race relations industry considered to be enlightened and progressive. In academic circles, the growing influence of cultural relativism ensured that notions of difference and of separate development would gain a sympathetic hearing. The term equality of opportunity can be interpreted in a variety of ways. It certainly did not mean the recognition of equality of people, since equality of opportunity recognised that individuals would use such opportunities differentially. The notion of equality of opportunity coexisted with individuals who were seen to have different and unequal capacities. That is why many supporters of racial segregation could live with the principle of equality of opportunity. They argued that separate development gave everyone the opportunity to advance, but in accordance with their own tradition. For this reason, although presented as a positive promotion of racial difference, the Lugardian synthesis should be read as a criticism of egalitarianism.

Certainly in the case of South Africa, Lugardian arguments were deployed in the 1930s in the form of a liberal segregationist policy. Alfred Hoernle's Phelps-Stokes lectures of 1939 combined the call for respecting different cultures with the policy of racial segregation.[28] In many cases the celebration of African 'race pride' and 'race difference' was also deployed to attack the policy of assimilation. Such views characterised the approach of the influential IAI. One associate of the IAI wrote at length about the need to improve the life of Africans economically as well as to promote their pride of race. These solutions were presented as a positive contribution to separate development.[29]

One of the clearest and most persuasive exponents of the Lugardian synthesis was the anthropologist Bronislaw Malinowski. Malinowski explicitly advocated this approach as an anti-doctrinaire standpoint. The new racial pragmatism presented itself as an alternative to racial supremacist philosophy. Malinowski was as scathing of Nordic supremacist theories as he was of ideas of race equality. Writing of these 'two hostile camps', Malinowski stated:

> One of them declares that race is everything and that there is an unquestionable supremacy of one race, the Nordic, to whom the dominion of the world belongs. The other view is in direct opposition to this: race matters nothing; everything is due to environment, and

we can make all people equal by giving them equivalent education and equal opportunities. Both doctrines are based on mere assumptions, and as all extreme views; they are untenable.[30]

This 'middle of the road' approach emphasised that races were different and all worthy of respect. It characterised racial pride as praiseworthy and accepted equal opportunities for individuals, but rejected social equality. So although formally it appeared to be an even-handed denunciation of the principle of supremacy and of equality, Malinowski's critique was principally oriented against the latter.

Malinowksi's relativist epistemology also led him to oppose the 'evil implication' of race mixing. 'Why not frankly state that the only sound policy is that of racial preserves: the policy, that is of indirect rule?' he asked.[31] In his article 'A Plea for an Effective Colour Bar', Malinowski insisted that the colour bar was a 'necessity' and justified his position on the grounds that races were naturally prejudiced against each other and unless they were segregated, conflict would ensue. 'I believe', he noted, that 'a great many members of other non-European races feel race prejudice as strongly as we do, and would welcome an effective colour bar protecting them from the European'. He added: 'those natives whom I know well and for a long space of time admit to a genuine dislike of our European smell, colour, features and manners, a dislike as pronounced as that manifested by some Europeans towards other races'.[32] This naturalisation of race prejudice, in effect, projected a European racial discourse on the rest of the world. In passing it is worth noting that Malinowski was inconsistent in his relativism. Somehow prejudice was raised above different cultures. It became naturalised and transformed into an essential condition of humanity.

Malinowski's defence of the colour bar, couched in terms of preserving different cultures, found a strong resonance among different currents of interwar thought, from hard-line segregationists to liberal and cultural relativists. Cultural relativists promoted the need to preserve the special qualities of different cultures. The editor of the *Spectator*, expressly argued against assimilation on these grounds:

And we have one word to say to the coloured folk, too. We will avoid talking or thinking of superiority and inferiority, but we need not fly in the face of common sense and ignore differences which are no fault of either side. Coloured people must accept these differences, for they will never annihilate them. Let them take a nobler path than aiming at any merging with the white races as though the differences could be ignored. Let them cultivate a noble pride in their own races side by side with the white races.[33]

This editorial was clearly open in its intent. In essence the *Spectator* offered a *quid pro quo* to the 'coloured folk'. In exchange for giving up any public declaration of superiority, the editor expected a renunciation of racial assimilation. Although couched in the fashionable relativist language of difference of the 1930s, a close reading reveals that the editor continued to adhere to the assumptions of racial superiority. When he warned against 'flying in the face of common sense', the implication was self-evident to his readers. And when he pointed to the differences which could not be ignored, the *Spectator*'s readers would have had no difficulty interpreting the statement as a reminder that the coloured races were not fit to assimilate into white society.

American race relations institutions were no less sceptical. Phelps-Stokes was ready to concede that since all races 'go back to the same human stock' there was 'nothing which should prevent their working together harmoniously'. However, he added: 'I do not believe that intermarriage between any widely separated racial groups is generally advisable, and think that in the interest of race pride of a good type the system of separate social life of different racial groups is normally advisable.' From this standpoint, inter-racial contact was acceptable as a formal and episodic arrange-ment. As Phelps-Stokes wrote, 'there is no reason whatever' why representatives of different racial groups 'should not meet occa-sionally to discuss their problems and to break bread together'.[34] According to this worldview, race relations could work if they were conducted at a distance and with a minimum of contact. This was common sense. Racial differences should be encouraged and assimilation should be avoided.

Hostility to assimilation expressed a clear commitment to hold some form of racial line. Outwardly assimilation was criticised because of its negative effect on the development of the races and because it was likely to encourage conflict. However, this focus on

racial conservation was not a disinterested one. It reflected the conviction that the white race was special if not superior. And although
pragmatism demanded that this should not be publicly stated, most
of the individuals involved in interwar race relations had little doubt
that this was so. Even the missionary lobbyist, J.H. Oldham, believed that history testified to the special qualities of the white race:

> In view of what the white man has actually accomplished in history it is
> evident that certain qualities that make for human progress are present in
> that race. The lack of historical achievement up to the present among the
> black people suggests that while they may possess other desirable quali-
> ties, those which have made white civilization possible may not be dis-
> tributed among them to the same degree. We cannot be certain that this is
> so, but it is possible, or, as many would say, probable.[35]

Terms such as 'possible' and 'probable' indicate that this was an
outlook that Oldham did not wish to pursue with vigour. Such
things were best left unsaid or noted only in passing. For the
pragmatism of this racial perspective was demonstrated through a
willingness not to dwell on topics likely to incite a reaction.

Advocates of indirect rule and racial segregation represented the
self-consciously conservative end of the relativist spectrum. But it is
important to situate their response within a wider climate of relativism. Racial notions of superiority and inferiority were gradually
giving way to the concept of difference. All shades of opinion –
including liberal and left – were strongly influenced by the consolidation of relativist intellectual trends in the interwar period. This
shift was evident in all areas of intellectual life. Kuklick's study of
British anthropology shows how this discipline moved away from its
concept of superior culture. Anthropologists 'no longer assumed
that the most technologically advanced and politically organized
societies would adhere to the highest moral standards'.[36] Many
anthropologists associated with the International African Institute
emphasised the difference of culture and, in line with the norms of
indirect rule, affirmed the importance of preserving native tradition.
Others, driven by a degree of despair with Western civilisation,
began to find positive qualities in other cultures. The British liberal
critic of Empire, Leonard Barnes, reminded his readers of the
'truths' that could be learned from Asia and pointed to the 'intimate

sense of brotherhood' that Africa offered.[37] C.T. Loram, a South African academic based at Yale, who established one of the first race relations programmes in the Anglo-American world, shared this worldview. He argued that the 'culture of backward people may be preferable to our own'. 'What would we Westerners not give for a society where every member of the group has a right and a duty towards every other member, where orphanages and old-age asylums are unnecessary, where "broken homes", as we call them, are practically unknown, where there are no unprotected widows and where there are even no old maids?'[38]

Most authoritative accounts of the intellectual history of the period regard the rise of relativism as essentially a positive and progressive reaction to racial theory. Kuklick, for example, has argued that interwar British anthropology 'became a vehicle for liberal criticism of Western society in general and colonialism in particular'.[39] Although Kuklick recognises the conservative inspiration for this critique, she nevertheless sees it as a positive development. In a similar way the rise of Boas's Columbia school of cultural anthropology has been interpreted by some as decisive for the discrediting of American racial theory. Persons has argued that Boas's cultural relativist perspective 'largely replaced the Anglo-American orientation' of the Chicago school.[40]

The overwhelming impact of cultural relativism on Western intellectual life in the interwar period cannot be denied. However, the problem of situating its role in the unfolding discussion on race is more complex than is generally recognised. As we have seen, a relativistic epistemology was fully consistent with the British imperial critique of equality. The incommensurability of culture was convincingly deployed to justify segregation and attack assimilation. Such arguments were also consistent with the affirmation of superiority. A re-reading of interwar anthropology shows that many who praised native institutions were in fact expressing the view that the African was not fit for British institutions. Moreover, the celebration of cultural traditions was quite consistent with a paternalistic imperial outlook. This standpoint was clearly expressed by the leading figures of the International Africa Institute. So, for example, Dr Margaret Read enthused about Africa because of the research opportunities it provided for Western scholars. Africa was a social laboratory for Read. 'The continent of Africa is in a sense a laboratory and experimenting ground for research in the social sciences, for all the nations, who administer colonies there', was how she put it.[41] In this paradigm, there were cultures that administered and those that were subject to others.

The interwar shift towards culture did not necessarily lead to the abandonment of racial thinking. Cultural characteristics could be presented as a variation of racial ones. This was precisely the trajectory of American race relations discourse as demonstrated in the work of Robert E. Park. Park, like many of his colleagues, did not so much write about racial traits as about temperament. Differences in temperament were accounted for, expressed in cultural terms. And the specific features of a particular culture – and not racial discrimination – could be used to explain the inferior social status of black Americans.[42]

Critics of racial thinking consider the shift towards culture to be an important blow to racism. George Stocking has argued that 'Culture',

> in its anthropological sense provided a functionally equivalent substitute for the older idea of 'race temperament'. It explained the same phenomena, but it did so in strictly non-biological terms, and indeed its full efficacy as an explanatory concept depended on the rejection of the inheritance of acquired characters.[43]

This attempt to free culture from inherited characteristics fails to address the issue. The notion of innate characteristics is only one aspect of racial thinking. Far more significant is the view that shared characteristics distinguish one group from another. These characteristics need not be biologically based to convey a sense of superiority/inferiority, and culture, regardless of how it is interpreted, contains within itself a tendency to include/exclude.

Sir Oswald Mosley, leader of the British Union of Fascists, stigmatised Jews as culturally different rather than racially inferior. He accepted Spengler's premise that there was a common European cultural heritage, which could not be made consistent with the idea of a universalist bond.[44] From this standpoint, Jewishness was necessarily an alien and non-assimilable force. The exclusion and isolation of Jews from British public life was the necessary conclusion of this viewpoint.

The Spenglerian perspective, which stressed culture's distinct identity, was by no means restricted to the far right. Many cultural relativists were attracted to Spengler's rejection of evolutionary progress. Ruth Benedict, a leading American cultural relativist, was enthusiastic in her praise of Spengler's *Decline of the West*. She wrote that, for Spengler,

> the 'destiny ideas' whatever they may be that evolve within a culture and give it individuality are what is dynamic and challenging in human life. These have differed profoundly from one another. Each great culture has taken a certain direction not taken by another ... and the full working out of this unique and highly individualised attitude toward life is what is significant in that cultural epoch.[45]

Benedict was a liberal anti-racist. What she drew from Spengler did not lead to Moseley's political stance. However, the interwar relativist consensus had an ability to include a surprisingly wide spectrum of political opinion.

During the interwar period, the apologetic use of cultural relativism was rarely engaged or criticised from an egalitarian standpoint. The only exception was in relation to the promotion of cultural relativism in the context of South Africa. In this case, the extreme manifestation of racial domination tended to expose the apologetic qualities of cultural relativism. It was in this vein that the American academic W.O. Brown remarked how in South Africa 'caste restrictions are fixed in customs and rationalized by a kind of theology of race relations'. He added: 'Whites naturally are anxious that non-Europeans be satisfied with their place and frequently express the pious hope that Natives and others will develop "along their own lines".'[46] In other circumstances, similar statements about the development of natives were still the norm. One of the earliest appreciations of the connection between the promotion of difference and segregation is to be found in the writings of the British anti-racist, Lancelot Hogben. He criticised anthropologists for their accommodation to the notion of separate development. '[They] have rediscovered the Beautiful Savage, and have upholstered Hertzog's segregation policy for starving out the Bantu by a pedantically sentimental plea for the right of the native to evolve along his own peculiar line of self-expression.'[47]

In South Africa, the insights of cultural and social anthropology were mobilised to explain the differential evolution of Africans. The shift towards cultures helped liberals avoid the thorny issue of assimilation. 'As disseminated through Bronislaw Malinowski (and possibly through Franz Boas), a popular notion of "culture" came to serve as a credible linguistic peg upon which the segregationist compromise was hung', argued Saul Dubow.[48] This symbiotic relationship between liberal relativism and proponents of separate development is truly intriguing. Nor was it simply a one-way affair. Many American liberal writers regarded the British policy of indirect rule as a model to be copied elsewhere. For example, the majority of American liberal cultural relativist contributors to a collection of essays, *When Peoples Meet: A Study in Race and Culture Contacts* (1942), clearly approved of indirect rule.[49]

Cultural relativism was often promoted as an argument for the maintenance of the colonial status quo. The view that Western institutions and values were inappropriate for colonial societies was, by implication, an argument against change. Such a perspective could be represented as a display of sensitivity to other cultures. William Elliot, a Harvard Professor of Government, argued in this vein:

> Any efforts to increase the consuming powers of the tropics must raise dubious moral issues. To confer on the native 'the benefits of civilization' is merely to lift him willy nilly from a state of culture anthropologically integrated with his character into one where his security is increased but the old savage freedom of self sufficiency is gone.[50]

This could be read as a plea for the protection of the noble savage. It could also be interpreted to mean that the native was not ready for modern life. Such flexibility was indeed one of the strengths of the new racial pragmatism.

As Economic Disadvantage

Racial pragmatism was not only flexible, it also transcended the ideological divide. Driven by the impulse to pre-empt a consciousness of racial grievance, it was prepared to accommodate a variety of influences. It was even prepared to concede that people of colour suffered from economic disadvantage. Racial oppression alone was its taboo subject.

There is considerable evidence that during the 1930s, contributors to the subject of race relations felt more comfortable with treating the issue as an economic rather than as a racial one. Critics of British imperialism demanded economic reforms and welfare measures; and liberal and left-wing writers concentrated on issues such as poverty and jobs. In retrospect, it is striking to note how much more willing writers were to discuss class rather than race. Even Marxist rhetoric was acceptable so long as race was suppressed. Liberal periodicals in the United States showed a clear bias towards articles on the theme of 'The Negro and the Unions' and demonstrated a preference for economic redistribution rather than racial equality.

Articles on the subject of racial grievances often expressed the hope that this was a temporary phase that would give way to a more normal economic one. Thus a study entitled 'The Possibility of a Distinctive Culture Contribution from the American Negro', published in 1938, concluded with the hope that class allegiances would cut across racial ones:

> Recent developments in the labour movement suggest the possibility of a new alignment which will cut increasingly across race lines and which may conceivably absorb the race issue in a struggle of a more inclusive character. It is also significant that the communist party is making a strong and not a wholly illogical bid for Negro support.[51]

The author did not reveal any communist sympathies and yet conveyed the distinct impression that he would prefer the consciousness of class to that of race.

Talking down the importance of colour and stressing the role of economic motives superficially resembled a radical Marxist approach. In fact, this was a defensive response for commentators who felt that economics was more susceptible to rational management than race. The fear of racial revenge, touched on in the last chapter, combined with the sentiment that this was a peculiarly explosive conflict, somehow inexorably led to economic conclusions. Even missionary publicists adopted an economic tone. Basil Mathews observed that in Rhodesia and Kenya 'the *cause of the conflict is economic'*, and added, 'it is their sense of injustice in regard to standards of labour and wages, land-holding and the vote' that helped forge race consciousness.[52] Elsewhere, Mathews proposed the thesis that racial hostilities were relatively unimportant compared to more fundamental economic tensions: 'My own strong conviction is that we put down to differences of colour and race emotions of hostility or repulsion or antagonism which are really, when analysed, the result of economic or cultural or ethical differences of standard.'[53] Clearly, Mathews felt far more comfortable with economic, cultural or ethical differences than with race.

Of course, the economic consequences of racial oppression were very real and class was not peripheral to the experience of domination. However, the emphasis on such matters was not inspired by a sudden rediscovery of redistributive justice. Rather, a re-reading of the literature suggests that economic rhetoric was unconsciously articulated to delay or evade what were perceived to be the racial adjustments required by the principle of equality. It is worth noting that this approach was even used by South African liberals. In the 1930s they often complained of the overemphasis on racial matters and, as an antidote, offered an economic analysis of problems. The South African economist Hobart Houghton argued that economic factors far outweighed racial factors. He bemoaned the fact that 'many natives are obsessed with the racial aspect and are apt to attribute their disabilities to European oppression'. '[It was] often not a matter of race but of economic forces' which created difficulties for black people. Houghton was prepared to concede that 'race prejudice may inflict social and personal hardship on individuals', but he insisted that 'most of the difficulties of the Bantu arise, not from the relationship of Black and White, but from the relationship of employer and employee'.[54] This focus on differences in class in a society dominated by racial segregation indicated how economic analysis could have an overtly apologetic content.

The conflation of racial oppression with economic exploitation was particularly common in the United States during the New Deal era. Jackson has argued that liberals believed that Afro-Americans had 'the same needs of many white Americans: relief, jobs, housing, education, and social security'. He cited Secretary of State Ickes who contended that the 'negro problem merges into and becomes inseparable from a greater problem of American citizens generally, who are at or below the line in decency and comfort from those who are not'. According to Jackson, white New Dealers advised blacks to 'concentrate on the attainable goal of economic progress and to postpone the challenge to segregation'. Such liberals assumed that the causes of racism were economic and this would diminish as 'whites rose out of poverty and blacks improved education and social standards'.[55]

The economic motif in American liberal literature was not merely one of emphasis. At times this literature seemed self-consciously to ignore the racial dynamic to make a case for a so-called class analysis. Peter Kellogg's authoritative study of liberal race attitudes provides important evidence of this response. His analysis of the content of the *Nation* and the *New Republic*, two influential liberal periodicals, helps illustrate this. In these periodicals, 'race was not so much a problem to be solved as a diversion to be avoided'. Articles on race relations repeatedly expressed a stubborn rejection of the role of racial motif. This approach was vividly illustrated in the discussion of lynching. Liberal journals regarded lynching as essentially an anti-working-class measure. During the New Deal, according to Kellogg, 'liberals saw blacks not as blacks but as Southern poor'.[56]

Kellogg's study raises an important question about the liberal response to the situation of Afro-Americans in the 1930s. Why was race so studiously ignored? Kellogg does not answer this directly. He remarks that they were 'not necessarily indifferent to the problems of Black Americans but thought those problems could best be solved under the broader category of class'. Kellogg himself is not entirely satisfied with this explanation for he offers other lines of investigation. For example, he argued that liberals ignored the quesiton of race in order to prevent Southern conservatives from benefiting from it. 'Attention to racial identity could in fact be dangerous for it provided conservatives with a weapon to divide the South's poor', was how Kellogg characterised a crucial component of liberal thinking.[57] No doubt such political calculations helped influence the development of a pragmatic attitude towards race.

While Kellogg was aware that the motives that shaped the liberal response were far from self-evident, other contributions are far less questioning. Kneebone's study of Southern liberal journalists also draws attention to their economic interpretation of race relations issues. However, Kneebone tends to accept the economic orientation of liberal journalists at face value. Kneebone believed that it was the overwhelming impact of the Great Depression which dictated an economic-oriented explanation of race:

> Hard times during the 1930s overshadowed problems of race relations and seemed to reinforce the assumptions behind vertical segregation. The Great Depression especially severe in its impact on blacks, forced Negro leaders and organizations to concentrate on economic rather than strictly racial issues. Naturally, emphasis on the economy also appeared in southern liberal thought. For many racial problems seemed the symptoms of the larger economic illnesses.[58]

No doubt the impact of the depression influenced the perceptions of contemporary commentators. But economic conditions, important as they were, did not lead directly to a consistent pattern of evading the issue of race.

The failure to confront race relations is all the more striking in that liberal commentators at the time were in no doubt that this was an explosive issue. It is to Kellogg's credit that his account gradually directs the reader to consider the racial fears of liberal writers as the main motive behind the evasion. He cites the example of Malcolm Cowley, editor of the *New Republic*, to illustrate this point. In 1936, Cowley criticised the American Communist Party for advocating an autonomous black belt on the grounds that the 'race problem in the South is slowly being transformed into a class problem'. However, two years later, Cowley was less certain. His review of Richard Wright's *Uncle Tom's Children* reveals a degree of caution regarding the emergence of such unity. Wright's stories illustrate the destructive dynamic of American race relations and three of the four stories culminate in black/white violence. Cowley's review was now more hesitant about class unity – it was presented as a desired objective rather than a real process. Moreover, he did not seem confident about the realisation of this objective. 'Wright makes us feel that the violence in the South will never end.' Not surprisingly, Cowley saw in Wright's book 'the expression of a racial hatred that has never had a chance to die'.[59] Cowley, like many others, preferred to ignore the uncomfortable realities of race, as revealed in Wright's stories. Their action was guided by the belief that it was easier to put right economic inequalities than to resolve age-old racial hatreds.

The desire not to confront race conflict was not only stimulated by the presentiment of impending danger. Expresssing concern with economic disadvantage was a compromise to the demand for equality. By recasting the issue of equality in economic terms, the question of racial assimilation could be avoided. Ultimately it represented a marriage of economic reform with the perpetuation of racial segregation. This standpoint was coherently expressed by the Southern liberal journalist, Virginius Dabney, who declared in 1933, 'it is entirely possible for a southern white man to be uncompromisingly in favour of justice to the Negro and uncompromisingly against intermarriage'.[60] Dabney's affirmation of segregation was by no means eccentric, for the American liberal intelligentsia explicitly avoided challenging the South's racial etiquette. There were many reasons for this, but their insecurity about the realisation of full equality was clearly at the heart of their response.

The compromise accommodation to the demand for equality coincided with an affirmation of the legitimacy of separate spheres of racial life. Accommodation rather than assimilation in the case of South Africa represented an apology for segregation. The liberal head of the South African Institute of Race Relations, Alfred Hoernle, justified segregation on the grounds that it would reassure those who might otherwise oppose economic reforms for Africans. He argued that 'in the conditions at present prevailing in South Africa, the barrier against race mixture is worth maintaining, so that we need not be deterred from a liberal native policy by the fear that race mixture throughout the community will be the inevitable result'.[61] This was a South African version of the case put by American southern liberals for vertical segregation. Anson Phelps-Stokes echoed this argument in the American context when he stated that desegregation in the United States should be postponed to avoid creating 'Southern antagonism'. He believed that 'we should aim at fundamental improvements which would bring about equality in educational facilities, civic rights and economic opportunities'.[62] Economic reforms in the American South, as in South Africa, were consistently promoted as an alternative to challenging the premise of segregation.

As Dubow pointed out, many of the intellectual authors of apartheid, such as Maurice Evans and Charles Templeman Loram, were strongly influenced by the experience of the American South. Evans' call for the 'separation of the races to an extent hitherto never attempted' to preserve their 'home life and race integrity' was viewed by British missionaries as a humane way of coping with the consequences of change.[63] Elsewhere in Africa, imperial publicists, missionaries and officials tended to view some form of segregation as essential for 'protecting' the Africans. As the historian Andrew Roberts noted:

> Mixing cultures made trouble; it was better to keep them apart. The crudities of a legalised colour bar might indeed be abhorrent, but more subtle forms of discrimination were not necessarily to be opposed.[64]

Paternalism was thus presented as reasonable compromise to ensure the healthy evolution of the Africans.

In Britain and the United States the case for segregation was justified on the ground that this was a matter of individual preference. An editorial in the *Spectator*, which concluded a series of articles on the Colour Bar, explicitly distinguished between the economic and personal aspects of the issue. According to the editor it was everyone's duty 'unceasingly' to help 'the coloured races', both 'politically and economically'. But 'socially each man and woman must judge for him or herself'.[65] In 1940, Eleanor Roosevelt put matters concisely when lunching with Ralph Bunche, an up-and-coming black American official: race problems were most 'effectively attacked on the economic front'. She added: 'social equality ought to be crossed out of the equation because that is strictly a personal and individual matter'.[66] By designating 'social equality' as out of bounds, Eleanor Roosevelt outlined the constraints to the accommodation to demands for equality. This accommodation, which sought to limit the disruptive consequences of racism, regarded the containment of conflict as its overriding priority.

The term 'social equality' itself deserves serious further research. In the 1930s and 1940s it was used to refer to personal relations and carried the premise of assimilation. The deliberate construction of a special sphere of 'social equality', where individual preferences could legitimately prevail, provided the foundation for the redrawing of racial boundaries. In this way the reform of race relations within wider society did not need to intrude into any sphere deemed to be personal.

Racial pragmatism embraced a variety of perspectives. It was a flexible approach that was influenced by anxieties about impending racial conflicts. It self-consciously avoided the adoption of strong views. So while it discouraged assimilation, it did not evolve a strong critique of assimilation as such. Rather, it warned about the consequences of assimilation. In pragmatic fashion it counselled restraint and patience. From the standpoint of today, racial pragmatism can be interpreted as a makeshift intellectual response which instinctively sought to avoid the consequences of racial oppression. As the next chapter argues, its main preoccupation was with the reaction to racism rather than with racism as such.

4   Reversing the Problem of Racism

The exploration of the evolution of racial pragmatism suggests that the theme of racial anxiety was fundamental to interwar deliberations on the subject. This approach to the history of changing ideas about race offers an interpretation whose emphasis is very different from mainstream academic contributions. In contrast to the emphasis here, most contributions on the changes to racial discourse in the 1930s focus on the intellectual reaction to Nazi racial science.

Many recent texts have as their focus the anti-racist intellectual reaction to eugenics, Social Darwinism and Aryan theories of race, particularly the Nazi variety. However, the reaction to such theories can not be equated with an anti-racist impulse. Only an insignificant minority responded to Nazi philosophy from an anti-racist perspective. Most critics of scientific racism were responding to the threat presented by German militarism. The target of their criticism was a particular German form of racist ideology and not its anti-egalitarian assumptions. Racial pragmatism condemned not only supremacist sentiments but also egalitarian principles. So someone like Julian Huxley, co-author of the influential 1935 critique of Nazi racial theory, *We Europeans*, could continue to be an apologist for British colonial policy. As late as 1944, Huxley was arguing against ending colonialism in Nigeria on the grounds that it would represent freedom only for 'the feudal Mohammedan Emirs or for the tiny minority of educated Coast negroes'. For Huxley there was no apparent contradiction between his trenchant attack on German race theory and his paternalistic view of Africans, who had 'for the most part' remained 'in an early stage of barbarism'.[1]

The liberal reaction to and criticisms of Nazi racial theories in the 1930s had little to do with combating racism. Thus, for example, at the 1938 Summer School for British Colonial Administrators, held at Oxford University, the participants expressed a distaste for such theories. Indeed one of the three recommended texts for the discussion on race was *We Europeans*. Professor Le Gros Clark's lecture took exception to the German and Italian versions of race theory, but not to race theory as such. Le Gros Clark took as given the prevailing notions of British superiority and African inferiority. In his lecture the 'retarded development of the Kenyan adult' was beyond doubt. The only question was whether this fact was 'fundamental, or in some way related to the environment'.[2] It is useful to note that Le Gros Clark was a highly respected anatomist and a member of the Royal Anthropological Society's 'Race and Culture Committee'. This committee, established in April 1934, was a response to the direction taken by racial theory in Germany. Barkan, in his discussion of the workings of this committee, situates Le Gros Clark in the context of the debates of the 1930s as an 'anti-racist'.[3] However, such retrospective interpretation can easily obscure the point that the dividing line between what is considered 'racist' and 'anti-racist' today was less clear-cut in the 1930s.

Recent contributions on the history of race discourse are understandably oriented towards an exploration of the more theoretically elaborated versions. The tendency is to examine scientific racism, the various eugenic and biological theories and, of course, the reaction to the Nazi experience. This preoccupation is quite understandable. However, there is a danger of reading contemporary concerns and insights into the events of the 1930s. Overwhelmed by the terrible events of the Second World War, it is easy to misinterpret the reactions and consciousness of the past. In particular, it is easy to focus on developments that appear to be intellectually linked to Nazi race theory. The central argument of this chapter is that the concern with racism and the reaction to it in the interwar period cannot be understood simply by studying the debates on eugenics and the various formal theories that explicitly engaged with the subject. For example, the controversy around scientific racism seems particularly important to us today. However, at the time, it was a sub-plot in the drama. The clash of views surrounding Nazi theory did not exhaust the deliberations on race relations. Moreover, there is a considerable body of evidence to show that those who were evolving a critique of racism were motivated not so much by the Nazi challenge as by the fear of the reaction to racism.

In recent studies of interwar race relations, the key texts of the period are examined. This narrow focus has ignored other material, which reveals a more complex story. Non-specialist literature, journals and the wider discussion on politics and international relations suggest that the scientific aspect of race discourse was relatively unimportant. The debate on science and race involved a relatively small number of specialists, but the much wider debate on race relations had a more significant audience. In this non-specialist literature, as well as in the deliberations of Anglo-American officialdom, the underlying concern was with the destabilising consequences of race relations. The term most widely found in studies of international affairs, as well as in the more specialist contributions of American sociologists and British social anthropologists, is 'race consciousness'. Although it has now fallen out of use, it was a central idiom of the race relations vocabulary of the period. Race consciousness was used to characterise the sentiments and attitudes of those who acted, spoke out or organised against white domination. It was almost never used to describe Western forms of racial thought. It referred to the consciousness of oppression. By inference, to be racially conscious was to be disruptive if not threatening.

The need to neutralise the development of race consciousness dominated the wider debate on race relations. That is why the literature that focuses on the controversy surrounding scientific racism misses this point. Thus both Nancy Stepan and Paul Rich have criticised Huxley and Haddon's *We Europeans* for not going far enough in offering an alternative. They also note the relatively minimal impact such attacks on race science had on public opinion. Barkan offers a more generous view of these critics of scientific racism and argues that the 'repudiation of racism by scientists was a crucial step in the growth of global egalitarianism'.[4] All these authors overlook the temper of the times because they concentrate on the intellectual history of racial theory. Anti-racism was simply not an issue. A small number of thinkers were disturbed by what they perceived to be a misuse of science by the Nazis. However, even the more anti-racist contributions were more concerned with confronting fascism than with addressing racial domination. Let us take the example of Cecil Dover, one of the more radical critics of racism during the 1930s. He argued that 'we must dismiss attempts to treat the main colour groups as distinct species because they are evidently inspired by political motives of the worst kind'. 'Fascism and imperialism have much to gain from this further separation of the so-called progressive and backward races', he added.[5] His call for race equality was justified not so much in its own terms, but by its contribution to the cause of anti-fascism.

In any case the reaction to Nazi race science, as important as it later proved to be, did not express mainstream preoccupations. Most contributors were far more concerned with the need to restrain the development of racial consciousness. This point is surprisingly understated in the literature on the history of race relations.

Contrasting research strategies and historiographical method-ologies may account for the different interpretations of race relations discourse in the interwar period. Most recent contribu-tions have tended to adopt an *internalist* as opposed to what is called an *externalist* approach. Internalist accounts tend to empha-sise the interplay of ideas in the generation of new paradigms, whereas the externalist perspective stresses the role of social experience. The role of intellectuals, academics and scientists in the formation of ideas about race is emphasised in the work of Barkan and Stocking. Many accounts of the development of an alternative to scientific racism in the United States, for example, assign a central role to the anthropologist Franz Boas. It is almost as if the changing climate of opinion was exclusively the product of a conflict of ideas. According to Gosett, 'What chiefly happened in the 1920s to set the tide of racism was that one man, Franz Boas, who was an authority in several fields which had been the strongest source of racism, quietly asked for the proof that race determines mentality and temperament.'[6]

Against such internalist perspectives, a few writers have focused on the role of social experience in the shaping of race discourse. John H. Stanfield, for example, has argued that there was a close connec-tion between the threat of instability and the evolution of race rela-tions theory: 'At least since the 1920s, black social scientists and historians have been in greatest demand when white elites perceive a crisis in racial authority.'[7] Such clear formulations of the relation-ship between developments in society and the demand for new ideas have become less and less accepted in recent years.

Even scholars whose work documents the interplay of experience and ideas have been reluctant to be identified with an
externalist perspective. Instead, they tend to adopt a position that
seeks to reconcile an internalist and externalist posture. Williams,
in his study *From a Caste to a Minority: Changing Attitudes of
American Sociologists Toward Afro-Americans*, attempts such a
compromise. He explains the demise of racial theory in the
interwar period in the following terms:

> These changes on the issues of race and race relations had taken place
> in sociology because external forces, such as significant economic,
> educational, and political progress, and internal forces, such as the
> drive for professionalization and the movement to adopt an empirical
> worldview, compelled sociologists to reassess the idea that blacks were
> inherently inferior and therefore unassimilable.[8]

The American sociologist, Thomas Pettigrew, takes a similar position. He argues that 'dramatic racial events were simply one of many
factors shaping the race relations field'. According to Pettigrew,
developments within sociology were no less important.[9]

Arguments that assign such importance to developments within
an academic discipline fail to explain why similar intellectual shifts
were occurring throughout society as a whole. In race thinking, as in
other areas, it is not possible to isolate developments from the trends
in society as a whole. Academics did not work in isolation from
public opinion and wider political and cultural trends. Paul Rich
recognises the importance of the wider social context, but nevertheless warns that 'a purely contextualist approach has weaknesses as
well since it is a fallacy to assume that a thinker or organizer of ideas
acts simply as a result of economic or political pressures'.[10] The reaction to context is probably inspired by the nature of the material at
hand. An emphasis on texts and the publications of various schools
of thought dispose the researcher to overemphasise the autonomy of
ideas. The relationship of theory to experience is far less transparent
than the reaction of one academic to another. Rich's separation of a
realm of 'pure' context testifies to a forced abstraction of the thinker
from the wider social trends.

This chapter seeks to transcend what is often an arid discussion
about the methodology of intellectual history. The counter-position

of different methodological perspectives does not address the question of what is the most suitable strategy for approaching the problem at hand. As with all dynamic relations, that between ideas about race and social experience is inexact. To grasp this relationship in the interwar period, it is useful to consider the forms through which the sense of race was represented. An examination of the mainstream literature at the time reveals reactions that were characteristic of the period. In order to approximate how public servants and policymakers defined the problem, their reactions will also be considered. Finally, these reactions will be considered in relation to the debates on race relations within the academic community.

Race Consciousness

The vocabulary of racial thinking has undergone many changes and modifications. Moreover, the meaning and significance attached to terms such as race have varied with the passing of time. Even a superficial comparison of the race vocabulary reveals shifts in preoccupations and attitudes.

It was during the course of carrying out archival research for another project that I first became aware of the shifting terminology of race discourse.[11] The term that occurred most often in official exchanges on the issue of race relations was 'race consciousness'. American and British officials tended to interpret this consciousness as a problem, or at least a potential problem, for white people. An examination of periodicals and journals confirmed that the same terms were deployed in the media. Terms such as colour consciousness and colour feeling were used synonymously with race consciousness.

The concern with colour consciousness was symptomatic of the political culture of the West. The problem was not racism – indeed this concept was not yet in usage. The predicament was that people who experienced racism would also react in a racial way. This was the underlying motif that would recur in the discussions on race relations on both sides of the Atlantic.

The term race consciousness was rarely elaborated. It was used as if its meaning was self-evident. Officials, academic specialists and journalist all used the term loosely.[12]

In some cases race consciousness was used interchangeably with 'nationalism' or 'national consciousness'. By implication racial assertiveness was interpreted as a variant of nationalist ones. Park and Burgess, in their influential *Introduction to the Science of Sociology*, treated racial conflict as if it were similar to the 'struggles of the European nationalities and the so-called "subject peoples" for independence and self-determination'. The demand for status and recognition united the most disparate reactions to the global status quo:

> Under the conditions of this struggle, racial or national consciousness as it manifests itself, for example in Irish nationalism, Jewish Zionism, and Negro race consciousness, is the natural and obvious response to a conflict situation. The nationalistic movements in Europe, in India, and in Egypt are, like war, rivalry and more personal forms of conflict, mainly struggles for recognition – that is, honor, glory, and prestige.[13]

Race consciousness was perceived as an unavoidable development in the global scheme of things.

The implication of the interwar discussion of race consciousness was that it was an international phenomenon. Although rarely spelled out, it was a consciousness that inspired all the so-called subject races against white domination. Although expressed in a confused and roundabout way, there was little doubt that the international conflict of colour provided the underpinning for the discussion of race consciousness.

The conviction that race consciousness had become a feature of international relations was seldom questioned. The only issue was the size of the threat this consciousness represented. Books and journal articles written by authors from across the political spectrum took the same line. The theme recurs in nearly all the texts on this subject recommended by the periodical *Foreign Affairs* during the interwar period. According to one of these texts, published in 1924, 'the consciousness of racial kinship is abroad in the earth'. The author, Ellsworth Huntington, warned that 'whether the present conception of racial differences is right or wrong, it seems destined to play a great part in the history of the next few generations, for it has become embedded in the world's equipment of ideas'.[14]

There was a number of variations of the argument that colour consciousness had become an international phenomenon. What united all the explanations was the conviction that this was a worldwide reaction to the white race. It was as if white global expansion had created a consciousness of colour among those subject to Western domination. According to Basil Matthews, another author recommended by *Foreign Affairs*, 'the Negro first becomes race-conscious when he confronts the White Europeans and Americans'.[15]

Although the concept of race consciousness tended to be deployed as an unreflected common-sense term, there were some attempts to elaborate its meaning. Robert Park, the foremost representative of the Chicago School of sociology, sought to endow the term with intellectual coherence. In his writings, black American race consciousness was represented as a reaction to exclusion from white society:

> It may be said that there is one profound difference between the Negro and the European nationalities, namely, that the Negro has had his separateness and consequent race consciousness thrust upon him, because of his exclusion and forcible isolation from white society.[16]

Park's discussion hints at a mild rebuke to its cause – that is, racial discrimination. 'Racial sentiment among the Negroes has sprung up as the result of a struggle against privilege and discrimination based upon racial discrimination.' It is interesting to note that despite his insights, Park tended to use the word racial to describe not only the dominant ideology of his society, but also the reaction to it. Park's acknowledgement of the reality of discrimination did not dent his belief that the prevailing 'democratic sentiment' absolved American society.

Park's views on race consciousness were further developed by William O. Brown, an American sociologist trained in the Chicago School tradition. Brown, who later became Chief of the African Section Office of Strategic Services (1944–46) and who served as an Africa expert in the Department of State, was always concerned with the policy implications of race relations. During the 1930s, he used the term racial to describe the response to white domination. For example, he warned the readers of *AJS*, in 1935, that there was 'emerging among South African natives an immature racialism which will ultimately grow into a matured race consciousness'.[17] Brown's contribution was premised on one of the central assumptions of the new racial pragmatism: that, in one form or another, race consciousness was bound to manifest itself in areas where two races interacted.

The inevitably of the growth of racial consciousness was predicated on the assumption that conflict was both its cause and the effect. So through 'race consciousness the members of a race become a historic group, acquiring a past, aware of the present and aspiring to a future' and therefore a 'conscious group' is a 'conflict group' and 'race consciousness itself is a result of conflict'. Brown sought to show how race conflict stimulated a reactive consciousness among blacks in South Africa. He identified three likely phases in its development. These were, first, the 'shift in mental attitude of the native with reference to the white man'; second, the 'emergence of expressional activities and organizations of various kinds among natives'; and third, 'the rise of specific movements attempting to mobilize racial sentiment to the end of elevating the status of the native'.[18]

Brown's schema is important because it was one of the few attempts at elaborating the concept of race consciousness. The elaboration helps reveal the assumptions and the concerns of those who used it. A careful reading of Brown's article suggests that what he offers is a racial interpretation of the reaction to colonial domination and racial oppression, and what he calls racial consciousness is any form of reaction – anti-colonial, nationalist, religious, civil-right – to Western domination. It is as if the very act of resisting the West is racially motivated. By implication what would be characterised as nationalism in a European context becomes racial in an African or Asian one. The term race consciousness was part of a vocabulary of double standards which prevailed in international relations. It said more about the intellectual outlook of those who interpreted events with this concept than about the subject of its analysis. Above all it revealed the 'racial consciousness' of its authors.

Since race consciousness was linked to a relation of conflict, there must be potential for tension in all situations where races interacted. The implication was that the international conflict of colour possessed an autonomous dynamic. That this was a problem which transcended particular societies and circumstances can be seen in the ease with which writers could shift from considering the interaction of black and white in the American South to inspecting the 'colour problem' in South Africa or India, or in any part of the European Empires. Moreover, American or South African specialists would study the effect of race consciousness in each other's societies to gain insights into what they considered to be a world-wide problem. It was as if relations between black and white constituted a subject independent of historical circumstances and social arrangements. American Foundations such as Carnegie and Rockefeller actively supported the exchange of ideas and of experiences between British, American and South African experts.

The interwar race relations industry regarded the problem as a generic one that could be studied in its own terms. In Britain, the key personalities involved with the International Institute of African Languages and Cultures often referred to the experience of conflict in Asia to make sense of the situation in Africa. Lugard argued his case for protecting the African from westernisation on the grounds that the 'effects of the impact between an old and new civilisation had been seen in Asia'. He warned that 'the same impact of two civilisations was taking place in Africa'.[19] If British experts understood Africa through the prism of the experience of westernisation in Asia, Americans understood international race relations from the standpoint of their Southern states. Visitors from American institutions to Africa lectured on their experience and exchanged views with local experts. Characteristically these discussions suggested that the participants believed they were discussing a common problem that manifested itself in different settings. Anson Phelps-Stokes reported from his African tour of 1932 that the questions that preoccupied his white audience were all too familiar.[20]

It was the generic conceptualisation of international race relations which influenced the research agenda of the Carnegie Corporation. In April 1932, it gave a grant to allow Anglo-Africans to study the educational work 'that is being done for the Negroes and Indians' in the United States.[21] Carnegie's decision was based on a proposal from Charles Loram, their South African adviser based at Yale. Carnegie's support enabled Loram to set up a race relations programme at Yale. In Loram's opinion, the subject involved the study of the impact of Western civilisation on the rest of the world. He explained the issues in the following terms:

> In the past, western civilization has been imposed upon non-western peoples without much forethought and with an almost complete disregard of consequences. While there can be no doubt that benefit has accrued to individuals and groups, the general result of this haphazard introduction of western civilization has been one of social, political, economic and religious disturbance of far-reaching and dangerous consequence. A glance at China, India and Africa today shows the extent of this disturbance.[22]

The international dimension of the danger to which Loram alluded was the pattern of Western impact provoking race consciousness.

It is important to note that the concept of race consciousness was not a neutral one. Western movements and peoples, with the exception of the Irish and the Jews, were seldom described as racially conscious. That was a term applied to them. Time and again, those who deployed the concept underlined its negative connotations. They stressed that this was a reaction rather than a positive assertion of identity. Snyder defined pan-Africanism as a 'negative movement brought into being as a result of white penetration into Africa'. 'Resentful, sullen, suspicious, he longs for the day of freedom', was Snyder's view of the African. It would be 'miraculous if under the circumstances, he did not eventually develop a racial consciousness'.[23]

'Oppression psychosis' was one of the most frequently used companion terms. This concept could be found in both academic and specialist literature and in political commentaries. The term had the merit of shifting the focus from oppression to the reaction it provoked. By equating the reaction to oppression to a psychological problem, the state of mind that was racially conscious was denigrated. One of the most widely cited texts on this subject was Herbert A. Miller's *Races, Nations and Classes, The Psychology of Domination and Freedom* (1924). Miller believed there could be no symmetry between those in a race relationship and he had little sympathy for the experience of oppression. 'An oppressed group is abnormally subjective', was Miller's diagnosis. Pointing to the Irish and the Jews, he noted that 'there is always a chip on the shoulder'. 'We know from experience in other countries not necessarily inhabited by coloured peoples, that nations striving for political freedom are apt to be hypersensitive and are prone to imagine condescension where none exists.'[24] Oppression psychosis was a pathology specific to the oppressed. The symptoms were those 'persistent and exaggerated mental states which are characteristically produced under conditions where one group dominates another'.[25]

Medicalising the reaction to oppression was to stigmatise the social action of the oppressed. The issue became that of a mentally unstable people. According to Miller, Jews and Negroes suffered from an 'inferiority complex'. Through focusing on the subjective disposition of the individual, the wider structural influences became marginal to the analysis. The main point of discussion was the mental state of the oppressed rather than the experience of oppression. Oppression psychosis, which masqueraded as a scientific description of mental symptoms, became a condemnation of those who questioned the legitimacy of racial domination. With Miller, the most banal of prejudices were recycled as a self-evident sociological observation. 'Hyper-sensitivity to insult is becoming characteristic of Negroes'; and he warned that this 'self-centredness or subjectivity is rapidly becoming pathological'.[26]

Miller was by no means extreme in his views. He had no difficulty in attacking the striving for racial domination. However, his objection to the psychology of domination was motivated by his fear of its destabilising consequences. As Fred Wacker usefully reminds his readers, although Miller 'opposed what he called the psychology of domination, it was not on the grounds that such psychology was undemocratic and oppressive but on the grounds that without tolerance it would be difficult to avoid conflict and revolution'.[27]

Terms such as 'oppression psychosis' show how the theorisation of race relations had shifted towards a consideration of the reaction to racial oppression. As we saw in the previous chapter, racial thinking had become increasingly defensive. The tendency was not so much to celebrate superiority as to point out the deficiencies of the inferiors. The constant reminders of 'their' inferiority complex was a mark of this preoccupation. Moreover, by pointing to the unreasonableness of the reaction of the oppressed, a consideration of the structure of racial domination could be avoided. Instead, the discussion could concentrate on the far more comfortable subject of what needed to be done to limit the global reaction to racial oppression.

Interpreting the Reaction to Racial Consciousness

Although experts such as Miller could openly write about the psychological deficiencies of the oppressed, Anglo-American writers were less than comfortable with the subject. The eruption of conflicts throughout the world confirmed the impression that the problem was under-researched. Revolts in the Empire and the discovery of racial tension in the ports of Britain usually prompted calls for more studies.[28] Sir John Simon, as Foreign Secretary, called for a thorough investigation of the 'colour question'. He wrote: 'I should like to see it analysed and worked out in advance, before the time comes when some of those peoples in Africa and elsewhere whom we are accustomed to call backward races claim more fully than they do now their full status as men and equals.'[29] Similarly, sociological inquiry into the subject was suggested by the public manifestation of the race issue in the United States. According to the pioneer black American sociologist E. Franklin Frazier, one of Park's students, the threat that blacks posed to stability in Northern cities stimulated his teacher to reorient and develop his ideas on race relations. The 1919 race riot in Chicago was particularly influential in this respect.[30] In all cases the calls for further study were justified on the grounds of anticipating potential difficulties in the relation between races.

The demand for more information was not a product of minds that were bereft of ideas or were neutral. On the contrary, it was precisely because the Anglo-American political classes believed in the importance of race, and feared the worst about likely developments, that they wanted to clarify matters. The demand for more information and study readily followed. The self-knowledge of the ruling class contained clearly defined ideas about race. Now these ideas had to be developed and reoriented towards conceptualising the reaction of people of colour. More specifically, innovative ideas were needed to manage the emerging consciousness of race. The objective of this chapter is not to re-examine the relationship of racial thinking with the dominant ideology of the ruling elite. There are already many interesting accounts of this subject.[31] The focus of this discussion is to examine the discourse of race consciousness.

The instinctive Anglo-American reaction to the rise of race consciousness was to emphasise its destructive dynamic. Virtually every account accepted that at the very least there was a potential for an explosion of race conflict. It is rare to encounter any positive assessments of race consciousness. Even the liberal editors of an American text on race relations – one of whom was black – could go no further then to apologise for it. 'Race consciousness on the part of minorities is an inevitable and pardonable reaction to majority persecution and disparagement', wrote Locke and Stern.[32] Most other writers stressed its harmful consequences.

The absence of positive or even neutral accounts of race consciousness was the result of an analysis that saw it as inherently dangerous. This was a consciousness that could have only negative consequences. One contribution, 'The Colour Bar and International Relations', published in the *Spectator* in August 1931, proposed the following argument:

> In the case of colonies where the colour problem is most critical, the feeling of subordination, coupled with colour prejudice, naturally develops into conscious racial hatred.[33]

The implication was that this was a consciousness that sooner or later would turn against the white race.

A clear correlation was drawn between those who were racially conscious and those who were anti-white. The one sentiment inevitably went with the other. From this standpoint, every manifestation of anti-colonial sentiment could be interpreted as a blow directed at the white race. Interwar missionary literature was saturated with this concern. Missionary periodicals such as *The East and The West* and the *International Review of Missions* were continually alerting their readership to this problem.[34] Similar sentiments were expressed by European and American publicists, who claimed a special knowledge of the colonial world.

The discussion of the potential anti-white dynamic of race

consciousness was linked to an expectation that the unity of the 'coloured races' was a practical possibility. It was as if the reaction to the white race had the capacity to unite all those who experienced Western domination. There was an implicit assumption that the 'coloured races' if nothing else shared a hatred of white people. So part of the Western reaction to race consciousness was motivated by the desire to prevent the emergence and consolidation of this unity of colour.

Today, when the continents of Africa and Asia are continually visited by strife and civil war, the notion that anti-white sentiment could provide a focus for unity appears far-fetched. However, in the interwar period, many American and British commentators were convinced that the West faced precisely such a threat. As noted in the previous chapter, signs of the impending growth of Pan-Africanism and Pan-Asianism were kept continually under surveillance.

Interwar studies of international affairs often alluded to the possible emergence of 'pan' movements or the unity of the 'coloured races'. One American study of the Paris Peace settlement asked, 'if the Western white races do not recognize the equality of the Asiatic races, will these Eastern races, which number half of the human race, be forced to a new kind of racial alliance?'[35] Most replies were in the affirmative. A discussion of the danger of Islam in the British periodical *Fortnightly Review* observed: 'nor must we lightly assume that because the Mahommedans are made hostile the Hindoos will be rendered more loyal, for there is a new solidarity afoot in India'. It warned against taking measures which might 'raise a point of racial equality' to 'which all Asiatics have become increasingly sensitive'.[36]

The fear of an anti-white racial movement consolidating was not restricted to sensationalist or eccentric accounts. Respectable officials and academics were touched by it. American studies of race relations in the 1930s often remarked on the development of a sense of identification amongst people of colour. W.O. Brown pointed to this international dimension of colour consciousness:

> The Negro in the United States who is assimilated to the ideology of race consciousness sympathizes with the struggles of the African natives, protests against the imperialism of the United States in the Caribbean, appreciates the nationalism of the Indians and Chinese and

is sympathetic generally with struggling minorities. The race conscious who belong to proscribed groups sense a spiritual unity and are
aware of a common cause.[37]

On the other side of the Atlantic, Bronislaw Malinowski, the
doyen of British social anthropology and a man not given to
verbal excess, was anxious about precisely the same point.
Malinowski feared that developments in the sphere of international affairs were uniting the world of coloured peoples against
Western influence.[38] Malinowski's warning directly echoed
Brown's, who noted that in 'the modern world the oppressed races
have a common foe, the white peoples of Western Europe and
their cousins of the United States'.[39]

As we have seen, discussions of anti-white unity were characteristically alarmist and had a tendency to inflate the significance of
every manifestation of anti-Western sentiment. This over-reaction
was the product of a sensibility which at some level expected that
those denied an equal place in the world were motivated by a
thirst for racial revenge. Race consciousness acted as a focus for
anti-white unity because of this desire. The Western sense of race
could only interpret the aspiration for independence and equality
in a racial form. Ultimately race consciousness was decoded to
mean a desire to settle scores. This insight influenced the thinking
of commentators across the political spectrum.

Many liberal and left-wing critics of imperialism in the 1930s
advanced the theme of racial revenge as an argument for a change
in policy. The radical British anti-imperialist Leonard Barnes's
The Duty of Empire was representative of this literature. Published
in 1935, the same year as *We Europeans*, it is seldom considered by
contemporary studies of 1930s race theory. Yet *The Duty of Empire*
expressed far more cogently the race concerns of the Anglo-
American intelligentsia of the 1930s than the specialist discussions on race science. Barnes projected the 'colour question' as the
main issue facing the British Empire. 'The crucial test of Empire
for this generation and its immediate successors is presented by
that vast complex of problems which we summarise as the colour
question.' Barnes believed that race relations was 'entering upon a
most difficult and dangerous phase', since some Asian nations
were in the position to compete economically and seek revenge

against their former exploiters. He had no doubt that 'when the men of colour, in paying off old scores, begin to strike at the markets on which western man has been brought up to regard himself as dependent for his livelihood, it is evident that undreamed of possibilities of inter-racial frenzy are being opened up'.[40] Barnes himself was ahead of British public opinion in his support of racial equality, but in his views on the dangers facing the Empire, he was part of a wider consensus.

The reaction to race consciousness was often overreactive. Terms such as 'peril' and 'catastrophe' reveal how the threat to the white race was exaggerated. The sociology of this reaction to race consciousness provides useful insights into the Western sense of race. As expected, the sense of race was particularly developed in societies in which social domination acquired a directly racial form. During the interwar period Western fears of racial revenge were particularly intense in the American South and in European settler colonies such as South Africa. In South Africa in the 1920s white politicians were gripped with the fear of the blurring of the colour line. One legacy of this, the Immorality Act, which banned sexual relationships across the colour line, was passed by the South African Parliament in 1927.[41] A similar process was at work in the American South. The revival of the Ku Klux Klan in the 1920s was one outcome of this 'overreaction'. According to a 1923 study 'the rising consciousness of the negro race' provoked something of a panic among white southerners. 'The southern Klansman' realised 'that if the modern negro has his way, the race problem of today is nothing compared to the race problem that will come'.[42]

At the time, the literature on race relations rarely addressed the main subject of this chapter: the issue of the white reaction to race consciousness. The few that did, considered it to be unproblematic – a natural consequence of prejudice, which was generally considered to be a natural phenomenon.[43] The literature was far more preoccupied with the growth of race consciousness and was itself part of the reaction to it. It would have required considerable self-questioning to have thought of the white reaction to race consciousness as a problem worthy of study in its own right.

The point at issue was the development of race consciousness. In some cases, commentators indicted those who were aggressively race conscious for stimulating white anxieties. There was little sympathy for the advocates of race consciousness. On the contrary, those who reacted to racial domination were criticised for provoking anxieties among white people, thereby undermining race relations. Edward B. Reuter, one of the leading American sociologist specialising in race relations during the interwar period, remarked that nationalist unity among blacks 'arouses fears and intensified the prejudices of certain white persons, thus increasing the difficulty of establishing and maintaining just and amicable inter-race relations'.[44] For Reuter, racial harmony and the preservation of the status quo were interdependent.

The most interesting work on the white reaction to race consciousness before the Second World War was John Dollard's pioneering study, *Caste and Class in a Southern Town* (1937). This work, which can be read as an anthropology of race anxieties, provides many useful insights into the racist culture of the American South. Dollard sought to uncover the passions that seethed under the surface and which helped to create such a racially charged atmosphere there.

Dollard was always surprised at the apparent overreaction of the white community to the threat posed by black race consciousness. Although he was sensitive to the assertion of black demands on society, and chronicled the different forms of this emerging revolt, he remained convinced that the white reaction was out of proportion to it: '[southern white people] show the greatest sensitivity to aggression from the side of the Negro, and in fact, to the outside observer, often seem to be reacting to it when it is not there'. His description of this white sensibility is most suggestive:

> it is very convincing to experience in one's own person the unshake-able conviction of the white caste that danger lurks in the Negro quarter. Only constant watchfulness, it is believed, and a solid white front against potential Negro attack maintain the status quo.[45]

What Dollard was describing was a silent race war, which required constant vigilance because a way of life was at stake. 'It is astonishing, when any little incident occurs, how unerringly aggressive intent on the part of the Negro is assumed', he remarked.[46] Every incident seemed to represent one more engagement in a never-ending battle.

It is to Dollard's credit that, unlike many of his contemporaries, he did not treat white anxieties as natural or unproblematic, but as a social question worthy of investigation. His main strength was his ability to interrogate the southern white self-image. His quasi-psychological approached was tempered by his awareness of local power relations. He was always clear that white reaction was inspired by a determination to retain the existing 'forms of social control' necessary 'for keeping the Negro in his place'.

Dollard argued that white people did not so much hate as 'fear Negroes' and offered two explanations for these fears. First, this fear was based on the belief that the institutions and political ethos of the United States encouraged the advancement of blacks. According to Dollard, this meant there was a challenge to the status quo which 'whites must constantly fear'.[47] This explanation of the structure of white fear is hardly convincing. No doubt many southern whites Dollard interviewed complained of Northern interference, but this may well have been their way of rationalising their situation. When the problem of social control is posed, it is not at all unusual to interpret the forces of instability as inspired by outside interests. Dollard himself did not pursue the argument. His second explanation of 'another form of fear' is much more relevant for understanding white overreaction.

So what is this other 'form of fear' which must be discussed? Dollard helped reorient the discussion towards those white anxieties that at first sight appear to make little sense. He emphasised that 'white people seem to be much more afraid of Negroes than there is any real reason to be'. He repeated this observation and added, the 'fright shown by white-caste members seems disproportionate to the threat from the Negro's side'. Dollard drew on his fieldwork to explain this. He argued that fear was based on the expectation of racial revenge. In other words, white people expected blacks to behave towards them as they did to black people. For Dollard, these fears represented an 'unconscious expectation of retaliation for the hostile acts of whites on Negroes'.[48]

The theme of racial revenge is central to Dollard's discussion of power relations between black and white. However, Dollard did not merely condemn this reaction; he also sought to reassure those who feared a changing balance of power. Whites 'realize the gains they are making from the Negroes and expect the Negro to react as they themselves would if they were arbitrarily assigned an inferior caste position'. But he added, 'they are mistaken in this assumption since there are other ways out of the dilemma than direct aggression'.[49]

Dollard's conclusion that white southerners had little to fear was based on the premise of black accommodation to a slowly evolving strategy. He hoped that there was enough time to make the adjustments necessary for stability: 'the negroes seem, in fact, to be rather well adjusted to the situation and to have, by and large, renounced aggression and organization as means of changing their status'.[50] Relying on the passivity of the oppressed, Dollard hoped that southern whites would come to terms with their irrational fears. When it came to practicalities Dollard remained very much part of the mainstream. Like Reuter and others, he saw the curing of race consciousness as the prerequisite for resolving the problem of race relations.

What distinguished Dollard was the open manner with which he addressed the silent race fears of southern white people. But he was no less certain that race consciousness had to be contained than those who were far more guarded about engaging the issues. Here too the problem of racism was reversed to the reaction to it.

Reversing the Racial Motive

Dollard's most relevant insight for this discussion was his observation about the manner in which white southerners attributed their racial motives to those they feared. In a similar, albeit more detached, fashion, Anglo-American publicists and officials continually insisted on interpreting responses to white domination as racially motivated. In this way the greater public acknowledgement of the indefensible character of racism need not have any direct implication for the self-image of the Anglo-American Establishment. The ostensible racism of colonial subjects or black Americans lightened the burden of responsibility.

It is not clear to what extent officials were conscious of their evasion of responsibility for the legacy of racial domination. During the 1930s they seemed to elide the distinction between the action of the oppressor and the oppressed. Demands for civil rights were seldom treated as legitimate aspirations, but as attempts to change the existing balance of racial power.

In the United States, the Federal Bureau of Investigation and other law enforcement agencies targeted the racially conscious. The black press in particular was monitored because of its capacity to challenge the existing racial calculus. J. Edgar Hoover disapproved of the black press because of its attempt to promote 'defiantly assertive' ideas about 'the Negro's fitness for self-government', 'race consciousness' and 'hostility' to the white race.[51] Black newspaper editors were held to be racially motivated troublemakers, who thrived on inciting black reaction against white people.

In American studies of the black press, the act of drawing attention to acts of racism was denounced as a threat to social harmony. According to one study, published in 1938:

> The Negro editor leads his group in being race-conscious. The value of reiterated discussion of the anti-lynching bill lies not so much in any changes it is likely to make in the lynching of negroes since the great majority of negroes know that they are in no danger. The value lies rather in the fact that the bill provides a definite issue about which race-consciousness can gather and become powerful.[52]

This unsympathetic image of the 'Negro editor', who artificially raises an issue such as lynching, cast doubts about the qualities of the race conscious. This view was also clearly expressed in a report on race relations funded by the American foundation, the Julius Rosenwald Fund. According to Bertram Scrieke, the author of this report, Negro editors were 'spitting and growling' at white domination, 'to the great glee of a race which rejoices at such impudence'. Scrieke was in no doubt that this was an 'expression of the inferiority complex'.[53]

The British establishment was relatively more subdued in its reaction to the demand for equality – at least in Britain itself – but it was no less scornful of the manifestation of race consciousness. The West India Royal Commission of 1938–39 indirectly blamed local newspaper editors for stirring up race consciousness. It concluded:

> In view of the very important and growing influence which many organs of the Press in the West Indies now exercise in the relation

between the public and the Civil Service, and on the important questions of colour prejudice and colour discrimination, we consider it most
important that the value of restraint and moderation should be fully
appreciated by those responsible for the conduct and tone of the Press.[54]

Such sensitivity to the colonial press became more and more
intense. By the 1940s the 'native press' and 'race consciousness'
were linked in Colonial Office memoranda.[55]

Privately, British officials were aware of the strength of white
racism. Following a series of exchanges about how to deal with
complaints regarding the operation of a colour bar in Britain, one
senior Whitehall mandarin noted:

> This is one of the most awkward of awkward questions that we have to
> deal with. There is no doubt that 'colour prejudice' *does* operate in this
> country to a most embarrassing extent. We are constantly hearing
> examples of it.[56]

The response of Colonial Office officials to this awkward question
was not to confront it publicly, but to try to prevent a militant reaction to it. Sir Alan Burns, Governor of the British Honduras, was
worried that the League of Colonial Peoples, who campaigned
against racism, might be captured by the 'Reds'. Others were critical
of the League being 'mainly preoccupied' with the colour bar.

The response of Sir Donald Cameron, who acted as a link
between the League and the Colonial Office, revealed the Whitehall mentality of the times. 'I have been preaching to them for
years that the one thing they should get rid of is their infernal
inferiority complex.'[57] For Cameron, public criticisms of Britain's
colour bar were not only a symptom of bad taste, but also of an
inferiority complex. He was far more sympathetic to the project of
getting 'rid' of this inferiority complex than in getting rid of the
colour bar.

In private, British officials were prepared to acknowledge the
prevalence of racism and also to concede that this was an
'awkward' question. At the same time imperial officials continued
to interpret events from a racial perspective. Any revolt against the
imperial status quo was regarded as either directly or indirectly
inspired by 'race consciousness' or 'colour feeling'. In their

worldview racialism was associated with movements against Western domination. The term might be applied to the contemporaneous Nazi movement, but certainly not to the British. In official correspondence, terms such as colour bar or colour prejudice were invariably placed within quotation marks, thereby revealing an embarrassment about their usage.

The imputation of racial motive behind anti-colonial sentiment was routine in British official correspondence on developments in the Caribbean. As early as 1924, the Inspector General of Police in British Guiana reported that the growing race consciousness and anti-white feeling were responsible for the militancy of plantation workers.[58] By 1930s such a characterisation was standard. In October 1935, the Governor of British Guiana reported: the 'mind of the African community is most powerfully affected by Italian–Abyssinian conflict which presents itself to them as a colour question'. A couple of months later, a series of strikes on the sugar plantations were explained away in similar terms. Disturbed minds and anti-white sentiment became the explanation for the high level of militancy of the strikers. The Governor reported:

> For a while, at least, every issue was regarded from the 'colour' point of view and the assaults and insults to which European overseers were subjected may be attributed largely to the resentment against the action of a European nation vis-à-vis one situated in Africa.[59]

The Commission of Enquiry into these strikes also blamed 'racial feeling' for the protests. A similar diagnosis was made of the causes of strikes during the subsequent years. The 1938 sugar workers' strike was described as a movement which was 'very largely of a racial character'. In 1940, the Governor reported the 'disturbing influence of racial antagonisms and prejudice'.[60]

The British view of race consciousness was also upheld by American diplomats stationed in the area. The American Vice Consul in British Guiana described Ayub Edun, a leading trade unionist, as 'inevitably anti-American since he was interested in the descendency of the white race and the ascendency of the colored race'.[61] The impression conveyed was of a white race always at the receiving end of racialism.

Western reactions were similar in Asia. In the years leading up to the Second World War, the Japanese were continually criticised for 'exploiting' the 'colour feeling' of Asians. One Foreign Office report observed that one of the impulses behind Japanese expansionism was 'colour and race-feeling, which, in so far as it is genuine, represents to a certain extent the psychological reaction of the Japanese to Asiatic exclusion policies in the United States and Australia'.[62]

According to the self-knowledge of the Anglo-American establishment, prejudice and racial antagonisms were sentiments typically expressed against Europeans. If one relied entirely on official correspondence, it would be easy to draw the conclusion that whereas Europeans tended to be colour-blind, everyone else was motivated by the sentiment of colour. Terms such as colour feeling and racialism were used as synonyms for the reaction to Western domination.

The racial interpretation of anti-Western protest became increasingly coherent in the 1930s. It helped establish an intellectual legacy that would question the legitimacy of the claims of Third World nationalism after 1945. Virtually every anti-imperialist outburst would be interpreted through the vocabulary of anti-white racialism. The reaction of the American Consul in the Gold Coast to the February 1948 demonstrations was paradigmatic. 'In my humble opinion of the native press, which had been preaching hatred of the whites and of the United Africa Company for a year was to a large extent responsible for the disorders that occurred last February and March.'[63] Racialism was now represented as something that motivated those who were challenging the West.

5   Crossing the Boundary:
the Marginal Man

The main interest of contemporary studies on the history of racial thinking in the 1930s is the debate on whether or not biological differences had social consequences. This was by no means the main concern of the race relations literature of the 1930s. As we saw in the previous chapter, interwar writers were far more concerned with the problems presented by the growth of race consciousness than with controversies about racial equality. A retrospective review of the presentation of race in American sociology textbooks in the 1930s concluded that the issues 'most popular of all' with sociologists were the 'phenomena of conflict, prejudice, race consciousness, and accommodation'.[1] Our own examination of the anthropological and sociological literature confirms this observation. The main preoccupation was with conflict, and in particular with the reaction of racially oppressed people to their circumstances.

The interwar literature often made reference to the issues of racial prejudice, which was associated with white reactions, and to race consciousness, which expressed a counter-reaction to differential treatment. Both reactions were represented as having similar qualities. Consequently, a symmetrical relationship was established between the two responses. By implication the one neutralised the other. Moreover, the sheer weight of the literature which directly and indirectly addressed the issue of race consciousness suggested that the central problem was this challenge to the status quo. Discussions would often begin with the reality of race prejudice as a prelude to considering and then attacking race consciousness. One contributor to *Social Forces* indicated that 'racial prejudice and segregation have had the effect of throwing the negro more and more upon his resources and, as a result, he is developing a racial consciousness'. According to the author, this development was leading to 'racial nationalism' and a 'racial psychosis', which he hoped would not go as far as to 'obscure' the 'fundamental identity of interest' between 'black and white'.[2] For this author the main question for research to answer was how to curb the race consciousness of American blacks.

The contrast between the literature on white prejudice and on race consciousness is striking. It is important to note, as Jackson observed, that research into race prejudice did not seriously begin until the 1920s 'when the debate over immigration restriction led to a heightened concern about reducing ethnic hostility in the United States'.[3] Moreover, for a considerable period, the literature on prejudice had a distinctly apologetic character. Often prejudice was presented as a natural instinct; sometimes race prejudice was treated as one of a number of everyday quirks, and thereby rendered banal.

The key sociological work on prejudice in the interwar period was the Chicago-trained sociologist Emory Bogardus' *Immigration and Race Attitudes*. Although directed at confronting prejudice, it was still very much within the naturalistic perspective. According to Bogardus 'race antipathy' was a reaction to 'differences in biological appearances'. He also considered that reactions 'against the odor of the body of members of "another race"' were 'uncontrollable'.

A race against whose members antipathy is aroused on sensory grounds cannot do much ... Particular attention to body constitution and appearance, hygiene and aesthetic measures, however, may accomplish something worth while.[4]

By the 1930s such a crude correlation between instinct and prejudice was giving way to more sociological explanations. Nevertheless, compared to the development of research into race consciousness, the study of prejudice remained relatively underdeveloped in the United States and Britain.

The fatalistic interpretation of prejudice and conflict in the interwar academic literature strengthened the conviction that a line between the races had to be maintained. Racial consciousness was itself presented as a product of too much contact between races. As a result, increasingly, attention was turned towards how to regulate or minimise such contact. Most contributors to a 1931 exchange on the colour bar in the *Spectator* supported some form of racial distance.

Even those who accepted that adjustment had to be made insisted on the maintenance of the colour line. As one of the contributors noted: 'the most favoured way of dealing with the problem at the present time is to readjust the dividing line between white and black and make it vertical instead of horizontal.' In other words, neither race would be economically superior to one other – they would just be living in a separate world. 'There would then be two pyramids – one wholly white, the other wholly black', was the helpful suggestion.[5] Other such sensible proposals insisted that regardless of what one thought of the problem, it was best to play safe and keep racial contact to a minimum.

Those who saw racial contact as the source of conflict invariably turned their attention to considering the human products of that contact. Such people were presented as by definition a problem, if not *the* problem, of race relations. Studies of westernised colonials and offspring of mixed-race relationships were symptomatic of an increasing interest in the sociology of crossing the line.

Drawing a Line – the Marginal Man

The widely held view that race consciousness was disruptive was ratified by the Anglo-American sociological tradition of the inter-war period. This perspective regarded colonial and racial conflict in terms of the *maladjustment* of individuals and groups to the conditions of change and modernity. From this standpoint the problem was not so much the impact of imperialism or of racism as the failure to adjust. It was proposed that those who could not adjust became racially conscious, anti-white or unstable. These were the uprooted products of the process of maladjustment. Neither rooted in their own society nor accepted by the West, the maladjusted individual lived between two worlds. The uprooted colonial intellectual or the racially conscious mulatto became symbols of the problem of instability. A review of the literature on maladjustment indicates that it soon turned into a sociological condemnation of race consciousness.

The model proposed by the thesis of maladjustment was based on the premise that the uprooted individual was an agent of subversion. According to this simplistic paradigm, westernisation, and in particular western education in the colonies, produced individuals with unrealistic aspirations. Educated blacks in America also suffered from the same pretensions. Since their aspirations would be inevitably rebuffed by European society, anti-white bitterness and hatred would be the most likely outcome. Rejection by the European was bad enough. However, the aspirant maladjusted individual could no longer return to his people. Such maladjusted individuals were doomed to a life of perpetual instability. Unable to live on either side of the cultural divide, they became a recruiting ground for troublemakers. The model of maladjustment suggested that they, rather than ordinary colonials, represented a danger to the existing racial lines.

Academic specialists, imperial officials, missionary intellectuals and Foundation lobbyists endlessly discussed the question of maladjustment. Sociological theories of maladjustment strongly influenced leading imperial officials. In turn, colonial administrators could draw on academics to provide an intellectual elaboration of their policy.

The British policy of indirect rule – colonial rule based on the conservation of tradition – was motivated by the imperative of avoiding the disruptive consequences of change. Lord Lugard, the author of this policy in Africa, was concerned to curb the expectations generated by modernisation and in particular regarded the 'educated native' as a threat to colonial order. The educated colonial subject in Africa, who aspired to Western standards in an environment which depended on the maintenance of racial and social distinctions, personified the problem. Such thwarted individuals were represented as impudent charlatans who aspired to be that which they were not. The literature continually emphasised the theme of envy and the absurd and futile attempt of the educated colonial to imitate the European. Such motives were proof of inferiority, but also suggestive of desperation. The very attempt to cross the lines between races, to seek to be what they were not, indicated that these individuals were capable of doing anything. Hence the counter-position between the traditional 'honest' native and the scheming 'detribalised' individual. According to Lugard these uprooted individuals were inferior to the traditional native:

The Europeanised African differs not merely in mental outlook from the other groups, but also in physique. Doctors and dentists tell us that he has become less fertile, more susceptible to lung-trouble and to other diseases, and to defective dentition.[6]

From this perspective such physical attributes were symptomatic of an underlying moral disease.

Lugard's indictment of the 'Europeanised native' was at once a condemnation of the blurring of the line that separates the races and a denunciation of the colonial intelligentsia. As proof of the futility of the policy of reform, he pointed to the example of the United States to demonstrate that despite educational opportunities, even black Americans had failed to progress. According to Lugard, the African educated person was even less likely to succeed. Such people were not to be trusted since they had lost touch with their own tradition and people. Lugard pointedly called into question their right to represent other Africans since they were 'separated from the rest of the people by a gulf which no racial affinity can bridge'. He described them in the following terms:

> Education has brought to such men only discontent, suspicion of others, and bitterness, which masquerades as racial patriotism, and the vindication of rights unjustly withheld. As citizens they are unfitted to hold posts of trust and responsibility where integrity and loyalty are essential.[7]

Such opinions were not the monopoly of officialdom. The American academic, Raymond Buell, in his influential survey *The Native Problem in Africa*, echoed Lugard's sentiments. 'The African "intellectual" is probably the most sensitive in the world', he wrote.[8]

In one of the most widely read and cited journalistic works on the subject of maladjustment, education was blamed for stimulating anti-Western sentiment. *Indian Unrest*, published at the turn of the century, argued that education acted on the 'frame of an antique society as a powerful dissolvent, heating weak brains, stimulating rash ambitions, raising inordinate expectations of which the disappointment is bitterly resented'. By way of contrast, the writer recalled *Les Deracines*, 'a remarkable French novel' about the 'road to ruin taken by poor collegians who had been uprooted from the soil of their humble village'. The writer added that 'in Asia the disease is necessarily much more violent, because the transition has been more sudden, and the contrast between old ideas of life and new aspirations is far sharper'.[9] During the next three decades social scientists would recall this 'remarkable novel' in their discussions of maladjustment.[10] In turn, the analysis of maladjustment would provide the point of departure for explaining the rise and consolidation of race consciousness.

American and British race relations institutions believed that people of colour would not benefit from Western education. Their educational experts advocated a system of education that emphasised practical rather than intellectual skills. Their proposals were couched in a relativist language of respecting peoples' traditions, but as Hetherington remarked: 'they also reflected the fear that broad Western education would promote subversive ideas'. This was a sentiment which sought to minimise the educational achievement of people since 'the process of educating the African might make him more easily indoctrinated with Pan-Islamic or Pan-Negro doctrines'.[11] Apprehension regarding the educated colonial converged with the reaction of moral condemnation.

Academics concerned with colonial matters and social scientists interested in the problem of change were increasingly drawn towards the study of the 'Europeanised' or 'detribalised native'. Such people who existed outside the conventions of tradition but who had not yet assimilated into modernity, personified the problem of cultural change. These 'Marginal Men' became an important focus for sociological discussion during the interwar period.

W.O. Brown, in his work on race consciousness, directly borrowed from the Lugardian perspective. He remarked that the 'native intellectual who formulates the grievances of the native is of importance for the student of race consciousness'. And echoing Lugard, Brown observed that the native intellectual's 'union with native culture is tenuous'. Because he belongs to neither the native nor the European world, 'he feels the pinch of the racial situation more sharply' and reacts more strongly than the 'average native'.[12] Similar formulations appeared in numerous publications during this period.

The interest that academics displayed toward the Marginal Man, the detribalised native, the mulatto or the half-caste was the product of their interest in the problem of change. There was considerable discussion about the capacity of the existing institutions to adjust to new circumstances. One of the most sensitive commentators on American race relations wrote in the 1920s that the 'rising consciousness of the negro race is slowly surpassing the capacity of present racial adjustments'.[13] Most analysts who studied the impact of conflict on institutions were particularly interested in the individuals who demanded change. Academics, involved in the study of the disruptive effects of colonisation and the prevalence of conflict, regarded such people as maladjusted. Maladjustment did not merely imply the difficulty of adapting to new circumstances. It also underlined a problematic mental state. Being uprooted and not being accepted in the dominant culture were seen to expose intense insecurities. The tendency to psychologise dissent by labelling it as oppression psychosis or an inferiority complex (noted in the previous chapter) dominated the literature. When one sociologist, in an address to the American Sociological Society in 1919, informed his audience that the condition of maladjustment led to a 'hyper self-consciousness', which, when 'carried far enough', could 'result in a definite neurotic condition, as is often seen among the Jews', no one voiced dissent.[14]

The interaction between colonial officialdom and British anthropology in the twentieth century is well known. However, the influence of imperial views on the subject of maladjustment went beyond that of a single discipline. Correspondence and collaboration between colonial officials and social scientists on both sides of the Atlantic was widespread.[15] It is often difficult to detect the origins of the ideas, but an inspection of reading lists distributed to colonial administrators and university students in the interwar period suggests that there was a strong current of cross-fertilisation.[16]

The American sociologist Everett Stonequist, author of *The Marginal Man: A Study in Personality and Culture Conflict*, was clearly influenced by these traditions. Stonequist was a student of R.E. Park, the leading representative of the Chicago School of Sociology. It was Park, drawing on the preoccupation of the European sociological tradition with the problem of order, who prevailed on Stonequist to embark on his thesis. Park was strongly influenced by the German sociologist George Simmel's ideas about the stranger, the early prototype for the Marginal Man.[17]

There were other influences on Stonequist. In the Preface to *The Marginal Man*, he acknowledged the influence of the Oxford academic and leading imperial publicist Sir Alfred Zimmern on his writing. But more pertinent for this discussion was Stonequist's debt to Lord Lugard. Stonequist wrote in his Preface that his interest in his subject matter 'began with a lecture given by Lord Lugard at the Geneva School of International Studies in 1925 describing the effect of European ideas and practices upon native life in Africa'. He noted in passing that he was particularly interested in Lugard's comments 'upon the detribalised'. This should come as no surprise: *The Marginal Man* can be read as sophisticated sociological defence of indirect rule.[18] Like Lugard, Stonequist considered the detribalised as a race apart. The Marginal Man suffered from 'personal maladjustment' and possessed a victim mentality.

The pathology of the Marginal Man recurred in the writings of many British thinkers. When Julian Huxley pointed to the detribalised African and declared that 'there is here the ill-regulated untidiness of the uprooted African', the Lugardian influence was unmistakable. The influential British sociologist Morris Ginsberg strongly praised Lugard's *Dual Mandate*. Ginsberg's *The Psychology of Society*, published in 1921, condemned the semi-educated intellectual: 'They are often capricious and despotic, and exhibit all the characteristics of the parvenu.'[19] This pathology of the Marginal Man – whether in the form of the detribalised native, the half-caste or the colonial intellectual – became an integral element of the self-consciousness of the British imperial mind. 'The pathology of wounded self-esteem reaches its acutest form in the new intelligentsia' was how Crocker described the condition of maladjustment.[20]

Sociological Contributions

It is worth noting in passing, that despite its conservative implications, many liberal social scientists felt at home with Lugard's approach. American cultural anthropology and the growth of relativism in the 1930s converged on crucial points with the policy of indirect rule. The preservation of tradition was consistent with the positive promotion of cultural differences. So, for example, in a collection of essays written by liberal social scientists in the 1930s and early 1940s on the encounter of cultures, every contribution sided with indirect rule as against assimilation.[21] British social anthropology was even more wholehearted in its promotion of indirect rule. This consensus on fundamentals may help explain the absence of a literature critical of the maladjustment thesis at the time.

The varied concerns and influences that shaped American and British thinkers meant that the ideas regarding the in-between person acquired different intellectual representations. In the United States it was the experience of racial tension which gave focus to the discussion. American sociology, in particular urban sociology, led the way. In Britain, the elaboration of ideas about maladjustment was stimulated by the experience of 'maladjustment' in the colonies. Here it was social anthropologists, for example the scholars associated with the Rhodes-Livingstone Institute, who elaborated the problem of maladjustment and of the uprooted individual.

The impact of the maladjustment thesis on British social anthropology was straightforward and self-evident. It was the direct result of collaboration with colonial officialdom and of the intellectual tradition. Malinowski warned the readers of the *American Journal of Sociology*, that the 'anthropologist recognizes more and more fully how dangerous it is to tamper with any part or aspect of culture, lest unforeseeable consequences occur'. Malinowski promoted the policy of indirect development in order to minimise the consequences of maladjustment. He was no less concerned with the 'African in transition', who 'finds himself in a no-man's-land, where his old tribal stability, his security as to economic resources, which was safeguarded under the old regime by the solidarity of kinship, have disappeared'.[22]

Malinowski feared that Europeanised Africans would rebel against the limits imposed on their ambitions by colonial society. Consequently he had profound misgivings about European education and the African intellectual. 'The European, instead of regarding all education or any education as an asset, might consider here that what the African takes from the European culture may be a handicap and a malediction, a blight or an injury, if it opens horizons, develops ambitions, raises him up to a standard of living which cannot be achieved', he warned[23] Ironically, others would hold up Jomo Kenyatta, one of Malinowski's former students, as the personification of the Marginal Man.[24] Later, the Mau Mau would be interpreted as proof of the dangers inherent in the state of maladjustment.

Most anthropologists regarded the 'educated native' with pity rather than an active dislike. Lucy Mair wrote of the responsibility that Britain had 'towards the educated African' since 'European policies have brought him into being, and the figure which they have created is in many ways tragic'. Others, such as Meyer Fortes, could barely contain their revulsion at the consequences of the 'insidious conflict of cultural values'. In no uncertain terms he vigorously upheld tradition: 'The religious and legal sanctions of right conduct have become ambiguous, and the common symptoms of a maladjusted social system – crime, prostitution, corruption, and unbridled acquisitiveness – have become prominent to an extent never known in the traditional social order.'[25] The sentiment that at the very least the detribalised were morally displaced dominated anthropological literature. According to Godfrey Wilson, urbanised men and women in Zambia found themselves 'morally and intellectually unprepared for the new conditions'.[26]

Most anthropological writing on the detribalised colonial was unsystematic. That individuals in transition were a problem appeared to be self-evident. There was little analytic elaboration of the concept. Many British ethnographers used the term detribalised as a synonym for such vague concepts as development or change. Wilson's imprecise use of the term was characteristic of the approach:

Moreover, as the change is taking place in an uneven manner the present situation is full of tension and maladjustment.

the historical process of adaptation to the new conditions – call it the process of civilization or the process of detribalisation, it is the same thing – is not yet complete; nor is it proceeding altogether smoothly.

Monica Hunter emphasised the tendency to the disintegration of tradition in her discussion. 'There is much talk of what is vaguely called "detribalization", or "the disintegration of Native society"', she reported. But for all its vagueness it continued to be used as if its meaning was self-evident.[27] A mixture of pity and revulsion is evident in the work of Westermann, a German anthropologist and one of the key figures in the London-based International Africa Institute. According to Westermann, the 'consciousness of an educated man that he is a member of an inferior race' required sensitive handling.[28]

The topic of the detribalised, uprooted colonial featured regularly in the deliberations of the missionary lobby. In Northern Rhodesia, throughout the 1920s, local missionaries had expressed serious concern about the dynamic of urbanisation. According to them, the mines disrupted local communities. Missionary thinkers believed that Africans who went to work in the mines would soon lose contact with their community, become detribalised and eventually fall prey to the temptations of the urban environment.[29] Local missionaries viewed urbanised Africans with suspicion and regarded the mine compound with scorn. These prejudices were regularly aired at conferences of missionary societies in Northern Rhodesia during the 1920s and 1930s.[30] Alarmist accounts of African immorality and of racial hatred were routinely despatched to the headquarters of missionary societies. Such reports clearly influenced missionary publications and the conceptualisation of the problem of social cohesion in Africa.

A conference of missionary leaders in November 1930 was devoted to a discussion of whether Northern Rhodesia provided an ideal site for the first major IMC research project. Here the development of the Copperbelt was problematised in a number of ways. Canon Spanton of the University Mission claimed that in some villages in Northern Rhodesia there was not 'a single able-bodied man' left. Another missionary stated that women were also leaving and that this 'double trend was most demoralising for the whole community'. He added that 'the whole effect of these contacts of the raw native with civilisation is disintegrating and demoralising'.[31] Missionary intellectuals lobbied the IMC to organise a research project on the impact of the Copperbelt on detribalised Africans. This conference 'agreed that the mining developments created a great human problem affecting the life of half a continent' and proposed that the department of Social and Industrial Research should undertake as one of its first major tasks a survey of the effects of mining in Africa with special reference to Northern Rhodesia. The investigation into the Copperbelt, eventually published as *Modern Industry in Africa*, and authored by Merle Davis, provided a paradigm for imagining and representing the demoralised in-between person. The discussion around the organisation of this project suggested that Merle Davis and his collaborators knew in advance what they wanted to say. The purpose of their research was to confirm their intuition and illustrate the pathology of maladjustment. The content of *Modern Industry in Africa* was largely anticipated in the preliminary discussions. For example, Merle Davis's preliminary report on his 1930 tour of Africa had touched on the themes reported in the subsequent survey. In this preliminary report, Merle Davis cited industrialisation and the growth of mining activities as the cause of the decline of Basuto society. He observed that in Basutoland, 'agriculture, stock, condition of land, health, morality and family, and family and tribal society have all definitely retrograded'.[32] Similar sentiments, which stressed the dangers of the urban environment for the African, were considered to be self-evident by IMC intellectuals. The depiction of westernisation as a direct danger to tradition and social cohesion was strikingly communicated in the portrayal of the urban environment as one of moral decay and disintegration.

Modern Industry in Africa provided a clear statement of the IMC agenda and presented a well-informed account of recent developments in the Copperbelt. But it was a story that interpreted events from the point of view of a Christian morality in crisis. Accordingly, culture contact created a problem of adjustment. Despite the presence of a sociologist on the research team, maladjustment was posed in moral terms. It regarded life in the newly established urban centres of Northern Rhodesia with a palpable sense of revulsion:

> The copper belts of Central Africa illustrate the moral and social confusion which attends the sudden meeting of widely contrasted cultures. Under these circumstances a marginal region, or moral 'no-man's land', develops in which the controls and sanctions of both cultures are weakened and the vices and licence of both reinforce one another.[33]

The Davis report confirmed missionaries' attitudes towards

'detribalised Africans'. Many missionaries regarded the urban Africa as a moral wasteland, where the urbanised African had become a depraved caricature of the European. As one missionary remarked at the July 1931 meeting of the General Missionary Conference of Northern Rhodesia, 'so now, we have a perfect black gentleman. He is dressed in silk, keeps a concubine ... [but] ... he is a stranger to his own village and he is detribalised.[34] Such sentiments were repeated in the survey. Although missionary intellectuals referred to their insights as 'scientific', their publications were essentially statements of morality rather than sociological analysis.

A more coherent development of this subject of maladjustment took place in the United States where sociologists were directly confronted with the problems of immigration and of race relations. The subject of assimilating immigrants from different cultures and of integrating the black population into the mainstream of American society stimulated a focus on the in-between individual. Many sociologists concentrated on the mulatto, the American deracialised equivalent of the detribalised African. Edward Byron Reuter's 1918 study *The Mulatto in the United States*, expressed concern that this group was tending towards agitation. His diagnosis of the educated mulatto 'agitator' was expressed in the following terms:

> The agitators voice the bitterness of the superior mulattos of the deracialised men of education, culture and refinement who resent and rebel against the intolerant social edict that excludes them from white society and classes them with the despised race.[35]

During the interwar period the discourse cast in racial terms gradually gave way to more sociological ones.

The Chicago sociologist, Robert Park, played a major role in reorienting this discussion from its early biological emphasis on racial mixing to a more sociological focus. Park's theory of the Marginal Man was the American equivalent of the detribalised native of the British anthropological tradition. Although Park was unusually sympathetic to his subject matter, he evoked the tragic dimension of the marginal way of life. There is a kind of ambivalence, which sees the 'mulatto' as a leader of the black population as well as an individual that could never be at ease with him- or herself.[36]

One of the consequences of migration is to create a situation in which the same individual – who may or may not be a mixed blood – finds himself striving to live in two diverse cultural groups. The effect is to produce an unstable character – a personality type with characteristic forms of behaviour. This is the 'Marginal Man'. It is in the mind of the Marginal Man that the conflicting cultures meet and fuse.[37]

Parks's disposition towards psychologising led him to formulate a personality type that was not the product of this or that experience but of all forms of culture conflict.

Consequently, with Park, the concept of the Marginal Man transcended the American situation. It was a generic concept that could be deployed to examine the dynamic of maladjustment in other contexts. Indeed, Park was concerned to emphasise that marginality was not reducible to racial mixing but encompassed a wider cultural and indeed moral dimension.

Ordinarily the Marginal Man is a mixed blood, like the Mulatto in the United States or the Eurasian in Asia, but that is apparently because the man of mixed blood is one who lives in two worlds, in both of which he is more or less of a stranger. The Christian convert in Asia or in Africa exhibits many if not most of the characteristics of the Marginal Man – the same spiritual instability, intensified self-consciousness, restlessness, and malaise. It is in the mind of the Marginal Man that the moral turmoil which new cultural contacts occasion manifests itself in the most obvious forms.[38]

Park's sociology of race relations provided a synthesis of the hitherto fragmented accounts of culture contact, maladjustment, race consciousness and the moral disintegration of the uprooted. Park himself was careful not to condemn the Marginal Man. The 'moral turmoil' of this mind is posed in relatively neutral terms. However, the symptoms that he identified, such as 'spiritual instability', 'intensified self-consciousness' and 'restlessness' were presented by others as a moral condemnation.

In previous discussions on the uprooted colonial there was a stress on cultural type rather than on personality. Park helped orient the subsequent research towards a more systematic consideration of a personality type. Increasingly, marginality became associated with a state of mind. This perspective readily lent itself to an apologetic interpretation, where the maladjusted mind rather than the problem of colonial domination or racial oppression became the problem. During the interwar period the discussion increasingly concentrated on the apparently unrealistic expectations of the Marginal Man. These individuals were extremely 'sensitive' and tended to 'overreact' to their situation. According to Western observers, they also tended to have an exaggerated sense of their grievances. These character traits were central to the discourse of the interwar sociology of the Marginal Man.

Articles on the subject of culture contact in the *American Journal of Sociology* were preoccupied with the condition of marginality. An account of the 'Eurasian in Shanghai' observed how this 'racial hybrid' tends 'toward exaggerated self-pity' and defensiveness. A discussion of Asian nationalism in the same periodical explained the problem of maladjustment in terms of a character flaw. 'An intellectual training had been provided which enabled them to understand Western ideas, but not the character formation which enabled them to function adequately in a dynamic competitive society.'[39] Elsewhere, the Anglo-Indian was targeted and condemned for his 'shabby and pathetic Britishness'.[40]

The American sociological periodical *Social Forces* was no less concerned. Articles on miscegenation and marginality paralleled the attitudes expressed in the *AJS*. The Anglo-Indian reappears as a demoralised individual prone to 'excessive drinking and gambling'. 'This demoralisation is reflected in the fact that in the large cities numerous Anglo-Indian women are to be found engaged in professional or semi-professional prostitution', the reader was informed.[41]

Either explicitly, or implicitly in the case of more detached observers, the character of the educated colonial was called to account. Considerations of maladjustment tended to shift back and forth between the moral and the psychological spheres. It was the psychological dilemma of having to negotiate living in between two worlds that shaped much of the reaction of the Marginal Man. In this way the reaction to racism of the educated colonial or the American mulatto or the Eurasian could be interpreted as the manifestation of a weak personality.

Stonequist's *Marginal Man* provided a synthesis of the sociology of the maladjusted individual. Although almost entirely derivative of the earlier discussion, the *Marginal Man* became one of the most influential works on the subject during the 1930s and 1940s. The concept influenced the work of Kenneth Little, who was probably the pioneer race relations academic in Britain.[42] The idea of marginality was not only part of the prevailing sociological tradition, it also influenced non-academic discussions. Stonequist himself was involved with the Institute of Pacific Relations and was Director of Research of the Office of War Information from 1944 to 1945. His *Marginal Man* combined the insights of the Chicago School with a Lugardian disdain for the educated colonial. From this standpoint the problem was not the colonial situation but the psychological reaction of the Marginal Man to it.

According to Stonequist, the state of marginality helped mould a character that was inherently unstable and oversensitive:

> Because of his anomalous position – not fully belonging to either parent race – he becomes more than ordinarily conscious of himself and conscious of his ancestry. There is an increase in sensitiveness.

Insecurity drove the Marginal Man to intensify 'his concern about status'. Stonequist argued that it is this preoccupation which explained their political involvement.

> His anxiety to solve his personal problems forces him to take an interest in the racial problem as a whole. Consequently he has an important part in defining and eventually changing the general pattern of race relations.[43]

In this model, anti-racist agitation was an instrument through which the maladjusted individual coped with life. Stripped of any principles or idealism, anti-racism was represented as a form of mendacious special pleading by self-centred individuals.

The Marginal Man thesis suggested that the reaction to racism or colonial domination was best understood as the reaction of the psychologically frustrated. The need to compensate for a sense of inferiority led to a 'new feeling of self-appreciation and even self-exaltation'. For Stonequist it is this feeling that 'heralds the birth of a nativistic or nationalistic movement'.[44]

The importance of Stonequist's contribution was that while he recognised some of the extreme manifestations of Western domination, his arguments called into question the legitimacy of anti-imperialist or anti-racist movements. Such movements were interpreted as the irrational action of the psychologically frustrated. The Marginal Man never acts; he overreacts. To give some examples:

> The hypersensitiveness of the Marginal Man has been repeatedly noted. [This] may result in a tendency to find malice and discrimination where none was intended ...
> The marginal situation produces excessive self-consciousness and race consciousness.[45]

By elevating the psychological state of marginality, there was a crucial redefinition of the issue at stake. It was not so much racism as the overreaction to it that constituted the problem. It was not idealism, conviction or political passion, but a psychological overreaction which drove Marginal Man's anti-imperialism.

For Stonequist, anti-colonial politics became the means through which maladjusted Marginal Man acquired self-esteem. Of course, this stress on adjustment left the colonial reality as unproblematic. Moreover, the detribalised native's character fault served to condemn him morally. The educated colonial was 'spiritually adrift', motivated by selfishness and envy. Thus it was not idealism, political conviction or nationalist motivation that drove anti-colonial movements, but the pettiness of the maladjusted personality.

Said's description of Western representations of the Orient focused on the recurrent theme whereby the

> oriental is imagined to feel his world threatened by a superior civilisation; yet his motives are impelled, not by some positive desire for freedom, political independence, or cultural achievement *in their own terms* but instead by rancour or jealous malice.[46]

The durability of this theme shows the vitality of the thesis of maladjustment leading to moral disintegration.[47] The focus on the psychology of anti-Western sentiment invariably distracts from the wider social and historical structures of Western domination.

By representing the reaction to racism as the pathology of the Marginal Man, sociological theories of race consciousness helped to discredit it intellectually. The widespread influence of this outlook in the 1930s and 1940s helps place in perspective the intellectual climate on race. Precisely at a time when scientific racism was under attack and when ideas of race equality were gaining currency, a rearguard action was successfully discrediting the reaction to racism. The emergence of a moral condemnation of race consciousness may well have helped the West postpone the time when it would have to confront the question of racial discrimination.

Holding the Line

The discourse on the in-between person was at once a discussion of maintaining existing social, cultural and racial boundaries. By his very existence the Marginal Man was seen to put into question the durability of these boundaries. By questioning these boundaries, the Marginal Man or the detribalised native threatened to encroach on the status of the European. That is why there was such a clearly articulated tendency to create a moral distance between the Marginal Man and the European. The insistence on moral difference represented an attempt to uphold a line and repulse those who claimed equality. Whatever they were, the Marginal Man and the detribalised native were not European. They might be in-between, but they were not conceptualised as a bridge between races. Mencke was surely right when he observed that in the United States, the discussion of the Marginal Man was interpreted by some as an argument to 'force mulattos back into the black race, at least morally'.[48]

A condemnation of miscegenation was almost always implicit in the literature on the maladjusted Marginal Man. The discourse continually fluctuated between arguments that stressed the racial and those that focused on the moral. According to academic specialists, the 'hybrid' that was produced was not just a racial but also a cultural hybrid. However, most studies either implicitly or explicitly assumed that it was the effect of racial mixing that was most far-reaching. As Wirth and Goldhamer noted, 'the mixed blood is sometimes assumed to exhibit the characteristic personality traits of the Marginal Man more clearly than the purely cultural hybrid'.[49] The premise of this assumption – that with race mixing there was no way back – was rarely spelled out.

Academic writers qualified their condemnation of race mixing with the caveat that the problem was not so much with the hybrid as with the circumstances which isolated such people from both the dominant and subordinate classes. Malinowski contended that the 'most dramatic, not to say tragic, configuration of racial relationships occurs' when 'whatever mixture takes place is socially degraded, and where in consequence, a rigid caste system comes into being'. But while Malinowski was sensitive to the way that society could stigmatise the hybrid, he himself had serious doubts about the wisdom of miscegenation. 'It is a questionable blessing when a lower race ousts or absorbs a higher, or when a distinctly inferior mixed race is formed', he concluded. Why? Because a 'mixed race does not rise to the level of the higher parent-stock'. Malinowski was pessimistic about the ability of a mixed-race society to progress:

> At best, we can hope, then, that the partly mixed, partly Europeanised population, such as the Negroes of the West Indies, will be able to hold their own and to establish a new polity and a new culture in their new home. The recent American invasion of Haiti is however, an ominous indication of the dangers which beset this type of solution.[50]

From this perspective, the avoidance of mixing and the strict maintenance of a racial line made the most sense.

Merle Davis's reports on the Caribbean combined an appreciation of the destructive effects of colonialism and discrimination with an almost emotionally driven revulsion against the immorality of a racially mixed society. According to Davis, this was a society where 'illegitimacy and superstition' reigned supreme. He reported that the 'West Indian rural community too often resembles a "no man's land", neither African nor British in its characteristics'. This was a 'grotesque world, distinct from that of either of the races to which destiny has linked it'.[51] It is worth recalling that Merle Davis stood at the liberal end of the race relations industry: the wisdom of holding the racial line was not a subject of controversy at this point in time.

In non-academic accounts the moral distancing of the Marginal Man was often strident and deliberately insulting. Hybridity was portrayed in unflattering terms and conveyed the warning: 'Do not presume to be like the white man.' Articles dealt at length on the alleged tendency of hybrids to imitate the European. Such pretensions were invariably repulsed and the reader was reminded that the products of race mixing bore the stamp of moral inferiority. The American writer Gertrude Marvin Williams observed that 'the most pathetic of India's minority groups are the mixed bloods'. As a mark of their pathetic state, she remarked that they 'always wear European clothes', and added:

> They fawn upon the English and make pitiful advances to them. They always speak of England as 'home' though they may never have been there, and they are forever vainly trying to include themselves with the British.[52]

It was the idea that those of mixed race and the English could share the same 'home' that Williams found particularly preposterous. Such an aspiration was unacceptable to the interwar racial imagination.

During the interwar period there was little criticism of the moral repulsion of the Marginal Man. White fears regarding race mixing were treated as natural and unworthy of critical reflections. This sentiment continued well into the 1940s. Anson Phelps-Stokes reminded his collaborators in 1946 that reports on the subject of race relations should avoid giving the impression that 'we favor inter-marriage'.[53] None of his associates took exception to this reminder. This was a subject on which no concession could be made.

One of the rare attempts to engage the moral condemnation of the Marginal Man was by the American writer Lewis C. Copeland. Copeland characterised 'moral distinctions' in race relations as the 'final rationalization of racial contrasts'. His analysis stressed the importance of moral distancing and moral repulsion against mixing in American racial thinking. He took the view that racial beliefs helped create 'two social orders and moral universes'. This outlook was rooted in white racial fears: 'There is a widespread fear of the invasion of the white social order by the black man.' Fear of social invasion was illustrated by the tendency of white people to react most to those black people who stood closest to them. Copeland believed that it was this reaction which motivated the 'defamation of the mulatto', for the person of mixed parentage was a 'moral anomaly' in the 'racial imagination'.[54] Copeland's concept of the 'defamation of the mulatto' clearly expresses the manner in which apparently neutral descriptions of the state of mind of the Marginal Man helped masquerade moral condemnation.

Copeland's insights help place in perspective the race relations discourse in the interwar period. Apprehensions about holding the line are not directly reducible to a desire to protect economic privilege. Such fears also expressed self-doubt and anxieties about the possible exposure of white pretensions. It was almost as if there was an expectation that nothing would be the same if other races came too close and saw the European at 'home'. The fundamental assumption was that the racial line had to be maintained otherwise white prestige would suffer. Thus the racial line existed in both a metaphorical and physical sense: even the existing world order was seen to depend on keeping everything in its place.

Lord Lugard's approach provides a striking confirmation of Copeland's analysis. The Lugardian perspective was firmly committed to the maintenance of racial boundaries. According to Lugard, too much inter-racial familiarity would have a detrimental effect on 'white prestige', and any weakening of this prestige would necessarily undermine global stability. It was from this standpoint that Lugard criticised those missionaries who pursued egalitarian ideals:

> That a white man should come to Africa to do menial work in the furtherance of an altruistic ideal is not comprehensible to ... [the native] ... and the result is merely to destroy the missionary's own influence for good, and to lessen the prestige of Europeans, upon which the avoidance of bloodshed and the maintenance of law and order so largely depends in Africa.[55]

In the final analysis the maintenance of racial boundaries symbolised order and stability. Those who crossed the line threatened to undo decades of painstaking empire-building.

The Panic About the Detribalised Soldier

The preservation of a Western-dominated international system depended on a system of control, and on the maintenance of a clearly defined race line. This would preserve imperial control in the colonies. From a Western perspective, it also reduced the problem of race relations by excluding people of colour from many parts of the world. This was the justification of the White Australia policy on immigration. In turn, theories of maladjustment provided a compelling argument against culture contact. Such contact was seen to generate conflict and to have a destabilising effect on race relations. From this standpoint, the possibility of a second world war was regarded with foreboding. It was feared that such a conflict, which would involve all races, would undermine the white-dominated international order. The impact of such a war would give maladjustment a new meaning, and concern was expressed about the survival of the prevailing boundaries of race. In the colonial context many of these preoccupations focused on the detribalised colonial soldier.

The colonial soldier was represented as a classical Marginal Man, but one in possession of a weapon. Moreover, such soldiers, having seen the world, became all too familiar with the ways of white people and developed aspirations about the future. 'What would happen to these soldiers when they demobilised?' was the question posed by many colonial administrators. In a sense the very experience of soldiering created the condition of marginality or detribalisation. One British propaganda officer in Northern Rhodesia noted that the *askari*, the African soldier, 'has become used to "direct rule" by a *Bwana*' and that moreover he was 'becoming "detribalized" in the army'.[56] According to this view, the African soldier was not only separated from his tradition but also from the conventional forms of white racial control. Colonial administrators believed that the experience of soldiering would have such a far-reaching impact, that the individual soldier would never be the same. Time and again reports warned that the returning colonial soldier would not be prepared to accept racial and social etiquette and would be potentially a force of subversion.

Throughout the Second World War, colonial officials in Africa were preoccupied with the potential danger which returning soldiers represented. One American intelligence officer reported that this was a recurrent topic of conversation among British administrators in East Africa.[57] Such conversations amongst European officials revealed deep anxieties about the danger posed by returning African veterans. 'God, so that's what we've got coming to us after the War', was the reaction of some Europeans watching a display of close combat by African troops in Northern Rhodesia in the spring of 1943. Dire predictions of future dangers were an integral part of casual conversations amongst Europeans in Africa.[58]

Reports by Captain A.G. Dickson, the head of a British mobile propaganda unit in East Africa, confirm the prevalence of these reactions. In a review of the situation in Uganda, Dickson noted that after Special Services troops dealt with a prison riot in Lugazi, it was an 'open joke' among the European officers at Kampala 'that their real "blooding" would have to wait till the Uganda troops returned home on demobilisation'. Dickson continued:

> Not one but almost every District Commissioner espoused anxiety regarding the return of troops ... This atmosphere of dread regarding the undisciplined African home from the wars dominated conversation. There was something unpleasantly sinister in the way Administrative Officers would frankly urge us to fire our weapons so that Africans might appreciate the futility of arguing with Bren guns.[59]

Throughout the continent of Africa similar white racial fears were evident. The American Consul in Accra reported that the 'Gold Coast Government is anticipating with some trepidation the return from the Far East of the thousands of its men now serving in the armed forces'. The fears were vague, though the underlying anxiety was highly concentrated. The warning issued by the Headquarters of East Africa Command in 1946 was typically indeterminate: 'the possibility of disturbances occurring, now that most of the troops have been demobilised will increase'.[60]

The language used to describe the problem conveyed the impression that the correspondents thought that trouble was unavoidable – 'bound to occur', to use the words of the American Consul, or 'inevitable' in the case of the Whitehall prognosis for West Africa. An editorial in *The Times* also had this alarmist character: 'the return of these men in their thousands – without their officers – may well jeopardise the whole fabric of indirect rule'.[61] That this trouble was likely to have 'racial implications' was one of the unstated assumptions. One of the ironies was that the vision of peril associated with the demobilised colonial soldier was in sharp contrast to the relative ease with which such troops were absorbed into society after the war. Imperial reaction to the returning soldier clearly had the air of panic. But what were imperial officials worried about?

The panic reflected deep concerns about losing control over individuals who had physically as well as morally crossed the existing social and racial boundaries. Everyone knew that when soldiers returned home from war they had usually changed. In the case of colonial soldiers, such changes were perceived to have far-reaching consequences. Colonial soldiers who travelled abroad were thought to be vulnerable to insidious influences. As a memorandum issued by the East Africa Command indicated, 'a large number of demobilised *askari* will have served in the Middle East where they have come into contact with ways of life quite different from those they knew before and which in many cases are undesirable'.[62] The term undesirable referred to the loss of control which the contact of East African *askari* with new and often unpredictable experiences implied.

The question of control often focused on the difficulty that a colonial society would have in absorbing those who had seen a different world. Having tasted freedom would these veterans accept white colonial authority? This question was posed with a particular intensity in the case of South Africa. As Louis Grundlingh's study of this subject indicated: 'the utilisation of black troops in areas outside South Africa such as North Africa, the Middle East, and Europe was a source of grave concern'. Soldiers' contact with everyday life in conditions 'vastly different from those in South Africa was seen as potentially dangerous because it might militate against the acceptance' of racial inferiority upon return.[63]

South African army reports on black soldiers continually referred to the problems that were created by their contact with the outside world. The most intense anxieties were focused on the potential for sexual contacts with white women. But even routine fraternisation between black and white soldiers was seen as a matter for serious concern. Colonel Stubbs, the officer in charge of black South African troops, complained that 'one of the great problems with which I am faced today and which does not tend to ease the position, is the fraternisation of European with non-European troops'. 'I am finding it very difficult to control them', he wrote. Stubbs noted that they have been 'allowed under force of circumstances a liberty, if not a licence, they have never enjoyed in this country, and on their return they apparently expect the same opportunities as they received in the Middle East'.[64]

Reports on African troops in the Middle East regularly echoed racial apprehensions about the consequences of crossing the existing boundaries. Stubbs objected to the use of black troops outside Africa on the 'ethical' ground of 'using Non-Europeans in purely European countries'. He also objected because he anticipated 'that when they return there will be grave difficulty in reorienting their minds to "differentiation" policy of the Union after their association with Europeans who know no colour distinction'.[65] Preventing black South African soldiers from getting round the colour line was an important priority for Stubbs and his superiors.

At one level the discourse on the colonial soldier involved apprehensions about his loyalty. But it also represented a presentiment that relying on colonial troops undermined white authority and exposed the weakness of imperial powers. Expressions such as 'loss of face' and decline of 'white prestige' recurred time and again in military reports. They probably said more about the state of white racial psychology than about the outlook of colonial soldiers. For example, American diplomats in Africa were convinced that white authority had declined. Joseph Touchette, the American Consul in Nairobi, reported that African soldiers had 'registered the fact that the Europeans have lost "face" in having to call upon black Africans to assist' in the war. British imperial officials believed that the moral authority of the Empire could be undermined by the experience of the war. Andrew Cohen, a leading policy-maker in the Colonial Office, directly linked the 'special problem of returned soldiers' to his conclusion that Britain was 'at the end of the period during which' it could 'rely on the white man's prestige to govern Africa'.[66]

Cohen's problematisation of white prestige reflected an awareness that the prevailing racial etiquette could not be maintained.

By implication it also represented an awareness that the race line could not be held much longer in its existing form. The colonial soldier, the personification of the Marginal Man, would not accept his allocated place on the other side of the boundary. This is what the discourse on white prestige was really about. It is difficult to find any elaborate discussions of white prestige in serious scholarly investigation, which is curious given its prominence in Anglo-American racial discourse. Such an omission is illustrative of a more general tendency to overlook the subject of white racial fears altogether.

White prestige implied the self-evident and self-confident affirmation of superiority. From this standpoint, colonial domination was represented as the product of white moral, intellectual and technical qualities. It was held, moreover, that colonial subjects readily recognised this superiority and more or less acquiesced to their domination. Fears about the decline in white prestige therefore expressed a real concern that relations of power could not continue as before. Accounts of what colonial troops saw, and why that would lead to the fall of white prestige, were characteristically vague. They tended to emphasise the point that familiarity with the white race would necessarily undermine that prestige. Who could be more familiar with the white race than African soldiers who 'have frequented brothels used by European troops and have had intercourse with white or near white women'. It is worth noting that this observation was made in a military report under the heading of 'What The *Askari* Has Learned Which Might Be A Source Of Danger On His Return To Civil Life'.[67]

One of the few attempts to elaborate the concept of white prestige is contained in a memorandum by H. McDowell on his experience as a European officer with the *askari* of the 11th Battalion of the Northern Rhodesian Regiment. In this interesting report, McDowell writes interchangeably of a 'prestige relationship' or the 'Bwana relationship' between the African and the European. 'This relationship so constituted, linked the otherwise separate social and moral worlds of African and European', he noted. The prestige relationship both regulated and maintained racial interaction through moral separation. McDowell argued that this relationship of superiority and inferiority depended on the belief 'that all white men were *ipso facto* candidates for a position at its upper end'. However, the war had created a situation where this pretence could not always be maintained. McDowell observed that during the war, African soldiers saw whites no longer as the stereotype *Bwana*. The African soldier 'fought on equal terms with white skinned Italians, and has no great opinion of them'. Experiences with Europeans scared under gunfire and with British Tommies who 'brawl' on the streets and do 'menial chores' and who 'above all does not consider himself, and still less proclaim himself to be, a superior creature' have meant that *askari* no 'longer knows who is a *Bwana*'. Such doubts, according to McDowell, had struck a fatal blow at white prestige. 'Once doubt about the validity of its assumption has begun to be felt, no prestige relationship in history has continued.' He concluded that 'automatic white prestige, as a mechanism of adjustment will continue to serve for years, but its fate is ultimately sealed'.[68]

McDowell's memorandum is important not so much for its analytic rigour as for its insights into the psychology of racial fears. In McDowell's scenario, the colonial soldier was represented as a direct witness of the white race at its worse. It was as if these interlopers had crossed the line and literally caught out the pretensions of white prestige. This consciousness of exposure was a testimony to the prevailing crisis of confidence about holding the line. The colonial soldier served as a reminder that something would have to change. The war had given culture contact and maladjustment theories of race relations a new meaning. It was no longer a one-way process of Westernisation. The whole world had been turned upside-down creating opportunities for new forms of contact. As the next chapter argues, the Second World War had a major impact on the transformation of international race relations. One of its rarely discussed but nevertheless important legacies was the erosion of racial boundaries, at least in the imagination of the Anglo-American elites.

Concern about white prestige and other manifestations of racial fears were not the only expression of the general consciousness of a loss of control of the Anglo-American elites. Nor was it necessarily the most important concern preying on their imagination. Imperialism in general was experiencing a crisis of confidence. This was the product of three interlinked and mutually reinforcing developments. The growth of anti-capitalist forces throughout the globe helped establish a radical alternative to the status quo. At the same time, a growing challenge from the South called into question the existing colonial arrangements. These factors contributed towards a crisis of self-belief – what has sometimes been called the moral crisis of imperialism.[69] This climate was hospitable to the growth of racial fears. In turn racial fears expressed apprehensions about control in general. It is worth noting that the problematisation of race mixing had two sides to it. In a sense, concern about race mixing also represented doubts about the lower classes of the white race. The so-called Poor White problem in South Africa was emblematic. As indicated earlier, reports on this subject were sensitive to the racial implications of too much contact between poor whites and blacks.

A 1944 report entitled the 'Condition of the Coloured Population in A Stepney Area', but actually about the effects of race mixing in this district of east London, manifested a strong sense of revulsion against the poor white. Concern about the moral fitness of the white poor was explicit. It complained that Negroes 'have no opportunity of meeting English people with good moral standards'. White women who took up with black migrants were described as 'prostitutes' or 'daughters of prostitutes'. The author of the report, Phyllis Young, stated that most of these women were 'below normal intelligence and, according to officials who have dealt with them, oversexed'. Young observed that 'these women have very little moral sense'. Her description of 'this tragic corner of Stepney' reflected deep anxieties about the 'erosion of the race line'.[70] In many ways the report was far less flattering about poor white people prepared to mix than about black migrants. The same sentiment was expressed by Canon H.M. Grace, a leading figure in the British missionary movement. In response to a demand for guidance as to how young English Christian girls should behave with black soldiers, he stated: 'I hope that as the races do gradually merge, marriage will begin in the higher social levels rather than the lower levels at first'.[71] This was a coherent synthesis of elite pragmatism. Canon Grace was reconciled to the inevitability of race mixing – but he still held out some hope that it could be regulated by those at the top of the social hierarchy. He was still hoping that somewhere and somehow some kind of racial line could be maintained.

6   The Second World War as Race War

As we saw in chapter 5, the Second World War witnessed the internationalisation of racial concerns. It was also a crucial experience for transforming racial thinking. According to one study of the attitude of American sociologists to race relations, 'perhaps more than anything else', this war was 'responsible for changing [the] attitude of sociologists'. Barkan's examination of the retreat of scientific racism also highlights the importance of the war for the 'discrediting of racism in international politics'.[1] Most writers have emphasised how the international revulsion against Nazism led to a new discourse on race. While this was an important motif in the recasting of racial thinking, it was by no means the most significant influence.

One of the most significant consequences of the Second World War was the erosion of the international colour line. This had important implications for international relations as a whole. Increasingly racial tensions in one part of the globe became interlinked with parallel developments in other parts of the world. One outcome was the growing rejection of the prevailing racial order in the colonies. Colonial subjects, who were asked to make sacrifices for a war that was not of their making, often reacted to new impositions on their lives. The war brought to the surface the grievances of those who were forced to live with the consequences of discrimination. Official censors throughout the British Empire continually pointed to the anger expressed against racism in the letters they handled. This indicated that even the most ordinary manifestations of the prevailing racial etiquette would soon be contested. A young woman from Bermuda, writing to her friend in Antigua in the summer of 1942, exemplified this reaction:

> In Bermuda young coloured girls and boys, men and women do not have positions like I heard in the West Indies. You could count the coloured lawyers, doctors and dentists here on your fingers and in all the big stores and numerous offices you see white girls and women. I

get so fed up sometimes to think why we could not work in the places and co-operate.[2]

Reactions such as this indicated that the old international order could not for long endure. Demands for a new, more equitable order were being voiced throughout the colonial world.

The experience of racial discrimination had an important influence on the anti-colonial movement in the Caribbean. Whitehall officials were aware of its importance and, by the early 1940s, feared that they could irrevocably lose the 'educated' Caribbean. The Information Officer stationed in Kingston, Jamaica reported that 'racial animosities are being vigorously stirred up' and predicted the growth of militant nationalism. American officials based in Jamaica concurred and, according to one account, feared the 'repercussions of conflict on the black population in the United States'.[3] The issue of racism pervaded all sections of Caribbean society: even troops recruited from the region exhibited a heightened awareness of the issue. It is instructive to note that when the British War Office offered to despatch the Caribbean Regiment to India, it warned that 'the men are extremely colour conscious and expect to be treated as white troops'. This sentiment was widespread in nearby British Guiana. An American State Department memorandum concluded that 'the Colony is seething with political movements based upon racial aspirations, economic discontent, and nationalist sentiment'.[4]

Even the relatively liberal missionary lobby was taken aback by the intensity of the colonial reaction to racism. Reports of outbursts of anti-white missionary revolts by African Christians were regularly discussed at meetings of missionary societies. Black African students at Fort Hare demanded 'religious liberty' and rejected the paternalism of European missionaries. One European missionary caught up during the 1940 Copperbelt riots described the shock of having to face black anger:

We were shocked and humiliated ... The room we were in was a mass of terrified Africans and several Europeans some of whom were in an abject state of terror. The humiliation of having to stand helpless during the climax of the tragedy, the dumb sorrow which seemed to hang like a pall over the Africans at Mindolo (we shall never forget the absolute silence of Wednesday night), our keen feeling that confidence had been lost and might be difficult to recover (perhaps it will never be completely recovered) in relationships between white and black – these and many other impressions will remain lifelong memories.[5]

This sense of rejection combined with a loss of confidence about managing the issue of race relations was widespread in missionary circles.

The rise of anti-colonial sentiment was only one dimension in the changing contours of the international situation. Another, perhaps the most significant development, was the crisis of white domination. As noted in the previous chapter, so-called white prestige stood exposed. As the prevailing norms of racial superiority came to be questioned, so even everyday conduct came under scrutiny. The erosion of the international colour line called into question the racial etiquette that was practised not just in the colonies, but also at home in Britain and the United States. A letter, written by an English woman, Kathleen Stephenson, asking church leaders for advice about how relations between her white English girls and black American soldiers should be conducted, is a testimony to a new dilemma. 'In Hull, as I suppose in many other areas, the colour problem has rapidly come to be a much more intimate problem than ever it was before the War', she observed:

> By helping in hostels and clubs provided by the American Forces, our girls are daily coming socially into contact with coloured men and of course dancing and other activities, which are shared and enjoyed by all, gradually tends to reduce any prejudice we might have had.

The question for Kathleen Stephenson was how far was it permissible to erode the colour line. 'Is it really harmful if friendship contracted in this way develop into deeper friendship of love and marriage, and if they do, what special problems will the people concerned have to face?' she asked.[6] The difficulty that her correspondent, as well as other church officials, had in answering this question was a testimony to the weakening of traditional racial certainties. Racially mixed dances, leading to romantic relationships, were new territory for everyone concerned.

Race had indeed become a dilemma. Even those who stuck to the previous norms of racial thinking felt uncomfortable with openly expressing their views during a war that was ostensibly against an ideology of extreme racism. However, the anti-Nazi ideology of the allies' campaign made it difficult to avoid discussing discrimination. The inconsistency of denouncing Nazism while ignoring racial discrimination was pointedly drawn by Gunnar Myrdal. He concluded that in 'this War the principle of democracy had to be applied more explicitly to race'. That meant that 'America had to stand before the whole world in favour of racial tolerance and co-operation and of racial equality'.[7] This inconsistency was so deeply entrenched that even a liberal American periodical, *Survey Graphic,* was able to separate its denunciation of Nazism from its support for eugenics in the United States. In one of its issues, the foreign correspondent John Palmer Gavit denounced Hitler's barbaric treatment of Jewish people, while a few pages later another author, R.H. Landman, argued for the adoption of German sterilisation programmes in America.[8]

The inconsistency to which Myrdal alluded reinforced the mood of racial uncertainty. Assumptions of racial superiority were too deeply entrenched for there to be a serious confrontation of the issue. However, in the new international climate, it was no longer possible to express such sentiments openly. As a result racial concerns continued to influence Anglo-American policy decisions and political life, but more and more covertly. The silencing of racial concerns became public policy, thereby widening the gap between racial practices and rhetoric. The deliberations of the American and British governments on the racial aspects of the war were highly secret and rarely intruded into the public domain. For example, officials sought to keep guidelines about the treatment of black American soldiers in Britain confidential. In turn, the notes issued by the British government emphasised the importance of not publicising racial incidents. 'Never pass on a story which would tend to create disaffection', was the advice offered by the official guidelines.[9] A similar approach was adopted in relation to the publication of an official report on post-war demobilisation. One official commented that the 'reference to the colour question' contained in the report 'might be considered objectionable' if it was published. He was reassured that the report would remain confidential.[10] This rule was widely observed by journalists covering the war. According to

Theodore White, an American journalist in China, 'the ethic of the time forbade one from reporting in terms of race'.[11]

The widely observed rule of silence may explain why this aspect of the conflict has received such scant attention. Even histories of racism underestimate the significance of the war in shaping the future of racial thought. Probably the most systematic exposition of the racial dimension of the war is to be found in the works of the British historian, Christopher Thorne. 'In one of its vital aspects, the Pacific War of 1941 to 1945 was a racial war', he noted. This was also the burden of Laurens' thesis, who has argued that the war 'raised the issue in a way that nothing else in history has ever done before'; and Akira Iriye has drawn attention to the way in which the war against Japan was interpreted through the prism of race by Western elites.[12] It is worth noting that these accounts have as their focus the more explicitly racialised conflict against Japan in Asia. However, this dimension was only the most explicit manifestation of the racial dynamic. As this chapter indicates, neither the racialisation of the conflict nor its perception as a race war was confined to the Asian theatre of war.

When the war broke out, sections of the Anglo-American elites were concerned about what they viewed as the explosive character of race. Many of them regarded the racial conflict in the aftermath of the First World War as a dress rehearsal for what was to come. Japan's early military triumphs in Asia and the positive response of colonial people to these achievements served as an unwelcome confirmation of this expectation. Deliberations held behind the scenes indicated that racial fears would influence official and informal policy. These fears, focused on demobilised colonial soldiers, are only one manifestation of this response. Apprehension was particularly intense in racially charged societies such as the American South and South Africa. The question of whether or not to arm black soldiers became a major source of controversy in white South Africa. The military went out of their way to prevent black soldiers from coming into contact with the white population in order to minimise the anxieties of Europeans. A leading military official demanded the postponement of a parade of black soldiers on these grounds. 'It has been the policy of the Government not to advertise amongst the European population of this country the fact that natives are being trained for military services', he wrote.[13] It was not only in South

Africa that the allied powers regarded their black soldiers with apprehension. Such sentiments prevailed within every level of the US military. Even the Secretary for War, Stimson, who regarded himself as unprejudiced, complained about those 'foolish leaders of the colored race' who objected to segregation in the Army. He dismissed their perspective as folly, since its goal was 'social equality' and this was impossible to achieve 'because of the impossibility of race mixture by marriage'.[14] Stimson, and the political class that ruled Britain and the United States, were not ready to concede social equality. But nor were they prepared to uphold racial supremacy. For them, social equality was a loathsome idea that could no longer be confidently rejected.

The fundamental dynamic behind the outbreak of the Second World War was not a racial one. It is not the intention of this chapter to argue that race was the defining feature of this conflict. However, the war brought to the surface a complex of racial concerns which helped to intensify white anxieties and strengthen the movement against racism. In the end, for a variety of reasons, this experience proved decisive in transforming racial thinking. The most important cause of the racialisation of this war was the self-conscious attempt by the Nazis to represent the conflict in racial terms. In response, those who opposed fascism became more sensitive to the destructive consequences of racial politics. In this climate, all forms of racist practices, including those of the Allies, eventually came under scrutiny. Vulnerable to such criticism, the Anglo-American elite often interpreted attacks on their own record as racially motivated. The Western powers adopted a variety of tactics to tackle this thorny question. However, there was little doubt that there would be important changes internationally in the way that race relations were conducted. We shall now turn to examining the different strands in this silent race war.

Racial Themes During the War

White Fears

All sections of the Anglo-American political class were apprehensive that the war might lead to a conflict of colour. Such sentiments acquired a profound sense of urgency following the setbacks which the Allies experienced in Asia. Japan's claim that it was fighting on behalf of the races of Asia lent the conflict an important racial dimension. Consequently, Western powers expected that the widespread manifestations of anti-colonial opinion would acquire a racial dimension. Such expectations were expressed with different emphases by liberal and conservative voices.

Liberal publicists, politicians and journalists argued that it was necessary to take pre-emptive action against racial discrimination. For example, the American periodical *New Republic* and the British *New Statesman* took the line that reform was necessary if a racial war was to be avoided. Articles in the *New Republic* focused their anger against the racist practices of the American South and accused Southerners of driving blacks into the hands of the Japanese enemy. 'Our Negrophobes from the South', wrote one columnist, 'have worked hard to keep 13,000,000 Americans isolated from our own community and to prepare them for Japanese propaganda'. It warned that American blacks saw in a Japanese 'a man of color'. The other theme on which the *New Republic* dwelt was the danger of what would happen when the 'new negro will return from the war'. 'He will have been taught to kill, to suffer, to die for something he believes in, and he will live by these rules to gain his personal rights', it warned. The same point was advanced by the *New Statesman*. It evoked the memories of 1919, 'when race riots flared as thousands of negroes sucked into the war machine were the first to be laid off into permanent unemployment'. It ominously noted, 'this time there are millions'.[15]

The need to attend to the problem of race relations was a regular topic in the deliberations of the Institute of Pacific Affairs (IPR). Many of the participants had an explicit racial interpretation of war. They regarded the reform of race relations as a vital aspect of the post-war settlement in Asia. Throughout the war, the IPR argued for an acceptance of the principle of racial justice in order to aid 'the better prosecution of the war'. 'Probably few of us understand how bitter the Oriental is about pre-war European imperialism', argued a submission from the American Council to a conference of the IPR.[16] One of the regular subjects of IPR discussions was the need to re-educate Western opinion on race. This view was also strongly upheld by missionary circles. American missionaries pointed out that poor race relations at home undermined the nation's image abroad. C.S. Johnson, the director of race relations of the American Missionary Association of the Congregational Churches, argued that the United States first had to 'clear its conscience on the issue of the rights of the common man' before it could 'take its rightful position on the high moral ground among the nations of the world'.[17]

The danger inherent in the racialisation of the war was an argument that some on the left used to advance the cause of reform. One prominent European member of the South African Communist Party informed an American diplomat that unless they solved the 'Indian Problem', it 'might become the tinderbox for starting another world conflagration, this time between the white race and the colored races'.[18]

Mainstream politicians and military leaders regarded the racial dynamic of the war not as a problem for the future but as an important influence over the conduct of the conflict. Their overall consensus was that such a war would weaken the power of the West. Some politicians believed that 'coloured nationalists' would use this opportunity to settle scores with their white overlords. Even before the outbreak of the conflict in the Far East, they regarded the coming war in explicit racial terms. By 1938, Anthony Eden, the British Foreign Secretary, was 'privately urging the need to "effectively assert white-race authority" in the Far East'. Sir Frederick Maze, the British Inspector General of China's Maritime Customs, saw the Tientsin crisis of 1939 as representing not merely a confrontation between Britain and Japan, but of 'Orient against the Occident – the Yellow Race against the White Race'.[19]

American officials were ever alert to what they referred to as the 'racial implication' of the conflict. A State Department memorandum of June 1942 feared that even if Japan was militarily defeated, it might obtain 'such a secure place as leader of the Asian races, if not the coloured races', that an allied victory 'might not be definitive'.[20] Officials feared that they could not count on the loyalty of the 'coloured races' in the Caribbean and in Africa. After the fall of Malaya, Rexford Tugwell, the Governor of Puerto Rico, wrote in his diary that the loyalty of his 'natives' was far from guaranteed. He was concerned to avert an act of 'betrayal'. 'I have been wondering whether it might not be strategic for the President to support a new status for Puerto Rico now', he wrote in his diary. Similar views were expressed by American officials stationed in Africa. 'I feel that our officers and men should be especially careful not to express their opinions on negro soldiers in public, in a country where every Arab has a drop of negro blood', observed one military official involved in public relations in Morocco.[21] Such reactions signified that Western supremacy had become uncomfortable with itself. That something had to be done to prevent a conflict that would inevitably work against the interest of the white race was the unspoken assumption of many of these exchanges.

White racial fears existed in a context of intellectual and psychological confusion. At the outbreak of the war, racial arrogance was still an acceptable style in the Anglo-American elites. Military leaders in particular seemed convinced about the merits of European superiority in face of enemy fire. When the British Commander-in-Chief in the Far East visited Hong Kong in 1940, he dismissed the Japanese soldiers that he encountered as 'sub-human specimens dressed in dirty grey uniforms', who would not be able to form 'an intelligent fighting force'. Even after the loss of Asian colonies to the Japanese, the British military still maintained their assumptions of superiority. General Cunningham concluded on the basis of the experience of the East African campaign that 'coloured troops with few exceptions, cannot stand up to the strain of modern warfare unless they are personally led by white officers'.[22] Similar assumptions were held by Lord Swinton, the British Government's key representative in wartime West Africa. 'Under white leadership the African is a good soldier, but will not only be completely ineffective, but will take no action at all, unless he has white officers or N.C.O.s to lead him', he argued.[23]

As the war wore on, confident manifestations of racial arrogance became increasingly rare. Many of the communications from Asia expressed not so much arrogance as demoralisation. The following report on Britain's débâcle in Burma summed up the mood of demoralisation:

It is a story of incompetence, panic and chaos ... The Chinese were the only forces really fighting. On my way out of Burma I met many a British soldier cursing his own officers, cursing the mismanagement of the campaign, cursing his equipment and the dud weapons he was given, cursing his lack of knowledge of the country.

The report contrasted the bravery of the Chinese fighting the Japanese. It noted 'the European element in my opinion, displayed appalling cowardice and selfishness'.[24] A similar shift is evident in the diaries of Sir Alexander Cadogan, an influential mandarin in the British Foreign Office. Cadogan routinely referred to the Japanese as 'beastly little monkeys' or as 'yellow dwarf slaves'. But on the eve of the fall of Singapore, his note of defeatism clearly outweighed racial arrogance. 'We are nothing but failure and inefficiency everywhere and Japs are murdering our men and raping our women in Hong Kong', he noted, before complaining that 'I am running out of whisky and can get no more drink of any kind'.[25] Reports of European failure and cowardice helped create a climate where the confident assertion of racial arrogance became less frequent.

White superiority was no longer unproblematic even to the most strident advocates of imperialism. The British surrender to the Japanese at Singapore had traumatised the imperial mind. This military catastrophe irrevocably diminished imperial self-confidence. Issues of control, loyalty and white prestige seemed to merge and tended to exhaust the imperial imagination. Setbacks in Asia disposed officials to expect the worst throughout all the colonies.

In practice, racial fears and assumptions of superiority existed in an uneasy relation with each other. The British War Office was sensitive to racial considerations – but the exigency of fighting the war forced it to compromise. While it accepted the view that 'neither West nor East Africans should serve in Europe, it could not guarantee the isolation of these troops from black Americans.[26] In Trinidad, the presence of American black troops produced a strong sense of apprehension among the white population. The American Consul reported that the whites showed symptoms of 'resigned petulance' because they recognised that 'their economic importance and their influence as a pressure group' were being reduced. The anxious white population organised a campaign for the expulsion of black US soldiers. They prevailed on the Governor to ask London to replace black with Puerto Rican troops. 'Though neither are wanted here Puerto Ricans would be preferable to United States' negroes', wrote Governor Bede Clifford.[27]

In turn, American military officials practised racial segregation not simply because they believed in white superiority, but because they feared the consequences of the erosion of the colour line. That is why they were unwilling to use Afro-Americans in front-line combat duties in certain theatres of war. In order to avoid facing up to the demands for race reform they were even prepared to underutilise black units. American military officials were quite sympathetic to the anxieties that colonial powers had towards the stationing of black American troops in their territory. At the same time they also feared the consequences of stationing such troops in French colonies on the grounds that it might undermine American racial etiquette. 'It is also possible that the social position accorded by the French, who in general are less color-conscious than Americans, to the handful of Paris-educated Africans in their midst might have some disturbing effects upon the morale of our own Negro soldiers stationed in the area.' Here, anxiety about the possibility that American soldiers might be treated like Paris-educated Africans by the 'less colour-conscious' French was interpreted as a potential discipline problem.[28]

The British were also concerned that colonial troops would develop loyalties along lines of colour. That is why Whitehall wanted to prevent colonial troops from being 'contaminated' with unacceptable ideas by black American troops. 'I imagine that in an ideal world we should certainly wish to avoid having British African personnel serving alongside American coloured troops', wrote A.H. Poynton of the Colonial Office. The considerable volume of correspondence on this subject indicated that Poynton was not alone. Administrators from different parts of the Empire were firmly against allowing their local soldiers to fight alongside black Americans. They were no less firm in their opposition to black Americans being stationed in the colonies. But this was not an 'ideal' world and colonial subjects could not be hermetically sealed against contact with black American soldiers. British Governors complained, and often blamed instances of unrest on the influence of black Americans on the local population. American officials were sympathetic. For example, the Intelligence Division of the US War Department reported that in Trinidad, the situation was stable until 'our colored troops disembarked'. It predicted that 'local disturbances' would ensue.[29]

Anglo-American officialdom regarded the overseas deployment of African troops as a problem for the future. It is worth noting that already during the middle of the war, plans were afoot to prevent the recurrence of this problem after the war. A report written in 1942 by a group of American race relations lobbyists, under the auspices of the Committee on Africa and Peace Aims, proposed that in future wars African soldiers should be restricted to their own continent. Almost all the American and British experts who were canvassed accepted this proposal. Malinowski expressed this consensus when he stated that 'the wise and imperative demand is made for the restriction of African troops to their own continent'. The only voice of dissent was that of the Afro-American intellectual, W.E.B. Du Bois. Du Bois retorted that 'African troops have as much right to fight outside of Africa for their vital interest, as white troops have to fight in Africa'. He reminded the authors of the report that the 'prestige of the white race' should not be a factor influencing their proposals.[30] None of the commentaries by white experts took exception to the proposal on African soldiers.

Regardless of fierce anxieties, during the war racial fears had to give way to the exigencies of warfare. Decisions had to be taken that violated the racial sensibilities of Anglo-American policymakers. Probably the most striking illustration of such uncomfortable decisions was to allow South African black soldiers to have access to weapons. When pushed against the wall, South African leaders were prepared to make all kinds of concessions. The most dramatic manifestation occurred in early 1942, when the strategic situation appeared to be desperate. The Japanese had broken into the Indian Ocean and South Africa was forced to prepare for an invasion. At this point, Jan Smuts, the President of South Africa, made his famous 'retreat from segregation' speech. He told Parliament that 'before Japan, before the enemy, takes this country, I shall see to it that every native and every coloured man who can be armed will be armed'.[31] Smut did not fulfil his promise. He didn't have to since the danger of a Japanese invasion soon passed. But by raising the possibility of arming South African blacks, Smuts helped to reinforce racial anxieties. Indeed, the very fact that the white elites were forced to arm those whom they feared must have given racial fears a new dimension.

The tension between racial calculations and the necessity for pragmatism in the sphere of policy-making was paralleled in the plane of ideas. The war also contributed to the crisis in racial thinking. Many writers have pointed to the contradiction between the prevailing anti-Nazi ethos and the practice of discrimination in areas under Allied jurisdiction. In these circumstances it was difficult for proponents of racial superiority to occupy the moral high ground. There was more than a hint of bad faith in the official correspondence of the time. In 1943, Whitehall officials recalled that in 1938 they were prepared to appease Germany by offering African colonies in exchange for a peace pact. Sir George Gater, the permanent under-secretary in the Colonial Office, wrote that 'out of fear of Germany, we were prepared to hand over large tracts of the colonial empire to Germany without consulting the wishes of the inhabitants'.[32] This acknowledgement that Britain was not beyond reproach expressed a vulnerability to the charge of inconsistency. On no other issue was the British Empire more incoherent than on that of race relations.

Racial Interpretation of the Demand for Equality

Throughout the war, American and British officials tended to interpret resistance against colonialism or discrimination as a manifestation of 'colour feeling'. It was believed that the war had internationalised the issue of race and had thereby contributed to the intensification of 'colour consciousness'. As a result the demand for equality tended to be situated in the context of an international challenge to Western domination. Moreover, the internationalisation of race presented itself as a direct influence in fuelling racial consciousness. The advocacy of racial equality was also defined as disruptive and potentially dangerous since it diverted energy from the conduct of the war. Those who nevertheless insisted on championing this cause were often perceived as dangerous subversives. From this standpoint, 'in appealing to the nationalist, anti-European feelings of the Asiatic peoples Japan has tried to turn her end of World War II into a racial war', was the conclusion of one study of Japanese propaganda.[33]

This racial interpretation of resistance to oppression often took the form of depicting the victim as the instigator of conflict. In many accounts those who exhibited symptoms of colour consciousness were the chief culprits for making race an issue. One American sociologist, H.R. Brearley, argued that the tendency of blacks 'to over-emphasise the racial interpretation of behaviour' has been 'reinforced by the recent world-wide development of race consciousness'. According to this argument the 'stirrings in India and elsewhere' have influenced the 'negro's conceptions of himself and of his role in human affairs'. 'Rather vaguely he begins to feel that he is part of a great social movement for the liberation of the dark-skinned peoples from the domination of the European.' From this perspective, the consciousness of race challenged not just the European but also the war effort. Even in the United States, 'The rapid increase of incidents of interracial violence among civilians during recent months [of the war] indicates that the American Negro has developed a belligerent attitude that is causing surprise and alarm, both North and South', wrote one author.[34]

Officials reporting from the colonies reported similar developments. Moreover the growth of 'colour consciousness' was sometimes linked to a decline in white power, prestige or even racial vigour. The advice of the American military was to treat such colour consciousness among African troops as an overreaction. A report entitled *Psychiatry Amongst African Troops* on West African soldiers stationed in India noted that 'emotionally they may be safely compared with school boys'. The report concluded with the following advice:

> Because he represents any trace of unfairness or discrimination to a degree unknown in Europe he must never be allowed to feel that he is being treated differently from his fellows, for he is very apt to sulk for days over some imagined slight.[35]

Despite its patronising tone, the burden of the report was to make concessions to a racially motivated demand for equality.

Throughout the Caribbean, the balance of power appeared to shift against white domination. A report written by a leading British colonial official on the problem of race in the Caribbean acknowledged that 'the feeling in regard to colour has been growing in recent years and this fact has to be faced'. He added:

> This feeling has been due to the challenge to the whites from the educated and more progressive elements of the middle class. With the

possible exception of those in Barbados and St. Kitts there is no doubt
that the whites in the West Indies lose physical and mental vigour and
indeed generally deteriorate unless their vigour is reinforced by
marriages with persons from Europe and North America.[36]

In line with the mood of the times, a zero-sum view of racial
competition informs the representation of political trends. The
obvious counterpoint to white decline was black ascendancy.

One of the underlying themes in this racial interpretation of resistance was the apprehension that an incident in one part of the
world would encourage a revolt against white domination in another. The view that race relations had become a relation of conflict,
which was reproduced on a global scale, acquired coherence in the
early 1940s. Consequently, discussions of a particular problem invariably raised the international dimension of this development.
Myrdal's *An American Dilemma* can be read as a warning to those who
remained indifferent to the global aspects of the race problem. He
believed that the 'time to come to an understanding on the basis of
equality is rapidly running out'; and he warned that in the end it
would be the whites who would pay the price. 'When colored nations
have once acquired power but still sense the scorn of white superiority and racial discrimination, they are likely to become indoctrinated by a race prejudice', which can only be satisfied 'by the whites'
humiliation and subjugation'.[37]

Although Myrdal was ahead of Anglo-American public opinion,
the view that one of the outcomes of the war would be the
diminishing of white influence was accepted in principle by
officialdom. This clearly informed the tendency to perceive
challenges to the international status quo in racial terms. Not
surprisingly the intuitive response to that challenge was to slow
down these changes.

The War as an Opportunity for the Racially Oppressed
The tendency to interpret the Second World War in racial terms
was also shared by advocates of black rights in the United States
and by those fighting imperial domination in the colonies.
Intelligence reports on the state of morale in British colonies
continually drew attention to the widespread sentiment that this
was a 'white man's war', which was of little interest to anyone else.

A report from Northern Rhodesia (now Zambia) observed that
educated Africans were expressing their response to the war in the
following terms:

> You want our help now that you are in trouble. But what have you
> done for us? What are you doing now for us? What are you going to do
> for us? You say German rule will be bad. How do we know? Yours is
> not so good anyway.

The Governor was at a loss to know how to respond to such sentiments. He observed that the 'African can see the "colour bar" which
in theory does not exist, working in practice'. Therefore there would
be little enthusiasm from this quarter for the war effort.[38]

Anti-German propaganda in Africa and the Caribbean often had
little impact on people who regarded colonial rule with hostility.
Many colonial officials were reluctant to promote the war as a struggle for freedom and democracy, in case people understood these
principles to apply to themselves. 'Colonial subjects', noted one leading Whitehall mandarin, 'might be tempted to say that they have not
much freedom to defend'.[39] Indeed, that was the consensus among
politically active people in the colonies.

Many nationalists regarded the war as an opportunity to wrest
concessions from the imperial powers. In the context of wartime
propaganda about the 'struggle for freedom and democracy' many
colonial nationalists believed that their time had arrived. In a
comment on President Roosevelt's speech commemorating the
anniversary of the Atlantic Charter, Ndame Azikiwe, the leading
Nigerian nationalist, pointedly asked 'whether President
Roosevelt had us in mind when he used the term "all Peoples"'.[40]
Azikiwe and other nationalist leaders continually drew attention
to the inconsistency of fighting for freedom in principle, while
tolerating its denial in practice. In a sense, the approach of African
nationalists was diametrically opposed to that of colonial officials.
Whereas colonial officials sought to keep silent on the issue,
anti-colonial nationalist continually drew attention to it. Anti-
colonial activists sensed that their opponents feared an open
high-profile discussion of racism. This point was retrospectively
noted by the British anthropologist Raymond Firth in relation to
West Africa. He contrasted the 'more violent opinions of racial

prejudice, as expressed privately by some Europeans' to its public manifestation by 'some organs of the African press'.[41]

Black activists in the United States also sought to promote the issue of racial justice as a key question of international relations. From their standpoint, the war had important implications for race relations. Many of them regarded the war as an opportunity to question the racial status quo. Black activists called for a 'Double V', victory at home over racism as well as victory over the Axis powers. From this perspective the goal of racial equality was seen as no less important than the prosecution of the war effort. The NAACP in the United States self-consciously linked the domestic race issue to the turmoil in India and the Pacific campaign. Its 1943 report declared that the war expanded 'the horizons of thinking people enormously, and sometimes painfully, widened with the realization that the United States cannot win this war unless there is a drastic re-adjustment of racial attitudes'.[42]

Reports by the Office of War Information (OWI)'s Bureau of Intelligence provided 'formidable evidence of the degree to which racial grievances have kept Negroes from an all-out participation in the war effort'. One survey conducted amongst Harlem blacks revealed that a significant minority of 38 per cent believed that it was more important to make democracy work at home than to defeat the Axis powers.[43] Many black leaders equated American racists with the Nazis and demanded fundamental changes to the institutions of discrimination and segregation. The war increased the bargaining position of black leaders. In exchange for delivering the co-operation of their communities they expected concessions and a reform of race relations.

Studies of black morale during the war indicated that the response of this community to the war was very different from that of the white population. It also indicated that the white community had no idea about the state of Afro-American opinion. 'Negroes express many grievances and dissatisfaction, yet the majority of whites think Negroes are generally satisfied.'[44] The division between black and white opinion was clearly reflected in their attitude towards Japan. Significant sections of the black community regarded the Japanese as fellow 'people of colour' who were beating the white man's civilisation.[45] The OWI called this current of transnational racial identification 'pan-colored feeling'.

Many stories in circulation provided vivid examples of how American blacks derived a quiet satisfaction from seeing the Japanese thrash their white opponents. Moreover, the perception of the war as one motivated by racial concerns was clearly communicated by the black media.

According to Kearney's important study of Afro-American reaction to Japan, 'the black press tended to view the war as a race war'. Kearney's analyses shows that black editors 'seemed anxious to explain war excesses on the part of Japanese as reactive' and they tended to be 'more condemnatory of atrocities on the part of whites'. The black press also argued that American policy towards Japan was racially motivated.[46] Articles in the black press drew attention to the racist insults heaped on the Japanese. It was suggested that a racist double standard was at work, which explained the virulent hatred that white Americans displayed towards the Japanese in comparison to their muted reaction to their European enemies.

Marjorie McKenzie, writing for the *Pittsburgh Courier*, drew attention to this. McKenzie noted that 'there is a quality of hate which Americans hold for the Japanese which does not compare with general sentiment about the Germans, even the Nazi leaders'. Kearney's study indicates that the Afro-American press continually pointed to the racial epithets which were thrown at the Japanese to draw attention to the racial motives behind the war. 'The use of the terms "yellow bastards", "yellow monkeys", "little yellow devils", or anything else with yellow affixed were generally deplored by blacks,' she noted.[47]

War-time reports on black morale indicated widespread disaffection and resentment. An influential study prepared by Kenneth Clark indicated that in comparison to the experience of the First World War, attitudes had hardened immeasurably. According to Clark, blacks could no longer be fobbed off with minor concessions; they had become 'more rigid' in their demands and were more militant and also more self-aware as a race. He added:

There is less eagerness and ability to identify themselves with the common cause (the goals and aspirations of the nation) ... There is evidence that this inability to identify with the common cause also involves an increase in the amount of racial ethnocentrism, which may probably be interpreted as a form of group withdrawal in the face of general and specific social frustration.[48]

It was this increase of what Clark called 'racial ethnocentrism' that would ensure that the war would be interpreted in racial terms by a significant section of the Afro-American population. Virtually every aspect of the way the war was conducted served as an affirmation of this perspective. The segregated America army was an illustration of how the conduct of the military was subject to the influence of race. Reports of German POWs eating in American restaurants that denied service to black GIs and the controversy surrounding the practice of segregated Red Cross blood banks helped fuel the resentment of the Afro-American population. The escalation of racial violence during the war – in 1943 alone, 242 racial battles occurred in 47 cities – indicated to black Afro-Americans that they had their own struggle to fight.

The consolidation of black racial awareness alongside mounting racial friction and violence had a major impact on the domestic scene in the United States. Until 1943–44, the American political class had sought to keep race off the political agenda. However, anxiety about the threat of a major outburst of black militancy and concern about its implication for the conduct of the war led to a change in approach. According to Plummer, the American political class began to take steps to contain this militancy. Individuals such as Edwin Embree of the Rosenwald Fund launched initiatives such as the establishment of the American Race Relations Council, to help prevent the radicalisation of Afro-American grievances.[49] Kellogg's important study of the liberal press provides compelling evidence that race was increasingly seen as a problem in its own right – an issue that the government had to address. One indication of this development was that at least in American liberal circles, race was less and less identified as the 'Negro Problem'; it was increasingly seen as a problem for whites.[50] The views expressed in Myrdal's *An American Dilemma* reflected this shift in attitudes. Those who contested Myrdal's stance did not question the significance that the war had for race relations. For example, the Southern liberal sociologist, Howard Odum, was sensitive to this development, but his reaction was to fear the worst. The difference between Odum and Myrdal expressed the two sides of the intellectual response to the issue. As Southern argued:

'Myrdal perceived the war as a vehicle for racial change, whereas Odum saw in the global conflict the spectre of racial turmoil.'[51] Although Myrdal was far ahead of American public opinion, he clearly anticipated its future direction.

The changing agenda of American race relations cannot be understood outside the context of a war that was seen by a substantial section of the Afro-American community as one motivated by racial concerns. The war eroded the line that separated the racial etiquette practised in the United States from the so-called international colour line. Whether Washington liked it or not, American race relations were now under international scrutiny. Racism in America had become a public relations liability for a power with pretensions to assuming global moral authority. Such international pressure contributed to the strengthening of a liberal attitude towards race relations. Undoubtedly this international conflict had far-reaching implications for the renegotiation of race relations. As Jackson argues, 'a new racial liberalism' emerged, which would dominate the discussion in post-war America.[52]

The Role of Japan and the War in Asia

It was the Japanese challenge to Anglo-American interests in Asia that constituted the most significant contribution to the internationalisation of the race issue. Other than the Russian revolution of 1917, the Japanese war effort probably constituted the most significant challenge to the Western-dominated world order. As a result it was widely perceived by all sides as a major blow against the prevailing racial balance. Despite its significance though, the central role of the Japanese challenge to the transformation of international race relations is rarely acknowledged.

The importance of the Japanese challenge is eloquently presented in Storry's study of Japan and the decline of the West in Asia. Storry has argued that 'in one way or another during this century in Asia the Japanese factor has been crucial'. He has advanced the convincing thesis that directly or indirectly 'the British withdrawal from India, the independence of Burma and Indonesia, Mao's revolution in China, Ho Chi Minh's in Vietnam, America's retreat in the Far East, were products of Japanese action'.[53] It can also be argued that the Japanese ascendancy did not have an impact on Asia alone. Kearney has argued that positive attitudes that Afro-Americans had towards the Japanese during the war 'in some measure contributed to a change of racial attitudes and patterns in the United States of America'.[54] Those subject to racial discrimination in the United States as well those experiencing the yoke of colonial domination regarded Japan's growing influence with enthusiasm.

In a number of important contributions Thorne has drawn attention to the racial aspects of the Far Eastern war and has contrasted the racial impact of the war against the Nazis with that of Japan. He notes that the conflict with Nazi Germany 'placed racist notions in a harsher light'. However, 'it was the Far Eastern War' which 'ensured that relations between whites and non-whites, and not anti-Semitism alone, became the object of greatly increased attention and passion'.[55] Thorne is right to argue that the war in the Far East undermined the narrow confines within which racism was problematised. There can be little doubt that the issue of race relations became highly charged and moved to the centre of international affairs as a result of the war. This outcome was the product not only of the racial motives of those who were directly involved, but also of the encouragement that Japan's success gave people of colour.

Officials in Britain and the United States were clearly aware that they could not effectively counter Japanese charges of Western racial discrimination. Their response to Japan was ambiguous and confused. On the one hand, the United States in particular conducted the war against Japan in racial terms.[56] At the same time policy-makers recognised that if the war was seen in racial terms, the Japanese would be the main beneficiaries. Consequently, official policy sought to deracialise the war with Japan. In both London and Washington, officials were grappling with the problem of how to concede the principle of race equality without losing face. A State Department document, written in February 1942, accepted that it had been a mistake to reject the principle of racial equality in 1919. And by early 1941, officials in Whitehall were discussing the possibility of issuing a statement which supported the principle of racial equality in order to improve relations with Japan.[57]

By 1944 a variety of official and semi-official institutions were discussing not if but when race equality would be accepted as a fundamental principle of international relations. It is significant that the reference point for these discussions was not the terrible consequences of Nazism, but the need to respond to the Japanese challenge to a Western-dominated world order. *International Safeguard of Human Rights* (1944), published by the American Commission to Study the Organisation of Peace recalled that 'we may be chastened by Wilson's rejection at Paris of the principle of racial equality – a rejection which embittered the Oriental world'.[58] This body of distinguished scholars and experts concluded that the principle of race equality had to be conceded to ensure a stable post-war order.

There can be little doubt that a major reorientation in official thinking on race relations was taking place. By the end of the war, Anglo-American officials believed that it was better to take the moral high ground and adopt the mantle of racial equality than to lose the initiative to others. The most significant influence behind this reorientation was Japan's success in transforming race into an international issue.

An International Issue

During the war, race relations became an international issue that required an urgent response. Japan had demonstrated a capacity to take advantage of the race issue and place the West on the defensive. This was an important lesson for the American elite, who realised that the country's rise to world leadership required a solution to its race problem. From the outset of the war, a minority of influential public figures recognised the 'far-reaching implications of the global war for American black and white-relations'.[59]

The issue of race became internationalised during the Second World War because a number of different developments converged to create a new climate of opinion. The intellectual retreat of racism and the inconsistency of practising discrimination while denouncing the Nazis placed the West on the defensive. This coincided with the growth of the anti-colonial cause and the militancy of Afro-Americans. The Japanese war machine exposed the pretensions of Western supremacy and, by its example, encouraged resistance against the existing world order.

One crucial factor in the internationalisation of race was the sense of loss of control by Western powers. This was particularly intense in the management of race relations. It seemed as if all the important racial norms and practices had become subject to serious modification. In the American South, white people were alarmed by the growing assertiveness of black people and by the anti-racist climate. Their insecurity was reflected through the circulation of rumours about the 'rise in black insolence'. Stories about how 'blacks planned to "take over" white women once white men went off to war' were widely circulated.[60] Fears about the management of racial affairs indicated a loss of confidence in the existing racial etiquette.

The race riot that erupted in Detroit in June 1943 indicated that racial insecurities were not confined to the South. It also called into question America's claim to occupy the moral high ground internationally. Washington's diplomatic offensive could have done without race riots in big American cities. Precisely for this reason, American diplomacy was defensive on this question of race relations. Pearl Buck, the well-known American liberal writer, attacked racism in the United States on the ground that it directly benefited Japan:

> The discrimination of the American army and navy and the air forces against colored soldiers and sailors, the exclusion of colored labor in our defense industries and trade unions, all our social discriminations, are of the greatest aid to our enemy in Asia, Japan.[61]

The implication of Buck's argument was that race relations in America could no longer be seen as a domestic concern. They now had to be approached from an international angle.

The intense insecurity of white people in the American South was more than matched by the demoralisation of the British elite over the collapse of its Asian empire. The fall of Singapore in February 1942, followed by the loss of Burma and Malaya, contributed to a moral crisis within the British Establishment.[62] The biggest shock for the British was the enthusiasm with which the conquering Japanese were greeted by local people. For many

Asians, the Japanese appeared as liberators from the white man's yoke. The trauma of this experience was recalled in numerous official memoranda in the 1940s. A 1947 memorandum written to the British Cabinet to justify the building of a high-powered wireless station in Singapore noted that 'all the nations of the Far East hate Japan, but all derived satisfaction from the ability of an Asiatic power to beat the West at its own game'.[63]

Britain's defeat had important reverberations throughout the Empire. After noting that *Colour Feeling* constitutes a particularly important problem', a report from Jamaica noted that 'particularly since the débâcle in the Far East there has been increasing questioning about British rule and the political future of the West Indies, some even regarding the Japanese as liberators'.[64] Similar reports from other colonies helped consolidate a strong sense of imperial unease towards the question of race relations. One official involved in the promotion of imperial propaganda stated that unless the Empire solved the problem of race relations, it would be 'broken by it'. Such fears were widely shared by those involved in the planning of the framework for the regulation of post-war international relations. 'Has the Foreign Office given any special study yet to this question of racial equality?: it is nebulous, but might become important', wrote Cecil Day of the War Cabinet Office.[65]

Day's characterisation illustrated the general lack of enthusiasm for this principle in Whitehall. Yet, this was an issue that was placed on the agenda of international affairs. How the reluctant Anglo-American political classes conceptualised their response is the subject of the next chapter.

Counter-Propaganda Towards 'Colour Feeling'

During the war, the issue of racism was one of the most difficult question facing American and British officials involved in propaganda work and psychological warfare. American officials felt uncomfortable defending their country's record on race relations. For British colonial officials, race relations had become an embarrassment which threatened to undermine the moral standing of the Empire. Even before the outbreak of the war, British officials knew that they were losing the propaganda war in Asia. In

Africa, British public relations experts found it difficult to attack Nazi policies without undermining colonial rule. They feared that attacks on Nazi policies of racial superiority and oppression could backfire and provoke the reaction from Africans that they were already suffering from racial domination.[66] The Colonial Office was reluctant to initiate an anti-German campaign among West Africans because officials calculated that such propaganda might encourage a revolt against white rule as such. 'Having been encouraged to hate one branch of the white race, they may extend the feeling to others', warned one memorandum on the subject.[67] This was a semi-conscious recognition that Britain did not possess any moral authority over Germany on the subject of race relations, at least in the colonies. Moreover, it recognised that by attacking the Germans, white prestige as such would be undermined. It is worth noting that British propagandists drew the conclusion that 'Above all, it is necessary to emphasise that this was not only a "white man's war", or a war of the Empire and United Nations, but a war of civilisation', as the 1944 *Plan of Propaganda to British West Africa* put it.[68]

The Allies' public relations battle on race relations with Germany was relatively unproblematic compared to its propaganda struggle with Japan. As against Germany, it was easy for the Allies to take the moral high ground. Japan was much more difficult, because it could legitimately expose Western hypocrisy on the issue of race. Moreover, Japan explicitly projected itself as an anti-white and anti-Western power. Japanese propaganda sought to harness anti-colonial grievances to its cause. As against this British propaganda was incoherent and defensive. Retrospective accounts all indicate that the British were clearly on the defensive in the propaganda battle.[69] A year before the fall of Singapore a major assessment of the Japanese challenge argued that the 'ground is favourable' for them since most Asians resented Western domination. Official reports written after the Japanese conquest of Burma clearly revealed that Britain had lost the argument. The official in charge of public relations for Burma in 1944 denounced the previous British propaganda campaign against Japan for being too defensive and ineffective.[70]

The inability of Britain to compete with Japanese propaganda was clearly spelled out in an American intelligence report. This report,

written in November 1943, warned that the 'nature of Japanese political control of Burma raises particularly difficult problems for the
United Nations in combating Japanese influence'. The problem alluded to was Britain's isolation from the Burmese population as a
result of Japan's psychological warfare victory. The report noted that
'it has been estimated that at least half the Burmese population was
not sorry to see British control removed' and that 'certainly no spontaneous pro-British movement provided a counterweight to the assistance given the Japanese'.[71]

Britain did not only lose the propaganda war to Japan. Its
humiliation on the battlefields of Asia irrevocably destroyed its
imperial pretensions in the region. The Japanese challenge put in
question all the basic assumptions of Western superiority. The
official in charge of British propaganda directed towards Burma
elaborated the problem thus:

> The Burman saw the British ignominiously driven from Burma in
> 1942. Hitherto, he had been brought up to believe in the invulnerabil-
> ity of the British. Now not unnaturally, he began to revise his ideas
> and think that Japan must be invincible. Ever since the evacuation of
> Burma, the Japanese propagandists have played upon this idea.[72]

Furthermore, Japanese public relations efforts clearly played up
the theme of race relations to isolate the Western powers in Asia.

America psychological warfare experts were concerned that
Japan's use of the race issue against Britain would work against
them as well. According to their analysis the Allies were in a 'weak
position in Burma'. They complained that the United States had
no distinct profile, because it was represented by Axis propaganda
'in the constantly recurring phrase "Anglo-American"'. In contrast, Japan presented itself as 'the standard bearer of Asia's
independence', a nation 'who has proved the weakness of the
whites at Singapore and in the Pacific'.[73]

Like the British, American psychological warfare experts were
at a loss to know how to counter Japanese propaganda. They
realised that Japan's success was underwritten by the appeal of
'Asia for the Asiatics'. They noted that 'appeals to racial pride in
the victories of the Japanese are frequent' and that they were
'reinforced by references to the racial discrimination practiced by

the British'. As against this propaganda, the Allies were 'at a severe disadvantage', partly 'because of the deep-lying disaffection' with British rule. 'Racial discrimination as practiced by the British' was one important legacy that American propaganda found difficult to neutralise.[74]

One possible response to Japanese propaganda was to tackle it directly. This was the course advocated by Pearl Buck, who also wanted America to tackle its own tradition of racism. Buck believed that the 'Japanese weapon of racial propaganda' was effective because it was 'presented to persons who have had unfortunate experiences with English and American people'. She added that America's internal record on race relations strengthened the hands of Japan. 'Every lynching, every race riot, gives joy to Japan', she argued.[75] Her conclusion was that if the United States was to compete with Japanese propaganda it would have to adopt an unambiguously anti-racist stance.

Since the United States was not yet ready to tackle its race problem, Buck's approach was never countenanced by officials involved in the propaganda war. Instead American psychological warfare adopted a more indirect approach. In practice this meant that either the discussion of race was avoided altogether or it was raised in the form of negative propaganda. In Africa, one official looking for ways to reply to charges of American racism concluded that 'my feelings is that counter-propaganda themes on this subject would be hard to find'.[76] However, a studied silence on race could not be maintained in every situation. This was the case especially in the Far East where Japan continually publicised the issue. The propaganda directed at Burma 'would have to be largely negative for the present', argued one American official. Such negative propaganda would 'stress racial differences between Burmese and Japanese'. It would also seek to 'expose Japanese views on their own racial superiority'.[77] The argument that the Japanese were in fact racists was a rather ineffective tactic designed to deflect attention from American racist practices.

Negative propaganda against the Japanese was unsuccessful. Attempts by the American public relations machine to accuse the Japanese of discriminating against Koreans and the Eta class of untouchables were easily countered. Hsinking radio in Manchuria replied to these accusations in July 1942 that Americans should 'look at home first' since 'their Negroes do not enjoy the life of citizens'. According to an American analysis of this propaganda battle, 'the race situation on our domestic front still makes us vulnerable as far as Japanese propaganda to India and Southeast Asia is concerned'.[78] Nevertheless there was little that the OWI could do in Asia, other than to evade the issues raised by the state of American race relations.

The orientation of anti-Japanese psychological warfare in Asia was an outgrowth of the perspective that the OWI adopted towards the 'Negro Question' at home. This was to deny or obscure 'pertinent realities about American race relations'. Through the promotion of symbols of American unity, it tried to portray race as incidental to the reality of being American. The aim of the OWI was to 'minimise racial consciousness'.[79] From this perspective the most effective propaganda was that which helped to diffuse the articulation of racial grievances.

The approach of British psychological warfare paralleled that of the United States. The official consensus was that 'colour feeling' had to be handled 'delicately' and never confronted directly. The conclusion of a July 1943 assessment in relation to the Caribbean was that the treatment of the 'colour question from the UK must be by means of indirect methods and must be handled most delicately if offence and resentment is not to be caused'. This point was reiterated on several occasions. 'There must be no reference to the existence of a colour problem in direct propaganda', argued a January 1944 public relations campaign document on the subject.[80]

It is worth noting that the only propaganda campaign designed to promote a positive representation of race relations in the Empire during the Second World War was never implemented. This campaign emerged from a series of discussions about how to frame the imperial message in the Caribbean. Proposals were formulated to assist the 'breaking down of colour feeling' in Jamaica. This plan suggested circulating literature to illustrate 'how the people of Britain and the Commonwealth are ceasing to be colour conscious, admitting coloured people from all parts of the Empire to full participation in all forms of citizenship'. As examples of this new attitude, 'Indians, Maoris etc. playing a prominent part in military or civil affairs' was proposed.[81]

Colonial administrators based in the Caribbean were horrified at the idea of mounting a publicity campaign around the issues of 'colour feeling'. As far as they were concerned any publicity would only make matters worse. Officials believed that they did not have a convincing case. Douglas Jardine, Governor of Antigua, was to the point, 'I do not think that the importance of avoiding attention being drawn to the existence of a colour problem can be exaggerated.' The tactic of suppressing any discussion of 'colour feeling' was swiftly adopted by the Ministry of Information. This approach is forcefully articulated in the MOI's 1943 *Plan of Propaganda to the British West Indies*. The plan advocated the promotion of a colour-blind image of the Caribbean. To avoid drawing attention to the problem of racism, it proposed using a colour-free vocabulary: 'we should refer to West Indians rather than to coloured men'. The aim was to avoid bringing into the open a problem with which MOI officials felt uncomfortable. The same sentiment was reiterated by the Colonial Office during its deliberations with the MOI: 'it seems to us clear that we should restrict to a minimum all references to colour discrimination and colour issues'.[82]

The difficulty of denying the reality of racial discrimination or of finding sufficient positive examples of multi-racial co-operation meant that Whitehall sought to avoid or to suppress the subject altogether. Imperial propagandists were in no doubt that race was definitely a weak point in the intellectual defence of empire. It is even possible to detect a sense of embarrassment during the course of deliberations on this subject. Officials were of the view that on this score Britain had something to hide. E.M. Jenkins of the Dominion Office put matters bluntly when he advised his colleagues in the MOI that 'the cards to conceal, play down, or explain are our racial arrogance, our former economic exploitation and our careless laziness'.[83]

Anglo-American war-time propaganda efforts on race relations had the character of a damage-limitation exercise. Its objective of minimising racial consciousness was promoted through trivialising the experience of racial domination. Such an evasive approach was based on the awareness that this was not a battle of ideas which the Allies wanted to fight. Anglo-American propaganda revealed a profound sense of ambiguity. Western public relations officials responded by elaborating a strategy designed to cover up the issue and to discourage others from debating it.

The Emerging Racial Calculations

The ambiguity of Anglo-American propaganda was reflected at the level of policy-making during the war. Racial thinking still influenced many of the people in charge of the war effort. At the same time, this sentiment could not be openly justified. This tension was clearly evident in the manner in which the war was fought against Japan. The racial character of the war in Asia was relatively open. Japanese propaganda stressed the propaganda theme of Asian unity against white domination. For their part, Britain and the United States responded to their military setbacks 'with an outburst of hatred which consigned the Japanese to the category of sub-humans'.[84] At the same time, public relations officials were attempting to distance the Allies from any association with racism. This was a confusing period, when old practices coexisted with the insight that important changes needed to be made. In one sense the war helped to clarify Western confusions about race relations. It became evident that the racial status quo could not be maintained and that sooner or later the principle of race equality would have to be accepted.

The acceptance of the principle of race equality did not come easily though. The war helped Western powers to appreciate that racism had become a destabilising force which could easily blow up in their faces. However, it was difficult to acknowledge responsibility for losing grip on the relation between races. It was easier for officials to come to this conclusion by portraying the problem as the fault of other Western powers. American officials criticised the British Empire in Asia for provoking the anti-Western sentiments that helped Japan. In a similar manner, many British officials were highly critical of America's poor record of domestic race relations.

Americans regarded Britain as a liability in Asia. They flattered themselves and believed that Asians looked up to the United States and regarded it as a friend. One American official stationed in Ceylon (now Sri Lanka) expressed his contempt for local people along with the belief that the United States was regarded with affection. He reported that 'we are admired and liked, so far as these feeble people admire or like anything, and if properly handled, the native elements would back American efforts.' However, he noted that 'frankly, in my opinion, they might sell out the British to the Japanese'. He concluded that the Ceylonese were a 'most cowardly lot' whose 'weakness must never be overlooked'.[85] The view that the British had undermined Western influence in Asia allowed some American officials to avoid coming to terms with the implications of the changing climate of race relations.

In Asia, American officials continuously contrasted the loyalty of their colonial people in the Philippines to the pro-Japanese sentiments that people expressed in the British colonies of Burma and Malaya. British officials were clearly sensitive to such comparisons. To deal with American propaganda, Field Marshall Sir John Dill asked for material 'to enable him to deal with comparisons, of the good behaviour of the Filipinos with what is happening in Burma'. Clearly, what Sir John wanted was information that would undermine American boasts about its positive record in Asia. Consequently, British officials were clearly heartened when they received news of American setbacks in the Philippines. 'One gets rather tired of quite inaccurate comparisons of the freedom of the inhabitants of the Philippines with the subjection of natives of Malaya and Burma', wrote one British diplomat from Washington. Pointing to American setbacks in the Philippines he added, this will mean that 'at any rate' there will be 'less of this'.[86] British officials also reacted to American criticisms by pointing the finger at racial realities in the United States.

American and British criticism of each other's record on race relations signified that something had changed. There was now an implicit assumption that the old ways could no longer continue. The very fact that they were pointing the finger at each other indicated that they hoped that the spotlight would be taken off their own track record on race relations. Official calculations about race relations continually ran behind events. Officials in London and Washington knew that the issue of racial equality would have to be considered in the post-war settlement. However, they hoped that the issue would not have to be explicitly addressed until after the termination of the war. This was the conclusion reached in the Foreign Office in early 1941, when the possibility of issuing a statement supporting the principle of racial equality was discussed. It would take almost four more years for a still unenthusiastic Whitehall to adopt such a declaration.[87]

The emergence of an anti-racist international consensus was reflected in the proposals made by China to include the principle of racial equality in the platform of the future United Nations. Sir Alexander Cadogan, head of the British delegation at the Dumbarton Oaks discussion on the establishment of a United Nations, telegraphed back to Whitehall that Britain had no choice but to accept the new consensus:

> Arguments strongly advanced is that it would be against our interest and tradition as a liberal power to oppose the expression of a principle, denial of which figures so prominently in Nazi philosophy and is repugnant to the mass of British and foreign opinion. Such action would moreover prejudice British and American relations in a sphere of great delicacy by supplying ammunition to critics who accuse us of reactionary policy in the Far East.[88]

Cadogan's reference to a sphere of 'great delicacy' highlighted the difficulties posed by the issue of race relations. The gap between egalitarian rhetoric and discriminatory practice in the Empire was one that Britain did not want exposed to international scrutiny. Cadogan still hoped that the acceptance of a declaration on racial equality would be a formality with few consequences. He indicated that such a declaration would not pertain to the sphere of immigration and that Britain should oppose any attempt that called into question discriminatory immigration laws. Cadogan argued for 'maintaining our view that recognition of racial equality is already part of the policy on which we govern our Empire, while immigration is the domestic concern of each sovereign state'.[89]

Cadogan's attitude was representative of the position taken by Anglo-American officialdom. Their approach was to separate the principle of racial equality from matters that came under domestic jurisdiction. In this way it was hoped that the acceptance of the principle would not have any immediate practical consequences. But, as Lauren has argued, once the principle of racial equality had been accepted it was difficult to carry on as usual.[90] Racial discrimination was difficult to justify and many members of the United Nations were quick to criticise those who practised it. Although Western powers did not have to make any significant alterations to their conduct of race relations, it was evident that more concessions would have to be made.

More than any other experience, the Second World War had helped discredit racism. In an indirect way, the international revulsion against Nazism undermined the racial thinking of the Anglo-American elites. In the realm of international diplomacy, racism was at least outwardly treated as a scandal. But such sentiments did not yet amount to an acceptance of equality. Consequently racist practices continued and often coexisted with anti-racist rhetoric. Race equality was treated as a worthy principle rather than as a guide to behaviour.

Anglo-American racial calculations had a pre-emptive character. However, as an exercise in damage limitation it provided only a provisional solution to the problem. The war had exposed the vulnerability of Western powers on the question of race. Their acceptance of the principle of racial equality did not mean that Britain and the United States had succeeded in neutralising their racial legacy. On the contrary, there was now widespread international interest in race relations. In the post-war period criticisms of racist practices in the United States and in the British Empire became widespread. The Soviet Union took it upon itself to place the issue at the centre of the Cold War agenda. In a sense, and probably inadvertently, the Soviet Union continued where Japan left off. The Kremlin understood that any international publicity about racial discrimination would boost its cause and place the West on the defensive. So whereas the Soviet Union adopted a high-profile diplomatic offensive on the subject of racism, the United States tried to prevent the emergence of race as an issue in the United Nations.[91] The Cold War ensured that racism would continue to be at the centre of international debate; and the strategy pursued by Britain and the Unites States was surprisingly similar to their strategy during the war. The main feature of their approach was to minimise racial consciousness and to depoliticise race. That is the subject of the next chapter.

7   As an International Issue

It was during the decade that followed the end of the Second World War that race relations emerged as a publicly acknowledged theme in the conduct of international affairs. That the issue of race would become a major question was already anticipated by key policy-makers during the war itself. A sensitivity to the future significance of this problem was evident during negotiations on the framework of the future world order and the establishment of the United Nations. However, those involved were far from clear about the long-term repercussions of their deliberations on a subject that hitherto had been rarely discussed formally by diplomats. As Laurens noted, the representatives of the leading Western powers still hoped to limit the impact of the widespread quest for race equality on international affairs.[1] They believed that general declarations on the subject of equality would be a sufficient response to the growing demand for an end to discrimination. They hoped that formal concessions to anti-racist aspirations would ensure that this would not become a source of tension in international affairs. Although Western diplomats knew that concessions would have to be made, they tended to underestimate the problems it would cause for Anglo-American diplomacy in the post-war period.

As it turned out, the two most important developments in post-war global affairs – the Cold War and the emergence of the so-called Third World – both contributed to the internationalisation of the question of race. To the surprise of the Soviet Union and the consternation of the West, resentment against racial domination was one of the few international questions that Moscow could use to bolster its moral authority. It is worth noting that at the time racial practices were directly associated with the Western world. South Africa was well on the way to becoming an international pariah. Racial discrimination in the United States, particularly the practice of segregation in the American South, had become a significant source of embarrassment for Washington. Britain too was defensive about the colour bar that prevailed throughout its Empire. The Soviet Union, on the other hand, was able to present itself as a society that was free from the curse of racial discrimination.

The contrasting image of a colour-blind Soviet Union and a West deeply implicated in discriminatory practices ensured that race relations would become intertwined with the Cold War. The existence of a society that boasted of its racial tolerance served as a visible condemnation of those powers that were still implicated in the culture of racism. Among Western diplomats, this produced the fear that the Soviet Union would be the direct beneficiary of the world-wide demand for racial equality. This perception, in turn, had the effect of creating an intense sense of insecurity in Western diplomacy. One symptom was an exaggerated assessment of the threat that the global reaction to racial domination represented to Western interests. During the 1940s, pronouncements by Western international experts and politicians often warned that racial tension was likely to be the source of global strife in the future. No one disagreed with Philip Noel Baker, the British Secretary of State for the Commonwealth, when he warned Parliament that the 'most probable and dangerous conflict' in the future would be 'between the peoples of Asia and Africa on the one hand and the peoples of European origin and culture on the other'.[2] In the 1940s such pronouncements were treated as unexceptional in the press.

Apprehensions about the international repercussions of racial grievances had important and direct implications for domestic practices. International pressure against racist practices was a decisive factor supporting the cause of race equality. Today, studies of race relations tend to underestimate the significance of the influence of the new mood of global anti-racism on domestic practice, but in the 1940s, most observers were sensitive to the impact of international factors on the direction of race relations. Characteristically, Myrdal's study ended with a warning that if Western nations did not abandon white supremacy 'colored nations might inflict "humiliation and subjugation" on the whites'. This theme was reiterated in numerous texts published in the 1940s. An important collection of essays by American observers of race relations in 1949 continually returned to the international dimension of the problem. Although the theme of the book was race relations in the United States, more than a third of the articles dealt with international themes. John La Frage, a prominent Christian thinker, was worried about how discrimination would undermine the Church. 'There is no point at which America's moral leadership of the world is more vulnerable no matter in which its decision is more crucial in the terrible spiritual warfare occurring at the present time, than our inconsistency in this regard', he warned. Others pointed to the negative impact that domestic racism had for America's military and strategic position. Adolf Berle remarked that the 'habit of race discrimination practised in considerable parts of the United States is the greatest single danger to the foreign relations of the United States and conceivably may become a real threat to American security'. Leading American sociologist, Robert K. Merton, pointed out that in 'a world riven by international fears' divisions between white and black 'cannot so, lightly be endured'. According to this standpoint, America had to sort itself out, if for no other reason than as a diplomatic expedient.[3]

The motif of international calculations continued to recur in the writings of prominent American scholars of race relations during the 1950s. When Dollard's renowned study of race and caste in the American South was reprinted in 1957, his new Preface expressed profound anxieties about the global aspects of the subject. He argued that American race relations were no longer a local matter. 'Our system is under world inspection', he noted and concluded: 'we shall go about solving the color problem ourselves, cost what it may, or it will be solved for us not to our liking'.[4] Dollard's appeal to the self-interest of white America was based on the premise that the balance of power internationally demanded an end to formal discrimination in the United States.

Preoccupation with the international dimension of race relations was not restricted to American specialists. One of the first British academic studies of the subject echoed the sentiments of its American counterpart. Kenneth Little's *Negroes in Britain* (1948) drew attention to the 'world-wide repercussions' of the colour bar in Britain. He was particularly concerned about how colonial students – who would eventually constitute the elites of their society – would react to their experience of racism in Britain. He noted that this 'may be a fact of some significance if, as some, possibly gloomy, prophets

predict, the main future alignments of mankind will form themselves on colour lines'.[5] At the time, most British contributions
tended to echo Little's gloomy prognostication.

The expectation of the international community that racist
practices would soon be eliminated directly influenced the deliberations of policy-makers. Politicians and diplomats alike accepted
that the prevailing racial etiquette had to change and were forced
to act accordingly. There can be little doubt that such considerations played an important role in the shaping of America's
domestic agenda on race relations. Laurens has argued convincingly that international pressure, particularly that of the Cold
War, played a significant role in accelerating the pace of change in
the race relations of the United States. The internationalisation of
concern put considerable pressure on the American political class
to act. It had little choice since it had become evident that this was
an issue that the Soviets could use to embarrass and even isolate
the United States. According to Laurens:

> This external pressure of the Cold War now began to play a
> monumental role in creating a new beginning for human equality
> within U.S. politics. Just as the Nazi experience had turned the mirror
> toward U.S. racial discrimination, so now the Soviet campaign
> effectively held up a magnifying glass and invited the rest of the world
> to look through it and see the United States at its worst.[6]

Studies of diplomatic papers suggest that the Cold War and the
associated fear that Africa and Asia might turn against the West
had a direct impact on the Anglo-American race relations agenda.

The progress made in the sphere of civil rights under the
Truman Administration was strongly influenced by international
pressure. Truman's decision to initiate a special Presidential
Committee on Civil Rights was motivated at least in part by the
need to respond to international opinion. It is worth noting that
when this Committee asked the Department of State how racism
at home affected US foreign policy abroad, the reply confirmed
the diagnosis that this was a source of diplomatic difficulty. The
path-breaking report of this Committee, *To Secure These Rights*,
expressed a clear awareness of the international implications of
American domestic racist practices. One of its arguments for the

reform of race relations was that 'throughout Latin America, Africa, the Near, Middle and Far East [the] treatment which our Negroes receive is taken as a reflection of our attitude toward all dark-skinned peoples', which in turn plays 'into the hands of Communist propagandists'.[7] According to Heald and Kaplan, the Truman Administration's civil rights policies 'were formulated in conscious recognition of the fact that the nation's treatment of its own minorities affected its standing in the eyes of the third world of colored, formerly colonized peoples'.[8]

The Eisenhower Administration was also alarmed by the negative international reactions that America's record on race relations invited. William H. Jackson, who headed a special committee appointed by Eisenhower to study ways of combating communist propaganda, cited the 'importance of military racial improvement for American success in the Third World'.[9] His Secretary of State, John Foster Dulles, was anxious to ensure that racial grievances did not provide a focus of unity for the emerging African and Asian states. Important reforms such as the celebrated civil rights case, *Brown v. Board of Education*, which led to the desegregation of schools, were strongly influenced by global factors.

Mary Dudziak has persuasively argued that the timing of civil rights legislation during the Truman and Eisenhower presidencies was substantially influenced by international concerns. This was a period of Cold War conservatism, when there was little attempt at domestic reform. Yet despite the mood of the times the government encouraged civil rights legislation. As Dudziak observed, 'during a period when civil liberties and social change were repressed in other contexts, somehow, some way *Brown* managed to happen'. The only plausible explanation, according to Dudziak, was international pressure. A US Justice Department brief written to influence the outcome of *Brown* argued that the case was important because 'the United States is trying to prove to the people of the world of every nationality, race and color, that a free democracy is the most civilized and most secure form of government yet devised by man'.[10] Most observers who have questioned the timing of civil rights legislation in the United States have pointed to the salience of international factors. This was certainly the approach taken by the leading American sociologist, Talcott Parsons, when he asked 'Why "Freedom Now", not Yesterday?'

According to Parsons, the 'world-wide significance of the American color problem' helped place the issue on the political agenda. His collaborator, Kenneth Clark, took the view that it was the threat of Soviet appeal for racial justice which forced the US to live up to its democratic ideals. 'America may have been caught with its ideals exposed by a new type of challenge in the world at large, by the emergence of an adversary which offered effective ideological, psychological, and military competition.'[11] The Soviet Union, by its very existence, directly influenced the race relations agenda of the United States.

Recent work by historians of international affairs has provided important documentation of the seriousness with which the US State Department took international criticism of America's record on race relations. A number of scholars now argue that the domestic reform of race relations was closely linked to the pursuit of foreign policy objectives. 'Coping with domestic racial problems and promoting the international prestige of the United States became, therefore, increasingly related activities during the Eisenhower years, as it became painfully obvious that America's problematic race relations were having a negative impact on US diplomacy', is the verdict of one interesting study of this subject.[12]

Race relations presented a complicated diplomatic problem for the United States. Washington did not merely assume global hegemony. It did so in the name of the superior morality of democracy. However, the inconsistency between this claim and the evidence of discrimination was difficult to reconcile in international forums. America's domestic record on race relations was probably the single most important factor undermining its moral authority. The problem was intensified by the fact that many leading American opinion-makers were themselves uncomfortable with America's double standard on this issue of freedom. A characteristically defensive posture defined post-war American policy-making on this subject. As Dean Acheson, Secretary of State during the Truman Administration conceded, 'racial discrimination in the United Sates remains a source of constant embarrassment to the Government in the day-to-day conduct of its foreign relations; and it jeopardizes the effective maintenance of our moral leadership of the free and democratic nations of the world'.[13]

It was not merely American official opinion that was conscious of the new internationalisation of race relations. Prominent Afro-American activists and politicians regarded international opinion as an ally with which to fight racism at home. Black activists such as A. Philip Randolph sought to exploit fears about national security to gain official action against segregation. No doubt, civil rights activists tended to exaggerate the threat of international opinion in order to boost their cause. Here was an effective argument that no serious figure in Washington could ignore. Many Afro-American intellectuals believed that improvements in civil rights were closely linked to international pressure. The writer James Baldwin saw civil rights legislation as the outcome of the rise of 'Africa in the context of the Cold War'. He observed that 'most of the Negroes I know do not believe that this immense concession would ever have been made if it had not been for the competition of the Cold War and the fact that Africa was clearly liberating herself and therefore had, for political reasons to be wooed by descendants of her former masters'.[14] The importance of Cold War competition and the emergence of the Third World as a new factor in international relations ensured that the issue of race relations could no longer be conceptualised as a local or domestic matter.

Apprehension about the diplomatic repercussions of race relations was not confined to the United States. British officials feared that the prevailing climate of international hostility to racism would compromise their hold over the Empire. At meetings of the Commonwealth, acrimonious debates about racial discrimination threatened to overwhelm the proceedings. Even at informal gatherings, such as the Commonwealth Relations Conference held in Canada in 1949, the debate on racism overshadowed the rest of the discussion. By the mid-1950s, many British observers feared that the question of race could destroy the Commonwealth altogether. *The Times* warned that since 'racialism provokes far more deep-seated passions' than any other, it could one day 'destroy Commonwealth Unity'.[15]

British officials were often taken aback by what they perceived as an unreasonable criticism of the Empire's record on race relations. This sense of disbelief, combined with the intuition that Britain had been caught unaware, was often evident in official proceedings. For

example, at a meeting of the Far East Publicity Committee in 1950, a
representative of the Foreign Office reported:

> Intense nationalist propaganda during the last year has led to a strong
> bias against Colonialism of all sorts. Any suggestion of racial discrimi-
> nation even against the black Africans for whom a certain scorn was
> felt, led to indignation.[16]

For many British officials, the new international 'bias' against
racism was an uncomfortable development. But whatever their
reservations, British officialdom had no choice but to acquiesce to
the mood of the times.

Like the United States, Britain was forced to adopt a new race
relations agenda. It was clearly the pressure of international opinion
that prompted the Colonial Office to reform race relations in the
Empire. The Secretary of State for the Colonies, Arthur Creech
Jones' 1947 circular on race relations was an attempt to pre-empt
criticism from the Commission of Human Rights of the United
Nations. Creech Jones was not ready to tackle the colour bar as such;
his aim was to eliminate the extreme manifestations of racial discrimination. 'I am far from suggesting that all discriminatory legislation can be swept away in the Colonial territories', he wrote. Such
hesitancy was not surprising. Creech Jones' defensive tone was dictated by the realisation that many British officials in the colonies
still regarded racial discrimination as basic common sense.[17] Official
claims of non-discrimination were continually undermined by
highly publicised examples of racial discrimination in the colonies.

The knowledge that Britain stood exposed on its race relations
record forced Whitehall to consider the public relations aspects of
this subject. So when in 1958 race riots broke out in Notting Hill,
London, the Whitehall publicity machine was able to go straight
into action. Concerned about the riots' 'effects on our reputation
abroad', British public relations experts were advised how to play
down the significance of the event. Whitehall officials feared that
international opinion would associate events at Notting Hill with
race riots in America. Whitehall publicity sought to minimise the
racial aspects of the riots and put out an 'all is well' message.[18]

Despite the international trend towards the elimination of
formal discrimination, there were still many instances when

attempts were made to slow change and hold the existing racial line. Both Britain and the United States sought to prevent the United Nations from having any jurisdiction over the domestic practices of member states and Britain and the United States sought to undermine any United Nations action directed against South Africa.[19] Many Western politicians hoped that change could be avoided by preventing international institutions from interfering in domestic racial affairs. Immigration policy was one matter which they hoped to keep out of the domain of international affairs. It was in this vein that Bob Menzies, the Prime Minister of Australia, complained to his British counterpart about criticisms made of South African domestic policies at meetings of the Commonwealth Conference. Menzies recalled, 'I pointed out at the time that if we were at liberty to discuss the internal racial policies of one member, it would be quite legitimate that at some subsequent meeting, to discuss for example, the Australian immigration policy which is aimed at avoiding internal racial problems by the expedient of keeping coloured immigrants out.'[20]

Menzies' actions, designed to preserve the status quo in race relations in Australia, required that the racial line be held globally. Such rearguard attempts went very much against the mood of the times. The dominant tendency of Western powers was to give way to the pressure for change only reluctantly. This was not a matter of conviction but of diplomatic expedience. American policy towards South Africa illustrated this. Ideally Washington hoped that South Africa could become an active ally in the Cold War. But in practice, Washington had to keep its distance from a state that had become the symbol of racial oppression. So even when the United States was looking for ways of preventing South Africa's diplomatic isolation, it sought to distance itself from Pretoria's policies. South Africa had become a diplomatic liability, and the State Department was forced to find a middle position between the Apartheid state and its critics, at least in public.[21]

How tangible was the pressure to reform race relations internationally at this time? It is difficult to define international pressure as a concept. In the 1940s the concept was used in a way that could incorporate virtually every tendency that questioned the global status quo. For example, the growing aspiration for independence in the colonial world was often interpreted as a demand for racial equality. Regardless of its intent, the growth of anti-colonial forces was often represented as a challenge to the prevailing regime of race relations. International pressure was also invited by the hesitant and defensive posture of Western powers on the subject of race. This was an issue that undermined Western pretensions to moral authority. The inability of the West to defend its race relations record had the effect of encouraging international criticism. Such criticisms, which were often motivated by *realpolitik* rather than the cause of anti-racism, helped create a climate in which a variety of grievances were expressed in a racial form. For its part, Western interests were more than ready to interpret challenges to the prevailing world order in a racial form. How Western powers imagined international race relations and how they responded to it is the subject of the rest of this chapter.

Imagining Changes in the World in Racial Terms

Fears regarding racial revenge and racial revolts, discussed in previous chapters, acquired a more intense focus in the post-Second World War period. Events such as the Chinese revolution and the growth of anti-colonial protest world-wide lent weight to the fear that the reaction to racism would now lead to war and conflict. These developments were often interpreted as a rejection of the West and, by implication, as a challenge to the white race. Even relatively moderate demands for independence and equality were depicted by Western diplomats as motivated by racial concerns. Reports from Western officials stationed in Africa, Asia and the Caribbean continually emphasised the racial motives of those who questioned colonial domination.

American diplomats stationed in the Caribbean in the 1940s stressed the influence of the racial factor on virtually every significant development. Perry Jester, the American Consul in Barbados, reported that no subject received more attention in the media than the question of racism: 'from this springboard discussion branched out to color discrimination in Great Britain, the United States, racial segregation wherever practiced including South Africa and racial relations between the white and black people in general'.[22] According to the American Vice-Consul in

Antigua, 'the question of color, and all that the term implies in frustration and discrimination remains a powerful psychological influence affecting a multitude of questions relating to the social and political future of the island'. His counterpart in the Gold Coast came to a similar conclusion regarding the problems faced by that colony. He concluded that the 1948 disturbances against British colonial rule were caused by the 'native press which had been preaching hatred of the whites'.[23] In reality, these disturbances represented the stirrings of a movement for independence. The perception of race hatred was shaped by an imagination that saw the revolt against colonialism as an attack against the white race.

There was a discernible tendency on the part of Western officials and observers to interpret the actions of nationalist and anti-colonial movements as anti-white. The regularity with which racial motives were attributed to the actions of such movements suggests that the fear of racial conflict was deeply embedded in the imagination of the official mind. It was as if the very strength of anti-Western reaction could only be understood as the outcome of some irrational emotion. Such emotion was usually diagnosed as the product of frustrated minds. The most widely discussed frustration was that of resentment borne of racial slight. As a result anti-colonial action was often interpreted through this prism of racial emotions. It was believed that even if there were no explicit manifestations of anti-white racism, this sentiment could be found just below the surface.

Sir Alan Burns, former governor of the Gold Coast and a Colonial Office specialist on race relations, was a prominent advocate of the 'racist under the surface' thesis. His argument was straightforward: 'in many cases "anti-colonialism" was merely a cover for intense racial feeling, a colour prejudice in reverse which reflects the resentment of the dark peoples against the past domination of the world by European nations'.[24] The belief that racial resentment was an active force bubbling under the surface informed official reaction to instances of colonial unrest such as that of Sir Hugh Rance, the British Governor of Burma, when he organised to deal with a police strike in 1946. 'I must ensure that all reasonable precautions have been taken, especially if developments should take a racial, especially anti-British turn', he wrote to his superior in London.[25]

The expectation that anti-colonial struggles would take a racial turn was based on the unspoken view that racial resentments constituted an exceptionally powerful, sometimes dominant, influence over those who questioned Western rule. Some observers even went as far as to suggest that racist sentiments were the overriding influence over outbursts of anti-colonial protest. This was the argument of an early analysis of anti-colonial protest in the Solomon Islands. According to its author:

> There was no question here as to the aims and desires of the natives; concern with economic rights and benefits, basic as it may have been, did not appear uppermost in their minds. Instead, there was envy and hatred of the white man – hatred so irrational as to resemble religious hysteria.[26]

The practice of interpreting events through the prism of race is evident in both American and British official correspondence.

David Gammon, the American Vice-Consul in Antigua, was a proponent of the 'pressure beneath the surface' thesis in his correspondence with the State Department. His colleague, Albert Rabia, Vice-Consul in British Guiana, took the same view. According to Rabia, those who agitated against the United States were 'interested in the descendency of the white race and the ascendancy of the colored race'.[27] Official dispatches from the Caribbean routinely warned that 'race awareness' represented the key problem facing American diplomacy in the region.[28]

British colonial officials also saw a racial motive in most instances of anti-colonial struggles. To take but a few examples.

In post-war Nigeria, the radical nationalist movement, the Zikists, were continually depicted as racist extremists. The leader of the movement, Ndame Azikiwe, was routinely accused of 'inflaming racial bitterness'. According to one authoritative account by a William Crocker, a former official in Nigeria, most of Azikiwe's writing could 'hardly have any appeal but to racial hatred'. This was also the assessment of a report on the Nigerian press submitted to the Colonial Office in September 1949. The report observed that the Nigerian press was not above exploiting racial feeling. According to one official account of the Zikist movement, this was a 'refuge of young semi-literate junior employees'. These Zikists were 'activated by envy in two senses, in that they envy any European because of his apparent wealth and because of his superior intellectual ability'. Since the racism of the Zikists had the character of a self-evident truth, such reports did not feel obliged to substantiate their claims.[29] Those reading this report in Whitehall would not have regarded the author's assumptions of superiority as racist. Such sentiments were usually associated with the resentment of white domination. In passing it is worth noting that throughout the period under discussion, active manifestation of anti-white hatred was conspicuous by its absence in Nigeria.

In the Caribbean, colonial officials appeared to be overpowered by the intensity of anti-white resentment. Governor John Shaw of Trinidad complained that 'normal social, class and economic problems are exaggerated and accentuated by the introduction of a colour or communal element'. In Jamaica, officials continually warned of the strength of racial resentment. 'This six month period has seen a noticeable growth in racial bitterness', reported the Governor of Jamaica in June 1950. A month later, he again drew attention to the 'disturbing increase of racial feeling'. An important report by W.H. Ingham on the tasks facing colonial propagandists in Jamaica reiterated fears about racial bitterness. According to Ingham, Rastas had 'the deepest possible hatred for whites'. He continued:

> Of late, other anti-white phenomena have appeared, such as the Coptic church, which for a period was active in Trinidad ... Mau Mau has also appealed in some way and been exploited to stir up race hatred. The author of this report also took the view that African nationalism was of a 'markedly racist character'.[30]

In Whitehall the electoral victory of the People's Progressive Party (PPP) in British Guiana in 1953 was depicted as a victory for racial hatred. Even though the PPP self-consciously eschewed all forms of racism, British parliamentarians were certain that the electoral triumph of this radical movement represented the triumph of anti-white prejudice. According to a government spokesman in the House of Commons, it was a 'tragedy that some members of the PPP have sought to introduce into a reasonably happy atmosphere, the pernicious theories of racial hatred'.[31] What British colonial officials perceived as racial hatred was in fact the uncompromising radical anti-imperialist agitation of the PPP.

The tendency to interpret North–South issues in racial terms led Western policy-makers to discover the motif of race in the most unlikely places. It was from this perspective that many British and American observers interpreted the 1955 Bandung Conference of non-aligned states. Officials regarded this conference as subversive of Western interests. In particular, they took exception to the fact that the West was excluded from an important international conference.[32] One important concern was the fear that the 'coloured nations' of the world would unite against Western interests.

The Bandung Conference marked an important milestone in the evolution of the Non-Aligned Movement. Although the delegates were clearly aware that this was a conference of nations which had experienced the yoke of Western imperialism, the issue of race did not figure prominently in the proceedings. According to the Australian ambassador to Indonesia, although the 'race and colour theme was present', it was not 'played up'. He reported that the conference was extremely 'moderate' and 'restrained' about race.[33] In the aftermath of the conference, Western diplomats privately acknowledged that the event was marked by moderation and pragmatism. Tensions between countries such as India and Pakistan also indicated that the unity of the so-called coloured nations was more apparent than real.

Despite the moderation and pragmatism displayed at Bandung, the event was interpreted in the Western racial imagination as a danger to white global influence. In the media Afro-Asian unity was presented as a new threat to the white race. Some observers emphasised the significance of the exclusion of the West from this conference. The *Christian Science Monitor* reported that the 'west is excluded' and the 'emphasis is on the coloured nations of the world'. It concluded, rather prematurely, that 'for Asia it means that at last the destiny of Asia is being determined in Asia, and not in Geneva, or Paris, or London, or Washington'. Other publications were even more sensationalist in their response to this event. *Newsweek* observed:

Everybody knows what must come to pass between Asia and the West, the *yellow and the white*. It is imbecile folly for us to close our eye to the inevitable. All the world understands that the gravest crisis in the destiny of the earth's population is at hand.[34]

Newsweek did not have to spell out what it meant by its statement that 'everybody knows what must come to pass between Asia and the West'. Terms such as 'inevitable' suggested that a kind of Social Darwinist vision of an inevitable conflict of races continued to haunt the Western racial imagination.

Even ostensibly more detached academic studies of the Bandung Conference tended to echo a concern with the racialisation of international affairs. The significance they attached to the outcome of the Bandung Conference is in many respects more interesting than the event itself, for the disproportionate official reaction to Bandung reveals more about the Western racial imagination than about this attempt to forge Afro-Asian unity. According to one study, the 'Bandung Conference of 1955 had been a turning point'. Why? Because twenty-nine 'African and Asian nations met in Indonesia, representing 36 per cent of the world's populations'. And, 'On this historic occasion, no white nations were invited.'[35] An American volume of essays on race relations, published in the aftermath of Bandung, also stressed the significance of Western exclusion for the future of world affairs.

The recent gathering in Bandung, Indonesia, of the political leaders from twenty-nine different countries of Africa and Asia highlights the urgency of tested knowledge on the theme of this book. The mere fact of calling a conclave of predominantly colored people, from which the former colonizing powers of the West were excluded, is itself a great moment to the future peace of the entire world.[36]

It is the continuous emphasis on the exclusion of Western powers that represents the most curious feature of the reaction to Bandung. That this elementary assertion of Afro-Asian autonomy could be endowed with such momentous significance reveals profound insecurity on the part of Western diplomacy. Just the 'mere fact' that it happened was enough to raise the alarm.

Bandung did represent an important development in the evolution of the Non-Aligned Movement. The emergence of this movement indicated that the so-called Third World had become

an important force in international affairs. But Bandung had little
to do with preparations for a race war. In so far as speakers raised
the issue of race during the proceedings, it was to denounce
racism. President Sukarno of Indonesia told the conference: 'we
are united by a common detestation of racialism'. Others, such as
Leopold Senghor, the President of Senegal, argued that Bandung
represented the 'death' of 'the inferiority of colonial peoples'.[37] It
was left up to the Western imagination to transform this event
into a portent of dangers to come.

If a relatively moderate proceeding like the Bandung Conference could provoke such alarm in the West, then it is not
surprising that more assertive expressions of anti-colonialism
would be seen as evidence of irrational anti-white hatred. The
Mau Mau revolt came to symbolise the rabid anti-white frenzy
which threatened the interests of Western civilisation.

Explanations of this epidemic of anti-white racial bitterness
generally focused on the psychology of resentment. Western
experts of African and Asian affairs stressed the negative, even
pathological, features of anti-colonial nationalism. They insisted
that this was a negative reaction, driven by jealousy and hatred of
the white race. Some contributors were of the view that the very
intensity of such racial hatred was the product of the inferiority
complex of the colonial subject. From this standpoint it was the
feeling of inferiority rather than the reality of racial domination
that provoked anti-colonial revolts. As a result, the pathology of
anti-racist resentment became a catch-all explanation of events.
The psychology of the highly volatile native provided an important theme for official reports. Racial inferiority became a subject
of study in its own right. Accordingly, the standard model of
analysis used to explain anti-colonial nationalism began with the
premise that the source of the problem was frustration, resentment
and a feeling of inferiority. It was held that these negative
sentiments led to a virulent type of reaction against the West,
which invariably took on an anti-white racist form.

Proponents of the inferiority complex model never considered
the possibility that it was their assumption of a psychologically
damaged and irrational Third World nationalist that was truly
racist. On the contrary, the very rejection of the West was held to
be the defining feature of racial prejudice. According to this

diagnosis, anti-colonial nationalism was the product of a disturbed state of mind, which was invariably susceptible to racist emotions. A Foreign Office report characterised it as 'a state of mind' in which 'any sense of grievance, injustice or inferiority is magnified out of all proportion'. In some cases this led to 'hysteria' and for some unexplained reason was seen to be 'highly infectious'.[38]

The link between resentment and anti-Western outbursts was rarely analysed. In most accounts it was simply asserted. Even in the specialist literature there was no attempt to explain why anti-colonial resentment would assume an intensely racial form. The arguments were put with such confidence that no discussion of the assumptions seemed necessary. In one account, the very resentment of Western racism is presented as the potential force behind a future Asian racism.

The resentment of Asia's democrats against racial discrimination is so profound that it can easily become a kind of racial chauvinism directed against Westerners ... This consciousness of racial discrimination provoked many Indians to believe that we used the atom bomb in Japan and not in Germany because much as we hated the Germans they were, after all, white men.[39]

By likening resentment to a potential racial chauvinism, the author problematised the reaction to racism rather than the prior reality of racial discrimination. It was the potential for an Asian racism in the future rather than the actual reality of Western domination that haunted this author.

A contributor to *Foreign Affairs* in July 1952 feared that anti-white resentment would fatally undermine Western diplomacy in Asia. He noted that the 'feelings of racial inferiority' were a 'serious hindrance to Western attempts to build bulwarks for freedom'. He added that 'racial hatreds have bred among many people in Asia and Africa profound distrust of all white peoples'.[40] The logic of this analysis was to interpret Third World nationalism as a force driven by racist sentiment. Some observers argued that the greater the racial difference, the more intense the nationalism. According to one Colonial Office expert, W.H. Ingrams, the growth of 'hysterical nationalism' was 'most acute on the part of Africans frustrated by whites i.e. in the case of the

greatest colour contrast'. Ingrams feared that 'circumstances in
Asia and Africa are causing racism to be equated with nationalism'.[41] By eliding the distinction between the aspiration for
self-determination with racial hatred, many Western observers fell
prey to their own obsessions. As a result, the significance of the
emergence of race relations as an international issue was experienced as a threat to white power.

The tendency to interpret resistance to Western domination in
racial terms indicated the continuation of the tradition of racial
fears. But it also had the effect of discrediting anti-colonial claims.
Insecurities about Western practices could be tempered by the
belief that those who were questioning the world order were
motivated by irrational emotions and intense racist passions. The
tendency to interpret the challenge to the status quo as racial had
the effect of casting the West in the role of the injured party. In
this way, Western officials could uphold the principle of equality
while dismissing those who demanded racial justice on the
grounds that their action was pathological. It would be wrong to
interpret such responses as the product of self-serving cynicism.
Rather, such an imagination was the outcome of a defensive
consciousness, which was unsympathetic to those who had
exposed the vulnerability of the West on race.

From the perspective of the Anglo-American elite, the transformation of race relations into an international issue was itself
unreasonable. The Anglo-American establishment was prepared to
accept formal declarations of equality. What they found objectionable was the transformation of those principles into practical
policy. Such intervention was perceived as disruptive. Since they
regarded race relations to be an explosive problem, any publicity
devoted to the issue was seen to be harmful. From their
standpoint those dwelling on the issue of racial discrimination
themselves contributed to the deterioration of race relations.
Consequently, those who publicised racial grievances were genuinely perceived as individuals who were disruptive and potentially
destructive.

The specialist literature of the 1940s and the 1950s continually
associated claims for racial equality with unreasonable motives.
Western observers professed to being shocked by colonial subjects
who had the bad manners to raise this subject. 'Foreigners visiting

India today are astonished at the coverage given in the Indian press to racial troubles from all over the world', wrote the author of one of the earliest studies of the 'Racial Factor in International Relations'.[4][2] This analysis even filtered into the pages of UNESCO publications. An introduction to a series of articles on race relations justified research on this issue on the grounds that 'coloured people' in the newly independent states have 'not forgotten the humiliations inflicted on them'. According to the author, 'they react either by developing an almost morbidly exaggerated nationalism, or by perpetuating an inferiority complex which saps their vitality'.[43] The implicit counterpart of this assessment was 'why do they go on and on about such an embarrassing subject?' Such sentiments were fully shared by British and American diplomats stationed in Africa and Asia. Their correspondence indicates that they were genuinely perturbed by what they considered to be unreasonable reminders of examples of Western racism. The American Consul in Antigua reported that black trade unionists were 'obsessed with racial discrimination in the United States'. His counterpart in the Gold Coast, Hyman Bloom, was also perturbed by the preoccupation of local Africans with race relations in the United States. His report advocated an active public relations campaign to counter the 'deep, wary almost psychotic concern with the whole issue of race-relations in America'. Bloom was of the opinion that this was a 'concern out of all proportion even to the admittedly profound importance of the Negro problem in U.S. affairs; a concern which seems always ready to believe the worst, however unlikely or even ridiculous that may be'.[44] Bloom's analysis expressed the sentiment of the prevailing official consensus that Africans and Asians who demonstrated an interest in race relations always had pathological concerns.

In reality, if there was any exaggeration or psychotic concern it was more likely to be on the part of Western officialdom's racial imagination. Its defensiveness on the subject expressed itself through an acute sensitivity to any airing of the subject. In part this response was influenced by the previously discussed tradition of racial fear, but it was also the outcome of pragmatic Cold War calculations. In this era of superpower competition, international concern and publicity with the subject of race relations appeared to place the West at a disadvantage.

The Fear of Losing the Third World

The acknowledgement of race relations as a significant theme in international relations was closely connected to the Cold War. The growth of anti-imperialist sentiment in Africa and Asia constituted a major challenge to Western diplomacy. The active intervention of the Soviet bloc in North–South affairs complicated matters and threatened to undermine Western influence further. There was a clear consensus among the political class in London and Washington that the politicisation of race relations would inevitably benefit the Soviet bloc. It was feared that Moscow would be able to use this issue to gain sympathy in the Third World and seriously undermine Western interests there. According to some experts, there was the danger that the conflict of ideology and that of colour would converge. This analysis was widely discussed in the most prestigious periodicals dealing with international affairs.

'The two great world problems of today are the racial problem and the class problem', wrote a contributor in the British periodical *International Affairs*, before pausing to ask rhetorically, 'perhaps they are to a great extent the same problem?'[45] The problem was posed in a similar fashion in the pages of *Foreign Affairs*: 'The two great conflicts of our world – the political issue between the Communist and democratic nations, and the division of race or, less inaccurately of color – are in danger of converging', wrote a well-known British expert on Africa.[46] This was by no means an eccentric observation. The possible convergence of ideological and racial conflict was a regular topic for discussion among the small group of official and unofficial specialists. In a keynote speech delivered at the Royal Institute for International Affairs, which argued for the establishment of a British Institute of Race Relations, H.V. Hodson warned that if the two conflicts 'became identified' as one, the West would be the loser. He told his audience:

> if Communism succeeded in enlisting most of the discontented or the non-European races on its side, so that the frontier between democracy and its enemies was racial as well as ideological political frontier – then the danger would be greatly multiplied, and the chance of our

eventually coming out on top would be so much poorer. To the extent that we solve the racial problem itself we shall of course be preventing that combination from coming about.[47]

For Hodson, it was the exigency of the Cold War that made the establishment of an Institute of Race relations a 'matter of urgency'. His anxiety was driven by the conviction that communism had a good chance of winning the allegiance of the anti-colonial movements of the South. The apparent success of communism in China, Korea and Vietnam suggested that the combination of radical nationalism and Soviet influence was a powerful combination to beat.

Many studies in the 1950s have explicitly pointed to the role of anti-communist fears in stimulating interest in the subject of race relations. St Clair Drake, a prominent black American specialist on this subject, argued that such fears were decisive in encouraging British liberals. 'While it cannot be proved conclusively, it is likely that concern over the growth of the Communist movement among colored people was one factor in stimulating humanitarian circles to begin acting on the color question in the early thirties', he wrote.[48] In the 1940s and 1950s, this consideration became even more important for those specialising in the subject.[49]

Unlike the West, the Soviet Union had every interest in placing racism at the centre of the international agenda. On paper at least, the Soviet Union had an enviable record on race relations. It preached a universalistic creed which was hostile to any manifestation of discrimination. The Soviet Union had no difficulty in representing racism as a distinctly Western problem. It could point to the practice of segregation in the United States, the colour bar operating in the colonies or the system of apartheid in South Africa. Soviet denunciations of these racist practices clearly placed Western diplomats on the defensive. They had little doubt that diplomatic battles fought on the terrain of race relations could not be won. Their main fear was that the goodwill which the Soviet Union earned in the Third World on the question of race could eventually be converted into a wider support for the communist movement in the Third World.

In retrospect it is evident that Western officialdom over-estimated the role that racial feeling had in stimulating Afro-

Asian support for the Soviet bloc. Many Western specialists believed that the success of the official communist movement in Asia was based on some kind of anti-white racial appeal. According to one account, this was a 'major, though concealed factor in the international Communist movement'.[50] In fact, the victory of radical nationalist movements allied to the Soviet Union was the outcome of a variety of complex factors. The tendency by Western diplomats to focus on the racial motif expressed a failure to grasp that the aspiration for self-determination and socio-economic advancement constituted a powerful force for change. Nevertheless, the racial interpretation of events made sense because on this question, unlike any other, the Soviet Union had a widely recognised claim to moral authority, while the West had only its record to hide.

Western officials and experts could do little to challenge the progressive image of the Soviet Union on this question. Attempts were made by anti-communist writers to indict the Soviet Union for its anti-Semitic practices. Well-known Cold War periodicals such as *Commentary* and *Encounter* regularly ran features which argued that Moscow's record on racism was far more brutal than that of the West. These articles claimed that Soviet oppression had 'no parallel in the history of European colonialism', and that colonial people should not trust them. But this propaganda was so explicitly driven by ideological concerns that it failed to separate fact from fiction. Accusations that Stalin was building alliances with 'chauvinist, fascist and Nazi groups' were unlikely to convince a critical readership.[51] Such clumsy Cold War propaganda failed to dent the progressive image of the Soviet record on racism in the 1940s and 1950s. On the contrary, it merely drew attention to the difficulties that Cold War publicists had in dealing with the problem.

Paradoxically, behind the scenes, Western diplomats even believed Soviet claims about its race relations record. They were so busy trying to cover up or to justify their own practices that they failed to interrogate the practices of their main international rival. It was as if diplomats felt that there was little point in fighting a battle that was already lost. According to the official documentation, Anglo-American policy-makers fully believed the essence of Moscow's propaganda on the Soviet Union's record. A report on this subject, circulated by the British Embassy in

Moscow in 1947, clearly overestimated the anti-racist culture there. 'It can safely be maintained that in the USSR the authorities try to avoid discrimination on grounds of race or sex just as much in practice as in theory', the report concluded.[52] This positive assessment ensured that Western diplomats would feel vulnerable on this question during the Cold War. Unofficial experts also accepted the claims that Moscow made about its race relations record. 'As matters stand the Russians practice non-ethnic nationalism much better than we do, and could make a stronger bid for the support of the non-white three-quarters of the world's population', argued a contributor in the periodical *Commentary*.[53] American academic periodicals regularly carried contributions which regarded the Soviet Union as a model for harmonious race relations. According to the accepted academic wisdom, 'the greatest asset of the Soviet power' was 'its policy of rigour and ruthlessly enforced ethnic equality'.[54]

The view that the Soviet Union had solved the race problem and was therefore winning support throughout the colonial world was an integral part of Anglo-American official opinion. This was certainly the working assumption of the British Colonial Office. They believed that communist ideology offered 'membership of a world order' in which race was 'irrelevant'. According to this thinking, the Soviet Union was able to gain the support of non-European people and directly benefit from any manifestation of racial grievances.[55] Investigations by the British government invariably concluded that the experience of racism directly contributed to the attraction of communism. One report on the impact of racial discrimination on colonial students in Britain noted that it greatly benefited the communists. It 'greatly increases anti-British feelings amongst Colonial Students and enhances the attraction of communism as a political creed which repudiates the colour bar'. Andrew Cohen recognised that the communists were 'in a far stronger position to influence these students than we are or anyone we encourage are'.[56]

Cohen's belief that race discrimination placed the West at a disadvantage against its Soviet rival had become a constituent part of official thinking on both sides of the Atlantic. Formulations like 'racial discrimination is capable of jeopardising the Western position of leadership and turning African thoughts towards

Moscow' were regularly used to warn of dangers in the colonial world. Racism had provided 'formidable ammunition' to Soviet propaganda. The West had to act![57]

Despite the recognition that something had to be done to improve the West's standing on race relations it was not clear how to proceed. Despite the recognition that open racism weakened the West's global position, there was a reluctance to take decisive counter-measures. Such hesitation is not surprising, since a genuine anti-racist commitment was absent. Racial thinking was still a factor in international affairs. This was particularly evident in actual conflicts. Western military intervention in post-Second World War Asia invariably demonstrated the persistence of racial thinking. For example, during the Korean War, the American media tended to represent the enemy as inferior human beings. The term 'gook' expressed the contempt with which a dehumanised Oriental was represented. According to arguably the most detailed study of the Korean War, 'barely a voice was raised against such racism'.[58] Such xenophobic militarism did not make good propaganda copy in Asia.

In practice, Western diplomacy was still influenced by racial considerations. British officials involved in the discussion of how to manage the relationship between the old white Commonwealth and the new African and Asian members accepted the principle of differential treatment. The Secretary of State for Commonwealth Relations reported that to preserve 'the closeness of partnership' between the old states, 'we may have to discriminate rather more in practice between these and other members in our relation with them'. In an aside he observed that this 'will only be the continuation of an existing tendency, and the experience with India, Pakistan and Ceylon has proved that such a discrimination can be managed without serious effects'.[59] The prevalence of discriminatory practices in diplomatic affairs tended to undermine those who sought to do something decisive and end the association of racism with the West. Consequently, the Western response to Soviet propaganda was hesitant and evasive. The fear of losing influence in the Third World did have a significant impact on Anglo-American diplomacy, but it led to the emergence of an approach that sought to depoliticise the issue rather than challenge it. When the Governor of the Gold Coast complained to

Whitehall that at 'present very little seems to be done to counter the Communist claims that only under their aegis will the coloured races advance to political freedom', he was missing the point.[60] A campaign against Soviet propaganda was the last thing on the agenda of officials in London as well as Washington.

Depoliticising the Issue of Race Relations

For American and British officials race relations were primarily perceived as a problem of presentation. Diplomats were careful to prevent any open expression of supremacist views. They regarded racially offensive behaviour as impolite and potentially destabilising. Expedience demanded a new racial etiquette. This though was more a matter of public relations than of any fundamental change of views. Officials, especially those involved in propaganda work, defined their task as conciliating those who expressed racial grievances. 'It is suggested that the British Council should engage in a two-way traffic flattering Asiatic opinion, by showing a deep interest in the cultures of the region in which it operates', concluded a strategy document on propaganda in the Far East.[61]

At times a distinct tone of cynicism was discernible in deliberations on the presentation of racial issues. Official exchanges reveal an air of condescension towards those who were demanding race equality. This mixture of diplomatic expedience and resentment about having to adopt a new racial etiquette characterised the British Foreign Office in the early 1950s. One official expressed this synthesis in the following terms:

> I think we should be most careful not to take a line which will give Asiatics an inferiority complex, i.e. we should not rub in the fact that these countries are still in their infancy socially and economically and that they are likely to remain so, so long as the people continue to breed like rabbits. It may be true, but Asiatics will not like us telling them so.[62]

This approach informed official discussions of African and Asian nationalism throughout the 1950s.[63]

However, cynicism about new racial etiquette was symptomatic of an underlying unease about how to handle the issue of race

relations in the Cold War. In practice, those involved in propaganda concluded that the best tactic was to try to prevent a public
airing of the subject. The role of Western propaganda was to
minimise international debate on the subject of race relations.

One approach favoured by propagandists was to divert attention
from 'colour' and 'race'. British officials continually sought to
present cases of racial conflict in a neutral, colour-blind manner.
That is why Whitehall officials continually insisted that the emerging problem of colonial immigration to Britain had little to do with
racism. 'We think it of the utmost importance that the problem
should not be treated on a "colour" basis', was the conclusion of one
Commonwealth Office memorandum.[64] A similar stance was taken
by British administrators in the colonies. It was in this vein that
Governor Arden-Clarke of the Gold Coast requested that publicity
on the Mau Mau should play down the racial significance of the
revolt. He took exception to the 'BBC presentation of early Mau Mau
news from Kenya' for giving 'rise to an impression that the struggle
was a racial one between Europeans and Africans'.[65]

This tactic was favoured by American and British information
officers stationed in Asia. During the early 1950s, regular meetings
were held between officials of the two countries to co-ordinate their
work. Time and again, the solution they advocated for dealing with
the Asian 'obsession' with racism was to try to deflect attention from
it. The head of the United States Information Service (USIS) in
Malaysia insisted that the two countries 'should do all that they
could to suppress references to racial discrimination as this was a
most dangerous subject damaging to both our interests'. Western
information officers sought to prevent, or at least neutralise, the
reporting of news of racial discrimination in the United States and
the British colonies.[66]

Whitehall mandarins also sought to suppress any public discussion of the subject. One official feared that public discussion 'would
merely exacerbate racial feelings'. Another argued against the publication of a survey on discrimination in the British Empire on the
grounds that 'the effect of publishing the survey would be very
damaging'.[67] News of racial issues in the Empire was carefully
communicated and often censored.

In practice, this proved unsuccessful. The mode of denial
placed Western propaganda on the defensive. The failure of the

British anti-Mau Mau propaganda campaign in the colonies showed that the issue of racial conflict could not be defined out of existence. 'My own feeling is that the less we say and hear about Mau Mau the better', wrote the Governor of Jamaica to the Colonial Office. Governor Foot argued that anti-Mau Mau propaganda was a waste of time in Jamaica since it only aroused suspicion about racial motives. He reported: 'the difficulty here is that amongst the great majority of the people there is a tendency to assume that injustice is being done to black people in Kenya and I very much doubt if anything that we can do or say will shake this belief'. Colonial realities overrode attempts to obscure the problems associated with racist practices. A Foreign Office inquiry into the impact of anti-Mau Mau propaganda in South East Asia suggested that 'the question is viewed there as of colour versus colonialism, in spite of the fact that we have tried to show that it is not a national independence movement'.[68]

Western propaganda could not distance Britain and the United States from their legacy of racist practices. Consequently, it was forced to adopt tactics that suggested that positive steps were being taken to eliminate racist practices. American information officers sought to project a progressive race relations image by employing Afro-American personnel in African and Asian societies. It appears that whenever USIS officers found it difficult to counter the charge of American racism, their standard response was to plea for a black American to front their campaign. Time and again, reports on the problem of dealing with racial matters concluded with the demand for black operatives. 'The assignment of a negro officer to every Consulate in the West Indies might work wonders towards the demonstration of progress in removing racial barriers to opportunity', was the solution of the US Consul in Antigua to counter the negative image of his country in the Caribbean.[69] Such a request proved to be unrealistic as there were simply not enough black officials to meet the heavy demand. Six years after this request, the demand for black American personnel was still frequently made. The US Consul in Barbados wrote a long memorandum on this subject in January 1954:

It is respectfully suggested, in the context of racial relations in this area, their pertinence to American interests and their connection with

our foreign policy as regards the Caribbean territories, that no chance
should be lost by the Department in exploiting the contact of
outstanding and representative American citizens of negro origin with
the people of this area.[70]

Finding such 'outstanding' citizens became an important activity
for USIS operatives working in the region.

During the early 1950s, the numerous official requests for delega-
tions of Afro-American public figures and diplomats far exceeded
the numbers that were available. American diplomats stationed in
West Africa, Asia and the Caribbean were often rebuffed by Washington. So, although USIS officials in Malaysia believed that a 'visit
from a negro or a negress would be most valuable', they were informed that there was no Afro-American USIS officer available.[71]
Whether such symbolic actions made very much difference is difficult to discern, but the very fact that the USIS looked to people of
colour to front its activities in Africa and Asia indicates its sensitivity to accusations of racial discrimination.

One way in which Western propagandists tried to depoliticise
the problem of race relations was through the attempt to present
racism as not a Western but a global problem. Information officers
were keen to alter the perception which associated racism with the
West. The argument which they sought to popularise was that
racism was a curse that affected all societies. The logic of this
argument was that no society was immune and therefore no one
could claim moral authority on this matter. By presenting racism
as an endemic problem the West could be relieved of the burden
of guilt.

Both the American State Department and the British Foreign
Office devoted resources towards the collation of racist practices
in other societies. In 1947, both Offices issued circulars asking
their diplomats to report on instances of racial discrimination,
which could be used as ammunition in international debates.
Laurens has noted that the 'Department of State needed something to throw back in the face of it foreign critics' and believed
that if it could show that racism was widely practised, America's
position would be strengthened. Whitehall adopted a similar
stance. Often diplomats expressed a mood of resignation when
they reported their inability to find convincing cases of discrimi-

nation. For example, the British Embassy in Nanking reported: 'we are sorry to say that we are unable to provide you with the sort of ammunition you would clearly like to have'. It added that in China 'there are thus unfortunately no specific discrimination enactments against subject races to which you could point'.[72] 'Sorry' and 'unfortunate' appear to indicate that the writer of the report would have been far happier if racial discrimination had been widely practised in China.

The search for ammunition on the racial etiquette of other societies expressed an attempt to present racism as routine, banal and widespread. The objective of this propaganda campaign was twofold. First it sought to discredit critics of Western racism for being hypocritical. Western information officers were keen to circulate stories about how rife racism was in African or Asian societies. The second and more important objective was to separate the practice of racism from its association with Western culture. For if racism could be understood as part of the human condition, it would cease to have any political significance. The eternalisation of racism meant that no particular nation could be singled out for special attention. In this way race relations would become depoliticised.

The tendency to depoliticise race dominated Western diplomatic action during the Cold War. However, it was not only diplomats who were travelling down this road. Unofficial experts and academic specialists were also caught up in this discussion. Indeed their contributions closely paralleled those of official thinking. As the next chapter argues, the evasiveness that characterised the race relations literature of the pre-war period continued well into the 1950s. The eternalisation of racism provided the ammunition sought by Western diplomats and endowed the policy of depoliticisation with an intellectual coherence.

8   The Silent 1950s –
Redefining the Issue of Racism

For Western diplomacy, race relations required delicate handling. Its commitment to the rhetoric of racial equality stood in sharp contrast to the day-to-day practice of discrimination. Assurances offered by the American foreign policy elite were often sabotaged by the realities of domestic compromise with segregationist politicians. Such tensions were strikingly confirmed in 1958, when the State Department sought to mount 'The Unfinished Business' exhibit at the World Fair in Brussels. The aim of 'Unfinished Business' was to show that Washington was determined to tackle America's civil rights and racial problems. However, as Krenn's study of this event showed, this initiative 'could not compete with the attacks by pro-segregationist forces in the United States and the administration's own dubious commitment to equality'.[1] In the end the exhibit was withdrawn and replaced by one promoting public health. The ignominious fate of one of the few attempts by Washington to project a positive public relations approach on race relations was a testimony to the difficulties it faced.

Anglo-American officials and their specialist advisers intuitively understood that it was difficult to win the battle of ideas on racism with positive arguments. Publicity campaigns promoting the progress of civil rights in the United States or of the ending of the colour bar in the British Empire were usually met with scepticism. There were too many embarrassing episodes to allow such representations to gain credibility. The information services of both countries were continually at a loss to know how to respond to instances of highly publicised acts of discrimination. Often, their instinct was to explain the problem away and present the incident as if it had little to do with racial discrimination. This was the perspective that tended to inform the public relations material of the Colonial Office. A Whitehall brief justifying the colour bar in shops in Zambia pointed out that 'African customers have a tendency to finger goods on display which quickly renders them unmarketable'. The brief concluded that the colour bar in this case was 'dictated by commercial and not racial considerations'. Oliver Lyttelton, the Secretary of State for the Colonies, used a similar approach in his justification of the colour bar in hotels in Bermuda. He noted that although the British Government was opposed to the colour bar, its maintenance 'in certain hotels is essential for the tourist trade'.[2] Such self-serving arguments indicated that the impulse to cover up far outweighed the desire to eliminate discriminatory practices.

The trivialisation of the experience of discrimination in Zambia and Bermuda reflected a tendency either to deny racist intent or to restrict the meaning of racism to its most extreme or grotesque manifestation. Time and again the argument was advanced that this or that incident had nothing to do with racism. Differences in culture, education or religion were advanced as explanations for various acts of racist discrimination. According to the restricted definition of racism, only its highly formalised form could be interpreted as discrimination. So-called personal or social forms of exclusion were interpreted as the natural response of people who wanted to associate with their own kind. This sentiment revealed a superficial anti-racism which found egalitarianism distasteful.

In the 1940s and 1950s the ideal of race equality was rarely attacked through the assertion of notions of superiority. Instead, the egalitarian ideal was challenged through the concept of difference. It seems that officials felt far more comfortable with conceding the right to be different than the right to be equal. They recognised that the right to equality demanded far greater changes to the prevailing racial etiquette than the right to be different. One Foreign Office mandarin commented in a discussion on human rights that the problem 'from the British Empire standpoint, arises over groups that wish to be assimilated, never the groups that wish to differ – we can be expansive about the latter'.[3] It was in this vein that Alan Burns argued that respect for racial difference did not have to mean assimilation:

> I see no reason why black men and white men should not live as fellow-citizens on terms of mutual respect and consideration, without either race sacrificing its identity. It is after all natural for those with

common interest to seek one another's companionship rather than the
companionship of those whose interest is different.[4]

In this way social exclusion was recast as the outcome of a
voluntary aspiration for the right to be different.

The right to be different did not challenge the fundamental
premise of discrimination, since difference implied non-
commensurability and, by implication, inequality. The implication
of this standpoint was rarely spelled out since proponents of difference wanted to emphasise their commitment to ending discrimination. However, from time to time, arguments would surface that
sought to question the apparently absurd idea that all human beings
were the same. H.V. Hodson, former director of the Empire Division
of the Ministry of Information, and one of the most influential voices
in the British Establishment on the subject of race relations, explicitly criticised those 'who proclaim that all races are equal'. In his call
for the establishment of an Institute of Race Relations in 1950,
Hodson argued that if we 'admit the concept of race at all, we admit
that races are different, and if different then unequal'.[5] What distinguished Hodson from most commentators on the subject was his
open defence of racial inequality. Nevertheless his premise that races
were different and therefore by implication unequal was the
accepted wisdom among his colleagues during this period.

In the South African context, the anti-egalitarian logic of the relativists' notions of difference acquired an open form and helped to
legitimatise segregation. Even liberal thinkers concerned with the
practice of discrimination justified separate treatment on the
grounds of racial differences. A group of Anglican bishops sought to
reconcile such conflicting principles by stating that 'in South Africa
there must be differences based on the racial characteristics of the
various groups composing the population, and on the various standards of culture and education and yet we are bound to condemn a
discrimination which is based solely on the colour of a man's skin'.
More sophisticated variants of this argument stressed the cultural
rather than the racial foundation of difference.[6]

In the post-war period, the official emphasis on the right to be
different could draw on strands of social science based on the
tradition of cultural relativism and pluralism. Such intellectual
contributions often sought to protect indigenous cultures from the

destructive impact of westernisation. Their liberal intent endowed cultural relativism with a progressive image. But, as Malik has argued, one of the consequences of this approach was to 'impute rational meaning to inequality'.[7] In the hands of those concerned with managing the international image of Britain and the United States, ideas of difference served the end of restricting the meaning of racism. For if indigenous culture needed protecting, then the dominant white culture could also justify its attempts to keep itself separate from others.

In the long run, the concept of difference would culminate in the institutionalisation of multiculturalism, but in the 1950s, this strand of thought helped provide an intellectual rationale for segregation and apartheid. It became influential in academic circles, but amongst the liberal intelligentsia, the inegalitarian consequences of cultural relativism were rarely explored.[8] At a time when demands for civil rights were increasingly heard in the United States, and when Soviet manifestos about the goal of racial equality were finding a resonance in the international community, the insistence on the right to difference had a distinctly apologetic air. Internationally, the demand for equal rights far outweighed the right to difference. Consequently, the emphasis of official contributions shifted towards what was portrayed as unreasonable demands for social equality. At the same time, propagandists attempted to undermine the widely held view that associated racism with Western society.

The Eternalisation of Racism

Throughout the twentieth century there has been a clear tendency to represent racism as an attitude that characterises the behaviour of all people. As the previous discussion on race consciousness has indicated, many Western observers have characterised the reaction to racism, that is *race consciousness*, as the principal problem. This perspective was also evident in the post-war period. However, the arguments developed in the interwar period were not adequate for engaging the international climate of opinion in the post-war period. In contrast to the 1930s, there was now a new international consensus which demanded nothing less than the equal treatment of all human beings. It was no longer sufficient to focus the discussion on those who were racially conscious. Even those officials who took exception to the unreasonable demands of those suffering from 'colour consciousness' were forced to pay lip-service to the ideal of equality. More specifically, discrimination in any form could no longer be openly justified. In response to this development, Western arguments about the problem of race relations underwent modification. In the post-war period there was a gradual shift from the focus on race consciousness to one that portrayed racism as a problem for which everyone bore responsibility. The logic of this representation was at once to implicate everyone and no one in particular. This discourse was rooted in the discussions of the interwar period, but in the 1950s it was systematically developed into a powerful theory of race relations. It provided a coherent defence for the negative argument that suggested that the West should not be singled out since everyone else was also racist.

As noted in the previous chapter, both the American and British governments looked for ammunition to support their stand in the experience of other societies. By publicising instances of discrimination throughout the world, Anglo-American diplomats sought to counter critics who condemned racist practices as a specifically Western phenomenon. This was often a cynical tactic designed to relieve the burden of guilt. However, interpreting racism as a natural mode of behaviour cannot be reduced to conscious cynicism. In many cases, this was an explanation which was arrived at almost instinctively. The need to respond to international criticism encouraged a reaction that sought to discredit the record of the critics. According to one account, the standard response of the American Consul in Madras to questions about the 'colour problem' in the United States was to answer 'Yes, it's almost as bad as it is in India'. The Consul claimed that 'this often caused such embarrassed confusion that the subject was immediately dropped'.[9] This approach was adopted throughout Africa and Asia. As the response was entirely negative, it did not attempt to defend Western racist practices directly, but suggested that others were complicit.

Even in the early days of the United Nations, Western diplomats often answered their critics by pointing out that discrimination was widespread throughout the world. As Laurens noted, in 1946, India's condemnation of racism in South Africa was countered with criticism of its caste system.[10] As India was one of the most vociferous critics of Western racism, the caste system became a repeated subject of Anglo-American criticism. Invariably, India was accused of gross hypocrisy. The caste system in India was represented as an intrinsically racist institution, which produced a far more intense obsession with race than anywhere else. 'No people are more colour conscious than high-caste Hindus', was the verdict of one observer cited by Burns.[11] Crocker insisted that African students faced far greater discrimination in India than in the West. He reported that the 'average Indian, beguiled by the diatribes of his delegates at the United Nations, and sharing the human frailty of seeing the beam in his colonialist neighbour's eye while missing the mote in his own, would be astonished to learn what thousands or so African students in India think about Indian race prejudice'.[12] Such reports contributed to an intellectual climate in which Western racism could be represented as unexceptional. It also helped undermine India's right to criticise the racism of the West.

The tendency to establish a moral equivalence between Indian and Western racism influenced both official and unofficial discussions at this time. Indeed official thinking was closely paralleled by the academic literature. Even before the Second World War, scholarly contributions pointed to the Indian caste system and its treatment of the untouchables to assuage Western responsibility. For example, the 1935 Report of the British Royal Anthropological Society, *Race and Culture*, dwelt on Indian 'colour consciousness' and its celebration of whiteness. It also reported that 'even among some primitive peoples differences in skin colour are made the basis for aesthetic judgement, with social repercussions'.[13] 'Even among Indians themselves I am told that parents arranging for the marriage of their daughters' select 'fair in preference to dark bridegrooms', was an often repeated homily.[14]

During the 1940s and 1950s, academic reviews of race relations rarely resisted the temptation of bringing the Indian caste system into the discussion. For example, one of the most influential British studies of race relations in the 1950s equated the Indian caste system with the 'so-called caste system in the Southern United States' and with the apartheid regime of South Africa.[15] Scholars continued to insist on the conceptual similarity between the Indian caste system and Western racial discrimination well into the 1960s. 'It should be evident that the range of similarities between caste in India and race relations in America, when viewed as relations among people, is wide and that the details are remarkably similar in view of the differences in cultural context', wrote a Berkeley social scientist in 1960.[16] British studies treated communal tensions in India and racial conflict in South Africa as if they were manifestations of the same problem. 'The integration of the Untouchables in India is just as much a 'racial' problem as the integration of the Negro in the United States', argued a paper read at a symposium organised by the Royal Anthropological Institute and the Institute of Race Relations.[17] One well-known American specialist took the view that the 'caste system of India' represented the 'most extreme system of color bar and racial prejudice'.[18]

Exposures of India's misdeeds rested on a fundamental reworking of the concept of racism. It involved an inflation of the meaning of racism to encompass literally all forms of group conflicts. Such an approach ignored the factors that were specific to the relation of power and of foreign domination. Instead, racism was reduced to a set of attitudes that influenced inter-group behaviour. In this way, racism was recast as a catch-all category that could be discovered in all cultures and was seen to define most relations of conflict.

India was by no means the only Afro-Asian society to be accused of racist practices. African critics of apartheid often faced the accusation that their domestic record was just as bad as South Africa's. An internal memorandum circulated by the British Conservative Party's Research Department proposed a propaganda campaign against Ghana to undermine the credibility of her denunciation of South Africa. The memorandum stated: 'if Ghana could be discredited and held up to world opinion as a Fascist dictatorship', then it would have 'no right to sit in judgement' on South Africa.[19] Discrediting the international critics of racism became the principal diplomatic tactic deployed by those concerned with defending the reputation of Britain and the United States.

It is striking just how far the specialist academic literature echoed the official line that racism was not the monopoly of white people. There was something compulsive about this desire to transform racism into a transcendental curse that afflicted all societies throughout history. In the 1950s, even UNESCO publications adopted the perspective that Western racism was one among many examples of racism. One paper, which presented the research agenda of UNESCO on race relations, was categorical on this point: 'Race prejudice has so far been analysed almost exclusively as exemplified by white people, though it cannot be said to be their preserve.'[20] While UNESCO publications were generally restrained about expanding on the subject of African or Asian racism, more apologetic contributions stridently blamed colonial critics for fanning the flames of racism. The British historian Max Beloff contended that colonialism had nothing to do with racism. He argued that the same situation develops whenever one society is settled by people from another. As an illustration, Beloff cited the case of Chinese settlers in Malaysia.[21]

The tendency to conflate Western racism with more general relations of conflict in other societies continued well into the 1960s. Many textbooks on race relations had the character of comparative studies in conflict resolution. The reduction of racism to a generic concept of conflict led many writers to conceptualise racism as a universal problem. Consequently, their conclusions invariably implied that Western societies bore no greater responsibility for racism than others. Hans Cohn's influential book provides a clear example of how racism was conceptualised as a sin afflicting the whole of humanity. After noting that a 'widespread popular error assumes that racial conflicts and color prejudice are confined to the relations between white and colored population', Cohn assured his reader that racism has been 'practiced by all races, white and coloured alike'. Cohn also advanced the view that white racial domination was relatively benign in comparison to that practised by Asiatic Mongols or African Bantus or American Aztecs. These societies, argued Cohn, 'have on the whole treated their subject races with much greater cruelty than the white man ever has in modern times'.[22] In this account, the distinct characteristics of racial thinking and racial domination are extinguished. Instead, diverse forms of human cruelty are abstractly compared, and not surprisingly, Western racism emerges with flying colours. Moreover, an all-purpose relationship of conquest and domination helps transform racial discrimination into a permanent feature of the human condition. Such an interpretation of history clearly minimised the significance of racial domination. It was reduced to a minor footnote, lost in the midst of dramatic accounts of bloody encounters.

Cohn's Who's Who of historic misdeeds exemplified a genre of writing on race relations, which survived well into the mid-1960s. Authors scoured history to construct a world in which racist practices were the norm. Thomas Melady, the American author of a widely read book *The Revolution of Color*, clearly illustrated this trend to demonstrate his thesis that racism is part of a universal human condition. The author introduced his catalogue of horror stories with an indictment of the Manchu dynasty: 'The Manchu conquerors of China enforced strict racial segregation and forbade all racial intermarriage.' He then turned to the Indian caste system and made the usual points. Melady then reminded his readers that during the Second World War, 'Japanese colonial administrators outdid Western colonial administrators'. To add a little balance, he commented that in India, American soldiers regarded natives as 'dirty and uncivilized' but added 'Hindu intellectuals looked down upon the Americans as boorish, materialistic, unintellectual and uncivilized.' Melady even included 'tribal' people in this list of inter-group hostilities, to show that everyone is guilty. 'Tribal man, confined to a small area among a small group of likes, regarded even members of a tribe as less than he, as subhuman, as savage.'[23]

An unflattering representation of human beings underpinned Melady's thesis of racism as an eternal condition. These were typically negative arguments which made no attempt to defend the race relations record of any society. Instead any special responsibility for racist practices on the part of Europeans was dismissed since all races were complicit. The eternalisation of racism also served to naturalise such practices. If even small tribes regarded their neighbours as sub-human, then it is only natural to dislike, hate and discriminate against others.

Although the tendency to eternalise racism had an obvious apologetic content, it is unlikely that it was the outcome of intellectual dishonesty. Rather, the literature reflected an instinctive reaction against the moral damage which the accusation of racism imposed on the West. This was a charge that could not be easily dismissed as the product of Soviet propaganda. The charge of racism exposed an important flaw in Western societies. Moreover, it was an accusation that many people in Britain and the United States conceded or at least found difficult to refute. One intellectual response – albeit that of a minority – was to accept the accusation and attempt to investigate the meaning of racism.[24] However, the dominant response was a defensive one. Most Western contributions on race relations felt more comfortable with discussing the discriminatory habits of other societies than with attempting to place under scrutiny the specific structures of domination in their own.

Above all, the mainstream race relations literature of the 1950s sought to counter the damaging consequences of the charge of racism. It was prepared to condemn the extreme manifestation of racism in cases such as Nazi Germany or South Africa, but it was not ready to examine the roots of racism in the social structure of Western liberal democracies. Instead, it preferred to treat racism as a bad idea that was inconsistent with the ideals and institutions of Western society. The literature was also silent about its own agenda. It rarely acknowledged its fears of racial revenge or its sense of unease with having to deal with the accusation of racism. Later a confident intellectual such as Daniel Bell would directly tackle the 'powerful negative affect in the accusation of racism',[25] but in the 1950s, such open presentation of the problem was rare. Writers preferred to discuss the inequities of the Indian caste system rather than engage in a direct confrontation with the charge of racism.

A Silent Subject

From a sociological point of view, race relations in the 1950s provide a subject in their own right. The race relations literature of this period was not only shallow and evasive, it lost much of the anger and dynamism that it possessed in the 1940s. In quantitative terms, publications on this subject ceased to grow. The decade was a period of intellectual hibernation. Serious research also slowed down. For example, the Carnegie Foundation, which supported Myrdal's project in the 1940s, provided no money for race relations research until the 1960s.[26]

An inspection of American and British academic publications in the 1950s suggests a loss of interest. This was particularly the case in the United States, where the number of articles on race relations published in important journals such as *American Journal of Sociology* and *Social Forces* fell during the 1950s. Richard Simpson found that between 1955 and 1959, the numbers of papers on race relations delivered at the American Sociological Association also fell.[27]

The decline in research interest was paralleled by a shift away from theorising about racism. John Stanfield's study of the history of race relations in the 1950s points to the narrowing of focus of this research. He has argued that there was no 'comprehensive theoretical work on American racial issues' during this period and that more 'macro approaches in race and ethnic studies would not begin to appear in the literature until the mid-1970s and 1980s'.[28]

This did not mean that there was no discussion of the subject. Rather, there was little attempt made to explore the underlying structures of race relations. In most cases racism was discussed as a phenomenon that was not directly connected, or was exogenous, to Western capitalist society. In many cases the subject of concern was race relations in places that were external to contemporary Western society. An examination of the *International Bibliography of Political Science*, published by UNESCO during the 1950s, indicates that most of the articles under the heading of race are about anti-Semitism or South Africa, and many of the articles on anti-Semitism concentrated on the situation in the Soviet Union. Serious discussions of race relations in Western liberal democracies were rare. The newly established journal *Race*, published by the British Institute of Race Relations, provided a striking illustration of this trend. It was preoccupied with overseas issues and rarely engaged with the question of domestic British racism. Clearly, Western race relations specialists felt more comfortable discussing problems in distant countries than with theorising about their own society.

During the 1950s race relations theory shifted its emphasis from the sociological to the psychological. Nothing was published that was in any sense comparable to Myrdal's study of American race relations. Probably the most significant race relations related publication of the 1950s was Theodore Adorno's *The Authoritarian*

Personality (1950). Adorno's work expressed a perceptible trend towards conducting studies of prejudice in terms of personality dynamics. As Banton remarked, Adorno's text 'influenced the social science of the 1950s, a decade when research into the socio-structural origins of prejudice ran the risk of being accounted as un-American activity'.[29] Banton was right to point to the dearth of structural studies of racism in the 1950s. Abstract speculation about prejudice and the reaction to it were conducted in isolation from any determinate social structure. Racism was interpreted as an attitude rather than an outlook-based structured practice and power relation.

Without wishing to attribute intent, the main project of race relations theory in the 1950s turned out to be an attempt to separate racism from its association with the West. Most contributors to this field did not try to evade the issues. They were sensitive to the explosive character of race relations and wanted to do something constructive to alleviate the situation. However, their impulse was driven more by racial uncertainties than by any egalitarian impulse. As a result, race relations theory opted for conservative interpretations of events. It sought to minimise racial tension and placed far less emphasis on the fight against racism. It thus contributed to the silencing of the issue in the 1950s. If anything, race relations theory ran behind the international acceptance of the principle of equality. It was defensive in tone and conservative in content. Like the prevailing official discourse, it had no wish to defend racism as such. Its project was to minimise the damaging consequences of the world-wide reaction to racism. It took the upheavals of the 1960s to transform the discussion on racism. Only then did racism itself become the main subject of concern for the field of race relations.

9 Conclusion

Throughout these chapters, one of the principal themes has been the way in which racial fears have shaped the discourse of race relations. This theme is by no means sufficient to tell the whole story of the evolution of racial thinking and of racist practices in the twentieth century. However, as the previous discussion suggests, such fears were crucial for understanding the story of how ideas about race, associated relations of conflict and even the academic study of the subject developed. The evidence of history indicates that throughout the twentieth century, race was a problematic issue for Western elites. One of the important paradoxes is that even before the emergence of anti-racist criticism, very few people were prepared to offer an intellectual defence of racism. Even the beneficiaries of the Western system of global domination sought to distance themselves from a celebration of race and were far more likely to fear the destructive potential of race conflict.

Racial fears have rarely been a subject of investigation. When observers have touched upon the problem, they have tended to do so outside any determinate relation of power. Often such fears are treated as the natural outcome of 'the juxtaposition of two divergent ethnic groups'.[1] In recent decades the focus has shifted towards the psychological, and more contemporary students have emphasised its imaginary qualities, which are seen to be shaped by the discourse of a particular institution, such as the media. There is little doubt that psychological and cultural influences have been decisive in shaping the form of racial fears. However, to understand the sociology of such fears it is necessary to situate them in history and in particular in relation to the changing balance of power. In *The Silent War*, international dimensions have been given prominence because it is at the level of global power relations that racial fears were most systematically articulated. In turn, anxieties about the changing balance of international power have had important ramifications for domestic practice.

Anxieties about control and power have been most vividly articulated through the concept of a race war. Discussants of this theme have hinted darkly at how the danger of race war is likely to increase in the future. Throughout the twentieth century, major events such as the victory of Japan over Russia in 1905, the upheavals precipitated by the First World War, the dislocations associated with the Second World War and the explosions of the 1960s have produced moral panics about global racial conflict. Such reactions always reflect a situation where the existing relations of power are contested. It is under such pressures that race relations have come to be problematised and invested with the quality of an impending peril. As one astute study indicated: 'since the middle of the nineteenth century' a 'redistribution of power has been in process and this has been conceptualized in part, at least, as a crisis in race relations'.[2] St Clair Drake, who wrote this statement, is careful in his choice of words. The redistribution of power is conceptualised, experienced or in a more contemporary vocabulary is represented as a crisis in race relations. In other words, the very discourse of race relations indicates a sense of crisis. Manifestations of this sentiment are evident at crucial moments throughout the twentieth century. Concern about the breakdown of white solidarity, the conscious-ness of demographic competition, the presentiment of racial wars to come, apprehensions about white prestige or the racialisation of the reaction to Western domination are symptomatic of an imagination that conceptualised the changing balance of power through the prism of race relations.

As long as the Western-dominated world order remained unchal-lenged, there was little interest in the relation between races. With the West dictating the terms, there was little need to consider the sensitivities of those experiencing its domination. It was the changing balance of power that forced the Anglo-American elite to think about the reaction of those it had regarded as inferior. Such an adjustment did not come easily. As Crocker remarked, 'the white races have had a long and remarkable innings, but the game is now coming to an end'. He added: 'one of the hard lessons that the white races have to learn today is that their innings is over'.[3] The manner in which thinking on race relations evolved testifies to a reluctance to come to terms with the end of the game.

The relationship between race and international affairs is not a straightforward one. The period when it probably had its most direct impact on the governing of the world order was during the last four decades of the nineteenth century. This was a time when a confident sense of race characterised the outlook of the elites of the expanding Western powers. The sense of race contributed to a sense of coherence and provided an outlook through which global affairs were interpreted, understood and regulated. It also led to the emergence of the so-called white consensus: an informal etiquette for the conduct of international affairs. As one useful contribution noted, at this time 'race functioned as a regulative force for maintaining stability both in the white-dominated states and the white-dominated international system'.[4] Since the turn of the century, the role of race as a regulatory force has been transformed into an element of instability. For Western diplomats it has increasingly come to symbolise a relation of conflict. And the knowledge that such conflict would weaken the position of the West helped fuel apprehensions. The manifest tone of defensiveness of the Western political class in turn had the effect of attracting international criticism. During the Cold War, anti-racism became one of the most effective ideological weapons against Western domination. A studied silence was probably the West's most effective response to anti-racist criticism.

Throughout the twentieth century ideas about race relations have reflected hesitancy, bitterness, scepticism, bad faith and above all the desire to slow things down. The development of racial pragmatism in the interwar period strikingly confirmed this tendency. It indicated that the conceptualisation of a distinct subject of race relations had as its problematisation the reaction to racism. Indeed until the 1960s, most of the insights, theories and concepts associated with race relations were oriented towards the explanation and containment of this reaction to racism.

The agenda of the official discourse on race relations was also driven by the exigency of containing the reaction of people of colour against racism. In every instance, the consideration of new norms and practices was perceived as concessions forced by circumstances. In virtually every situation, where race relations were the subject of official deliberation, the objective of the participants was to avoid coming to terms with the legacy of racism. Archival records indicate that reluctant officials felt compelled to do something about a subject which they would have far rather ignored. Time and again the question was how to slow down the pace of change. Often this question was assessed with brutal frankness. One official was prepared to bury an embarrassing report on the state of race relations in the British Empire, even though he acknowledged that he was 'doubtful whether we shall get away with it indefinitely'.[5]

The issues of timing, prevention, containment, damage limitation and deception far outweighed any genuine commitment to reform. In the post-Second World War period, the principle of equality was only grudgingly accepted. And even then the rhetoric of equality was rarely allowed to impact on old practices. One prominent official in the British Civil Service had no problem in reconciling the promise of equality with the reality of discrimination. After noting that people of colour had the right to compete for civil servant positions, he indicated that they had little chance of being appointed, since the 'great majority are obviously not "qualified by knowledge and ability" for the positions they are seeking'.[6] The forced acceptance of the principle of race equality helped foster a climate where dishonesty became a cornerstone of the institution of race relations.

As time ran out, the sentiment that it was not possible to fudge the issue indefinitely was a recurring theme in official deliberations. Such attitudes could be found well into the 1960s, when the success of anti-colonial forces and the American civil rights movement provoked another round of discussion about the need to avert impending race wars. Snyder, whose pronouncements on this subject in the 1930s have already been considered, returned to this theme in the 1960s:

> With population explosion in Africa and Asia, with Western colonialism dying, with China pursuing a belligerent position in its 'great leap forward', it may be that the great conflict of the late twentieth century will be dominantly racial. In that case, racialism could well replace nationalism as the most important force in the world, more important than civilization, decency, kindness, pity; more important than life itself.[7]

Barbara Plummer has documented the emergence of 1960s' race war rhetoric. She noted that in the United States, the 'imagery of impending racial conflict found its way into a substantial amount of journalism, social commentary, and speech writing of the time' and that 'commentators offered insights and proposed solutions that they believed would help avert disaster'.[8]

The final, albeit hesitant, acceptance of the principle of equality in the 1960s is not the subject of this book. It is worth noting that with this further erosion of the line of race, the sentiment of racial anxieties has become even more silent. As Fanon noted, a stage has been reached where 'racism no longer dares appear without disguise'.[9] As I shall argue in another book on this subject, this disguise has confused many contributions on this issue.

The Legacy of Containment

In the end, racial pragmatism had to give way to a formal acceptance of equality, but by the time this occurred, decades of racial pragmatism, and the practices associated with it, had helped create a climate where the West could minimise the damaging consequences of its racist tradition.

The intellectual legacy of racial pragmatism continues to influence the literature. Over a period of time the race relations paradigm has contributed to the redefinition of the problem. As a result racism has been gradually separated from its association with the West and also from relations of power. The tendency to reverse the problem of racism, discussed in chapter 4, was not merely an intellectual exercise. American and British officials and propagandists spontaneously focused on the racially conscious rejection of Western domination, and the media continually represented racism as an attitude that afflicted everyone. Indeed the more that racism became discredited the more there was a tendency to orient the discussion towards the reaction of the oppressed. 'Rather unexpectedly, the racist group points accusingly to a manifestation of racism among the oppressed', observed Fanon.[10] Their rejection of the culture of domination is recast as a fanatical form of prejudice. One of the consequences of the legacy of containment is that the term racism has become increasingly contested. Everyone and no one is implicated as a racist; instead of racism, we now have a plurality of racisms.

Throughout the twentieth century, the legacy of race has tended to be experienced as a problem and a liability by Western elites. During the Cold War such sentiments became more focused since the association of racism with the West directly contributed to a loss of moral authority. Unable to defend their record on race, Western elites were forced to distance themselves from their own past. In the short term, this approach had the effect of undermining the self-image of the Anglo-American elites. But the abandonment of racial thinking did not lead to the acceptance of an egalitarian ethic. If anything, the loss of moral authority, which the abandonment of racial thinking implied, was intensely resented by Western leaders. Such resentments were reinforced by the ascendancy of the Third World in the 1960s.

The heroic moment of the Third World was experienced as a rejection of the authority of the West. The capacity of the Third World to command moral authority – even amongst the youth of the West – struck a direct blow against the old coherence of the superior Western self-image. The sensitivity of Western liberal and conservative intellectuals was demonstrated by their obsessive concern with this problem. During the 1960s and 1970s Cold War-inspired books and articles on a variety of subjects lashed out against the Third World. Liberals and student radicals were denounced for their gullibility. The leading American sociologist Daniel Bell sought to limit the damage by attacking those who sought to manipulate 'liberal guilt about racism and exploitation'. Bell's attempt to lighten the burden of American foreign policy by pointing to the 'savageries' of 'Rwanda, Burundi, or Uganda' anticipated by more than a decade a central theme in North–South relations.[11]

Since the 1960s, attempts to repair the damage to Western moral authority have almost always taken an indirect form. There has been only a minimal attempt to defend the race relations record of the West; instead the emphasis has been on indicting the actions of Third World societies. The ending of the Cold War has facilitated this moral rehabilitation. Since the 1980s, it has been possible to represent the societies of the South as not racially but morally inferior to the North. The failures of the South, particularly of Africa, often serves as a retrospective vindication of the legacy of imperialism.

The moral condemnation of the South in the 1990s allows Western elites to settle scores with the uncomfortable 1960s. The corollary of this new sense of superiority has been the creation of a two-tier system of international relations. The world is governed through a system of double standards, but this time its form is moral, not racial. Japan is formally treated by Western powers as an equal partner. Indeed, successful Asian economies are held up as models in the Western press. But Asia's acceptance by the West is not yet complete: attention is often drawn to differences in culture and morality.

Increasingly the vocabulary that is applied to the South is morally different from that which is used in relation to the North. Many societies of the South, especially those of Africa, are treated in pathological terms. Africans are routinely represented as devoid of moral qualities. Many accounts of the conflict in Rwanda have pointedly argued that its people simply do not know right from wrong. According to one report, 'Rwanda is a society where deception and dishonesty are the most highly esteemed values'.[12] Others have condemned societies of the South for breeding too fast and for being the nursery of terrorism. Terms like fundamentalism are used to distance such societies from the North.

The new moral equation between a superior North and an inferior South helps legitimise a two-tiered international system. It is a system that lacks the optimism and certainties of the old world of Western empires. But for all that it is a system that, for the time being, remains unchallenged. Race no longer has a formal role to play since the new global hierarchy is represented through a two-tier moral system. Gradually, the old silent race war has been replaced by moral crusades and by 'clashes of civilisation'. But that is a story for another book.

Notes

Introduction

1. Tinker (1977) p. 131.
2. Park's article 'Our Racial Frontier on the Pacific' was originally written in 1926 and reprinted in Park (1950). See T.F. Pettigrew, 'How Events Shape Theoretical Frames', in Stanfield (1993).
3. Adorno (1969) p. 24; and Jencks (1992) p. 99.
4. Adorno (1969) p. 8.
5. Dollard (1957) p. 319.
6. PRO: FO 371/6684, 'Racial Discrimination and Immigration. Memorandum by F. Ashton-Gwatkin', 10 October 1921.
7. See the discussion on this subject in PRO: CO 859/165/1, especially 'Minute by G. Foggon', 9 May 1950.
8. Gong (1984) p. 51.
9. H. Bull, 'The Emergence of a Universal International Society', in Bull and Watson (1984) p. 125.
10. M. Howard, 'The Military Factor in European Expansion', in Bull and Watson (1984) p. 31.
11. PRO: PREM 11/3665, 'Prime Minister Harold Macmillan to Robert Menzies', 15 January 1962.
12. See Hofstadter (1955) p. 192; and J. Huxley, 'Colonies and Freedom', *The New Republic*, 24 January 1944.
13. Stepan (1982) p. 139.
14. Barkan (1992) p. 30.
15. See PRO: CO 111/756/60358/38, 'Minute by Mayle', 18 October 1938; and CO 1/770/60270/1940, 'Governor of British Guiana to Secretary of State for the Colonies', 12 October 1940.
16. Tinker (1977) p. 131.
17. E.B. Reuter, 'Review of Race: Science and Politics', *The American Journal of Sociology*, January 1941, vol. 46, no. 4, p. 621.
18. Gossett (1971) p. 174.
19. These themes are admirably discussed in Rich (1986) chapter 5.
20. See Barkan (1992) pp. 280–1.
21. Hogben's *Dangerous Thoughts* represents one of the first attempts to mount a critique of racism from an egalitarian standpoint. See Hogben (1939).
22. Myrdal (1962) p. 1019.
23. PRO: CO 875/11/1, 'Note by Edmett', 30 December 1941.

24. PRO: FO 371/40716, 'Earl of Halifax, Washington to Foreign Office', 19 September 1944.
25. For the British discussion, see PRO: CO 967/143, 'Minute by Mr. Seel to Lloyd', 28 January 1949. For the American deliberation, see M.L. Krenn, '"Outstanding Negroes" and "Appropriate Countries": Some Facts, Figures, and Thoughts on Black U.S. Ambassadors, 1949–1988', *Diplomatic History*, vol. 14, no. 1, 1990, p. 131.
26. PRO: FO 924/147, 'Education and Racial Tolerance' by A. Sommerfelt, 12 February 1945.
27. Sewell (1975) p. 53.
28. For a discussion of this initiative, see A. Metraux, 'UNESCO and the Racial Problem', *International Social Science Bulletin*, vol. 2, no. 3, pp. 385–6.
29. Percy E. Corbett; 'Next Steps After The Charter', *Commentary*, vol. 1, no. 1, p. 27.
30. Lauren (1988) p. 159.
31. Vincent, 'Racial Equality', in Bull and Watson (1984) p. 252.
32. For this interesting exchange of views see PRO: FO 317/27889, 'R. Butler to Sir H. Seymour', 3 March 1941, 'Minute by Ashley-Clarke', 6 March 1941, 'Minute by Sir H. Seymour', 12 March 1941; and 'Minute by R. Butler', 12 March 1941.
33. K.B. Clark 'Introduction: The Dilemma of Power', in Parsons and Clark (1966) p. xiv.
34. Blacker (1952) p. 323.
35. Rich (1986) p. 117.
36. Barkan (1992) p. 395.
37. Jones (1988) p. 72.
38. Vincent, 'Racial Equality', in Bull and Watson (1984) p. 252.
39. Gong (1984) p. 87.
40. Ibid.
41. See Tinker (1977) p. 43; and Dower (1986).
42. Cited in Lauren (1988) pp. 143–4.
43. Lauren (1988) p. 144.
44. See H. Bull, 'The Revolt Against the West', in Bull and Watson (1984) p. 221.
45. Myrdal (1962) pp. 1020–1.
46. Kohn 'Race Conflict', in *Encyclopedia of the Social Sciences*, vol. 13 (1934) p. 40.
47. Myrdal (1962) p. 1021.
48. K.B. Clark, 'Introduction' to Myrdal (1962) p. xiv.
49. H. Hodson, 'Race Relation in the Commonwealth', *International Affairs*, vol. 26, April 1950, p. 305.
50. F. Wunderlich, 'New York's Anti-Discrimination Law', *Social Research*, June 1950, vol. 17, no. 2, p. 219.
51. PSF: Box 37 Folder 5, 'The Atlantic Charter and Africa from an American Standpoint' by The Committee on Africa and Peace Aims, May 1942, pp. 1, 19 and 103.

Chapter 1

1. For an overview of these concerns, see Banton (1987) and Miles (1989).
2. See the interesting discussion 'Social Darwinism, Racial Theory and Fascism', in Lukács (1980); and the 'Legacy of Social Darwinism', in Jones (1980).
3. Langer (1951) p. 85.
4. Toynbee (1948) p. 206.
5. Cited in Rich (1984).
6. See Iriye's concept of international relations as intercultural ones in Iriye (1981) p. vii.
7. Cited in D. Lavin, 'Lionel Curtis and the Idea of Commonwealth', in Madden and Fieldhouse (1984) p. 113.
8. R. Preiswerk 'Race and Colour in International Relations', in *The Year Book of World Affairs* (1970) p. 55.
9. *The Times*; 3 July 1882.
10. Sir A.C. Lyall, 'Introduction', in Chirol (1910) p. ix.
11. Vincent, 'Racial Equality', in Bull and Watson (1984) p. 240.
12. IMC/CBMS: Box 1211, Rev. A.M. Chirgwin, 'Christian Missions in Relation to World Movements', July 1931.
13. Hailey is cited in Walton (1997) p. 16.
14. PRO: FO 371/6684, 'Racial Discrimination and Immigration'.
15. Cited in Hitchens (1990) p. 110.
16. PRO: FO 371/6634.
17. Cited in J.M. Winter, 'The Webbs and the Non-white World: a Case of Socialist Racialism', *Journal of Contemporary History*, vol. 9, no. 1, January 1974, p. 190.
18. Snyder (1939) pp. 284–5.
19. Cited in L. Grundlingh '"Non-Europeans Should be Kept away from the Temptations of Towns": Controlling Black South African Soldiers During The Second World War', *The International Journal of African Historical Studies*, vol. 25, no. 3, 1992, p. 540.
20. Grundy (1983) p. 39.
21. Willcocks (1904) p. 194.
22. H. Bull, 'The Revolt Against the West', in Bull and Watson (1984) p. 220.
23. Wm. Roger Louis, 'The Era of the Mandates System and the Non-European World', in Bull and Watson (1984) p. 211.
24. See A. Ruger, 'The Colonial Aims of the Weimar Republic', in Stoecker (1986) p. 322; and IAI: Box 37, 'Notes by Dr. Margaret Read Regarding Possible Activities of the Institute During the War', undated, circa early 1940.
25. CCA: Box 298, 'E.R. Embree to F.P. Keppel', 5 March 1933.
26. V. Palmer, 'The Empire and Asiatic Immigration', *Fortnightly Review*, July 1919, p. 558.

27. Gregory (1931) p. 70; and Willoughby (1923) pp. 226–7.
28. See Wright (1939) p. 264.
29. Crozier (1988) pp. 122 and 273.
30. *The Times*, 21 August 1935.
31. Cited in Dutt (1936) pp. 187–8.
32. Q. Wright, 'The Government of Iraq', *American Political Science Review*', vol. 20, 1926, pp. 752–3 and 768.
33. A.H. Steiner, 'The Government of Italian East Africa', *American Political Science Review* (APSR), vol. 30, 1936, pp. 886 and 900.
34. See Henderson (1962) p. xii.
35. Putnam Weale (1910) pp. 98 and 112.
36. Vincent 'Racial Equality', in Ball and Watson (1984) p. 240.
37. Pfaff (1993) p. 144.
38. Fryer (1984) pp. 319–20.
39. Money (1925) pp. 88–9.
40. See Wm. Roger Louis, 'The Era of the Mandates System', in Ball and Watson (1984) p. 211.
41. See Ruger, 'The Colonial Aims', in Stoecker (1986).
42. See J.H. Franklin, 'The Two Worlds of Race: A Historical View', in Parsons and Clark (1966) p. 61.
43. PRO: PREM11/3665, 'H. Macmillan to R. Menzies', 3 February 1962.
44. Ibid.
45. R.J. Vincent, 'Racial Equality', in Bull and Watson (1984) p. 241.
46. Cited in Lauren (1988) p. 83.
47. Griswold (1966) pp. 251–2.
48. Nicolson (1933) p. 145.
49. Griswold (1966) p. 247.
50. B. Aston, 'Annual Report, 1919', in Bourne and Cameron Watt (1991) p. 4.
51. See H. Kohn, 'Race Conflict' (1934) pp. 36 and 41.
52. See S. Naoko 'The Japanese Attempt to Secure Racial Equality in 1919', *Japan Forum*, April 1989, pp. 94–5.
53. Cited in Füredi (1994) p. 27.
54. Cited in Lauren (1988) p. 141.
55. See PRO: FO 371/35949, 'Japan and the Issue of Racial Equality at Paris, 1919', 3 February 1942.

Chapter 2

1. Cited in Füredi (1992) p. 164.
2. Orwell (1950) p. 6.
3. P.A. Means, 'Race Appreciation and Democracy', *Journal of Race Development*, vol. 9, no. 2, October 1918, p. 180.
4. M. Ellis, 'Federal Surveillance of Black Americans', *Immigrants and Minorities*, vol. 12, no. 1, March 1993, p. 8.
5. PSF: Box 27, Folder 4, 'A Sane Approach to the Race Problem', by

The Stabilization Fund of the Commission on Interracial Co-operation, 1930, p. 5.

6. 'Notes', *Journal of Applied Sociology*, vol. 7, no. 6, 1923, p. 291.
7. Institute of Pacific Relations (1925) p. 13.
8. Snyder (1939) p. 5.
9. See Snyder (1939) pp. 281 and 298.
10. Snyder (1939) p. 302.
11. Kohn, 'Race Conflict' (1934) p. 38.
12. Coupland (1935) p. 21.
13. Institute of Pacific Relations (1925) p. 13.
14. Stanley (1990) pp. 135 and 168.
15. T.Z. Koo, 'A Chinese View of Pacific Relations', in Institute of Pacific Relations (1925) p. 70.
16. A.L. Dean, 'The Approach to Pacific Problems', Institute of Pacific Relations; *Honolulu Session, 30 June–14 July 1925. History Organisation, Proceedings, Discussion and Addresses*, Honolulu, 1925. Mathews (1924) pp. 28 and 30. See also J.L. Barton 'The Effect of the War on Protestant Missions', *Harvard Theological Review*, vol. 22, January 1919.
17. W. Paton, 'The Jerusalem Meeting and After', *The International Review of Missions*, vol. 17, no. 67, July 1928, p. 437.
18. A.L.P. Dennis, 'Exploitation of Underdeveloped Areas', in Turner (1923) pp. 29–30.
19. Dower (1986) p. 163.
20. See E.M. Manasse, 'Max Weber on Race', *Social Research*, no. 2, vol. 14, 1947, p. 191.
21. Cited in Lauren (1988) p. 68.
22. Cited in Tinker (1977) p. 39.
23. Lord Weardale, 'Introduction' to Spiller (1911) p. viii.
24. G.B. Johnson, 'A Sociological Interpretation of the New Ku Klux Movement', *The Journal of Social Forces*, vol. 5, no. 4, May 1923, p. 442.
25. For a discussion of this post-war malaise, see Füredi (1992) pp. 162–7.
26. Myrdal (1962) p. 91.
27. See Stoddard (1920).
28. See 'Communication' by Professor Caldecott in *Sociological Review*, vol. 3, no. 3, July 1910, p. 241.
29. Iriye (1981) p. 81.
30. Matthews (1926) p. 31.
31. Coupland (1935) p. 22.
32. CCA; Box 281, Oldham J.H., 'Memorandum of Conversation with Colonel Arthur Woods, Dr. Ruml of the Laura Spelman Foundation, 26 and 28 October and 5 November 1925'; and Malinowski, 'Introduction' to Kenyatta (1938) pp. x–xi.
33. PSF: Box 31:2, 'Racial Conditions in America and Africa', by T. Jones, 27 April 1927.
34. A.K. Holt, 'Is Race Friction Between Blacks and Whites in the United States Growing and Inevitable?', reprinted in Pettigrew (1986) p. 26.

35. Park and Burgess (1926) p. 578.
36. J. Dowd, 'Race Segregation in a World of Democracy', Papers and Proceedings: Fourteenth Annual Meeting, 29–31 December 1919, *American Sociological Society*, vol. 14, 1919, p. 179.
37. PSF: Box 31:2, Laura Spelman Rockefeller Memorial, 1927, 'A. Phelps Stokes to T. Jones', 5 May 1927.
38. Crocker (1931) p. 13.
39. Coupland (1935) p. 16.
40. H. Kohn, 'Race Conflict', in *Encyclopaedia of the Social Sciences* (1934) p. 41.
41. F.G. Detweiler, 'The Rise of Modern Race Antagonism', *The American Journal of Sociology*, vol. 37, no. 5, March 1932, p. 746.
42. Snyder (1939) p. 313.
43. Gong (1984) p. 87.
44. See Freeden (1986) p. 87.
45. For a discussion of this point, see L. Wirth, 'Problems and Orientation of Research in Race Relations in the United States', *The British Journal of Sociology*, vol. 1, no. 2, 1958, p. 117.
46. See the discussion in Gossett (1971).
47. Himmelfarb (1985) p. 327.
48. Jones (1980) pp. 144–5.
49. Cited in Jones (1980) p. 145.
50. Malik (1996) p. 111.
51. For a discussion of this point, see Nye (1975).
52. Masterman (1960) p. 79.
53. See the discussion in R. A. Nye, 'The Bio-Medical Origins of Urban Sociology', *Journal of Contemporary History*, vol. 20, 1985.
54. Webb (1907) pp. 17–18.
55. Bagehot (1872) p. 117.
56. See Nye (1975) p. 51.
57. CCA: Miscellany – Volume 12 – Africa, 'Report of Dr. Kenyon I. Butterfield on Rural and Sociological Problems in South Africa (1929)'; and 'Report to the President and Secretary as to an Educational Program in Africa', 20 October 1927.
58. Carnegie Commission (1932) , vol. 1, pp. xix, vol. 5, pp. 38, 39, 40, 106.
59. Spengler (1938) pp. 36–7.
60. Park and Burgess (1926) p. 636.
61. Buell (1965) p. 376.
62. *Rand Daily Mail*, 25 June 1918.
63. L.F. Neame, 'The Real South Africa Problem', *The Quarterly Review*, no. 483, January 1925; and *The Times*; 29 September 1924.
64. IMC/CBMS: Africa general. Box no. 206, 'J.H. Oldham: Memorandum: The Population Question in Africa', undated, circa February 1925.
65. *Cape Argus*, 13 August 1946.
66. Dr Chandrasekhar, 'Population Problems and International Tensions', *International Social Science Journal*, vol. 1, 1949, p. 55.

67. See Himmelfarb and Baras (1978).
68. See for example G.D. Foster et al., 'Global Demographic Trends to the Year 2010: Implications for U.S. Security', *The Washington Quarterly*, Spring 1989.
69. Teitelbaum and Winter (1985) p. 17. Teitelbaum and Winter's work on strategic demography provides many useful insights into how relations of power are experienced through the prism of population in the Western imagination.
70. See Carr-Saunders (1936); and Thompson (1929).
71. Carr-Saunders (1936) p. 45.
72. D. Kirk, 'Population Changes and the Postwar World', *American Sociological Review*, vol. 9, 1944, p. 32.
73. See Donaldson (1990) p. 18; and Symonds and Carder (1973) p. 96.
74. Chandrasekhar, 'Population Problems', p. 61.
75. See E.A. Ross, 'The Menace of Migrating Peoples', in Turner (1923).
76. See, for example, G.F. McClearey, 'Australia's Population Problem', *The Milbank Memorial Fund Quarterly*, vol. 20, 1942, p. 32.
77. Carr-Saunders (1936) p. 219.
78. See, for example, J. Donaldson, *International Economic Relations: A Treatise on World Economy and World Politics*. Published in 1928 ostensibly about international economic relations it, contains a chapter entitled 'International Economic Aspects of the Problems of Race and Population'. Similarly books with titles such as *Danger Spots in World Population* (Thompson, 1929) are about the problem of racial competition for land and resources.
79. E.A. Ross, 'The Menace of Migrating Peoples', in Turner (1923) pp. 102–5.
80. C. Gini, 'The Future of Human Populations', *American Journal of Sociology* (AJS) , vol. 36.
81. Myrdal (1962) p. 69.
82. Kirk (1942) pp. 60–1.
83. Kirk (1942) p. 1.
84. S.J. Holmes 'The Increasing Growth-Rate of the Negro Population', *The American Journal of Sociology*, vol. 42, no. 2, 1936, p. 203.
85. Carnegie Corporation Archives (CCA): Box 295 Population Investigation Committee, 'Frederick Osborn to Keppel', 21 May 1937.
86. Cited in Lagemann (1992) p. 127.
87. Myrdal (1962) pp. 167 and 169.
88. Myrdal (1962). See footnote, p. 179.
89. Rockefeller Archive Center (RAC): JDR 3, Box 44, Folder 1, 'Dr. Thomas at Academy of Science: Conference on Population Policies, Evening Session, 21 June 1952'.
90. See for example Crocker (1931); and Thompson (1929).
91. Myrdal (1962) p. 1019.
92. D. Kirk, 'Population Changes and the Post-war World', *American Sociological Review*, vol. 9, 1949, p. 35.

Chapter 3

1. Johnston (1920) p. 61.
2. Chirol (1924) pp. viiiix, 207, 210–13.
3. The term Orientalism is used here in Said's sense of the term. See Said (1985).
4. Cited in Gossett (1971) p. 334.
5. American racist writers such as Lothorp Stoddard, Clinton Stoddard Burr and Dr Charles Conant Josey are often cited as examples of the interwar contributions. These writers were part of the post-war outburst of literature. However, their social influence was relatively marginal. Our concern is with the assumptions of race contained in the more mainstream literature.
6. G. Young, 'Europeanization', *Encyclopedia of the Social Sciences*, vol. 5, 1931, p. 630.
7. PRO: FO371/6684, 'Racial Discrimination and Immigration. Memo. by F. Ashton-Gwatkin', 10 October 1921.
8. See Matthews (1964).
9. Oldham (1924) p. 12.
10. Coupland (1935) pp. 16–17.
11. 'The Year 1920', *International Review of Missions*, vol. x, no. 37, January 1920, p. 59.
12. W. Paton, 'The Jerusalem Meeting and After', *The International Review of Missions*, vol. 17, no. 67, July 1928, p. 437.
13. H.T. Hodgkin 'Memorandum on Missions', in Preliminary Paper Prepared for Second General Session 15–29 July 1927, Institute of Pacific Relations, 1927, pp. 9–10.
14. See Institute of Pacific Affairs (1925) pp. 7–14.
15. C. Kendall, 'Peace in the Pacific', *Current History*, November 1936, p. 77.
16. G.M. Fisher, 'Relations between the Occidental and Oriental peoples on the Pacific Coast of North America' in *IMC* (1928) vol. 4, p. 201.
17. Cited in Kohn, 'Race Conflict', p. 40.
18. PSF: Box 31:2, 'Racial Conditions in America and Africa', 27 April 1927.
19. Ibid.
20. Robinson and Gallagher (1981) pp. 10–11.
21. Cited in Nye (1975) p. 59.
22. See Füredi (1997) p. 11.
23. RHL: J.H. Oldham Papers, Mss. Afr. S.1829, Box 2 File 2, 'Memorandum on Colonial Research', December 1927, B. Malinowski.
24. CCA: Box 196, 'Diary of Visit to South Africa', 22 August 1927.
25. See L.T. White, 'The Church in International Relations', *Journal of Applied Sociology*, vol. 10, July–August 1926, pp. 566–7.
26. Sir F. Lugard , 'The Problem of Colour in Relation to the Idea of Equality', *Journal of Philosophical Studies*, vol. 1, no. 2, April 1926, p. 213.

27. CCA: Miscellany – Volume 12: Africa, 'Report to the President and Secretary as to an Educational Program in Africa', 20 October 1927.
28. For a discussion on Hoernle, see Rich (1984) chapter 3.
29. Westermann (1939) pp. 336–7.
30. B. Malinowski, 'Race and Labour', the *Listener*, 16 July 1930, supplement, p. viii.
31. Ibid.
32. B. Malinowski 'A Plea for an Effective Colour Bar', the *Spectator*, 27 June 1931.
33. The *Spectator*, 12 September 1931.
34. PSF: Box 18:18, 'A. Phelps-Stokes to Ralph Bunche', 15 August 1939.
35. Cited in Hetherington (1978) p. 81.
36. Kuklick (1991) p. 265.
37. Barnes (1935) p. 97.
38. Yale University Library (YUL): Loram Collection, Box.1 folder 27, Memo: 'The Education of Backward Peoples: A suggested program', 1933.
39. Kuklick (1991) p. 265.
40. Persons (1987) p. 147.
41. IAI; Box 37, 'Notes by Dr. Margaret Read Regarding Possible Activities of the Institute During the War', undated, 1940.
42. The view that black American culture is in some sense responsible for the perpetuation of weak family ties, which is then responsible for economic and social failure, continues to surface in contemporary discussions of poverty.
43. Stocking (1963) p. 230.
44. See Thurlow (1987) p. 18.
45. R. Benedict, 'Book Review', *American Anthropologist*, vol. 27, 1933, p. 427.
46. W.O. Brown, 'White Dominance in South Africa: A Study in Social Control', *Social Forces*, vol. 18, no. 3, March 1940, p. 409.
47. L. Hogben 'Preface of Prejudices', to Dover (1937) p. 9.
48. Dubow (1989) p. 35.
49. See Locke and Stern (1942).
50. Elliot (1932) p. 176.
51. T.G. Standing, 'The Possibility of a Distinctive Culture Contribution from the American Negro', *Social Forces*, vol. 17, no. 3, October 1938, p. 106.
52. Mathews (1930) pp. 121 and 71.
53. B. Mathews, 'The Colour Bar', in the *Spectator*, 25 July 1931.
54. IMC/CBMS: Box 1230, Central and Southern Africa, D.H. Houghton, 'Some Economic Problems of the Bantu in South Africa', November 1938.
55. Jackson (1990) p. 6.
56. Kellogg (1971) pp. 3, 9, 68.
57. Kellogg (1971) p. 1.
58. Kneebone (1985) p. 95.

59. See M. Cowley, 'Long Black Song', *New Republic*, 6 April 1938, cited in Kellogg (1971) pp. 68–9.
60. Cited in Kneebone (1985) p. 91.
61. R.F.A. Hoernle, 'Race-Mixture and Native Policy in South Africa', in Schapera (1934) pp. 265–6.
62. PSF: Box 27:4, 'A. Phelps-Stokes to G.B. Johnson', 15 August 1944.
63. See Dubow (1989) p. 26. For a positive assessment of Evans' views, see A.S. Cripps, 'An Africa of the Africans', *International Review of Missions*, vol. 10, no. 37, January 1920, p. 99.
64. A.D. Roberts, 'The Imperial Mind', in Roberts (1986) p. 50.
65. *The Spectator*, 12 September 1931.
66. Cited in Jackson (1990) p. 126.

Chapter 4

1. J. Huxley, 'Colonies and Freedom', *The New Republic*, 24 January 1944.
2. IIOR: M/3/476, 'Prof. W.E. Le Gros Clark, "RACE", in *Oxford University Summer School on Colonial Administration, Second Session – 1938*'.
3. Barkan (1992) p. 289.
4. See Rich (1986) p. 114; Stepan (1982) pp. 140–1; and Barkan (1992) pp. xii and 289.
5. Dover (1939) p. 16.
6. Gossett (1971) p. 423.
7. Stanfield (1985) p. 6.
8. Williams (1989) p. 146.
9. T.F. Pettigrew, 'How Events Shape Theoretical Frames', in Stanfield (1993) pp. 172–3.
10. Rich (1993) p. 8.
11. The result of this research was published as Füredi (1994).
12. Much later, in the post-war period, this term would be used by some as the consciousness which when heightened gave rise to racism. Leo Kuper wrote, 'in heightening racial tension, the technique is to heighten race *consciousness*, by so weaving racial classification into the perception of the individual, that the basic definition of the widest possible range of situations is in racial terms'. See L. Kuper, 'The Heightening of Racial Tension', *Race*, vol. 2, no. 1, November 1960, pp. 24–5.
13. Park and Burgess (1926) p. 578.
14. Huntington (1924) p. 3.
15. Matthews (1924) p. 121.
16. See R.E. Park, 'Racial Assimilation in Secondary Groups', in R.H. Turner (1967) p. 130 (originally published in 1914).
17. W.O. Brown, 'Race Consciousness Among South African Natives', *AJS*, vol. 40, no. 5, March 1935, p. 571.
18. Ibid., pp. 569 and 572.

19. IMC/CBMS: Box 205 Africa General 'Minutes of the Sixth Meeting of the Executive Council of the IIALC', 19–20 December 1928.
20. PSF: Box 34:20, African Tour of Anson Phelps-Stokes 1932, 'A. Phelps-Stokes to T.J. Jones', 10 October 1932.
21. CCA: Box 298 Education of Primitive Peoples, Resolution B97J, 19 April 1932 of Carnegie Executive Committee.
22. PSF: Box 298 Primitive Peoples. Ed. of, 'Memorandum on Research and Training in the Introduction of Western Civilization to Non-Western People', May 1932 by C.T. Loram.
23. Snyder (1939) pp. 280–6.
24. See the *Spectator*, 14 February 1931.
25. Miller (1924) pp. 35 and 32.
26. Ibid., p. 155.
27. Wacker (1983) p. 51.
28. See, for example, 'Coloured Families in English Ports', in *The Nation and Athenaeum*, 9 August 1930.
29. Sir J. Simon, 'Frontiers', *International Affairs*, vol. 12, no. 6, November 1933, p. 712.
30. Cited in Williams (1989) p. 110.
31. See, for example, Hitchens (1990).
32. Locke and Stern (1942) p. 529.
33. The *Spectator*, 1 August 1931.
34. For example, see 'The Year 1920', *International Review of Missions*, vol. X, no. 37, January 1920, p. 59.
35. Baker (1922) p. 234.
36. Constantinople and India', *Fortnightly Review*, March 1920.
37. W.O. Brown, 'The Nature of Race Consciousness', *Social Forces*, vol. 10, no. 1, 1931, p. 96.
38. See Malinowski's 'Introduction' to Jomo Kenyatta's *Facing Mount Kenya*, in Kenyatta (1938) pp. x xi.
39. Brown, 'The Nature of Race Consciousness', p. 97.
40. Barnes (1935) pp. 301 and 302.
41. See Rich (1993) p. 25.
42. Guy B. Johnson, 'A Sociological Interpretation of the New Ku Klux Movement', *The Journal of Social Forces*, vol. 1, no. 4, May 1923, p. 444.
43. See the interesting discussion on the nature of prejudice in the British periodical *Notes and Queries*, throughout the year 1934.
44. Reuter (1927) p. 420.
45. Dollard (1957) p. 288 (originally published in 1937).
46. Ibid., p. 288.
47. Ibid., p. 317.
48. Ibid., p. 319.
49. Ibid., p. 288.
50. Ibid., p. 319.
51. Cited in O'Reilly (1989) p. 14.
52. F.G. Detweiler, 'The Negro Press Today', *AJS*, vol. 44, no. 3, 1938, p. 398. See also the discussion of the Negro press in *Social and Political*

Forces in the Dependant Areas of the Caribbean – Papers 229–276, NARA:RG.59.

53. Schrieke (1936) p. 150.
54. Cited in Burns (1948) p. 142.
55. For example, the Nigerian press was denounced for 'appealing to anti-European prejudice' and one official commented on a publisher: 'I am afraid he has ample opportunity to stir up and inflame racial bitterness without running any risk of conviction.' See PRO: CO 537/4631, 'Governor of Nigeria to Secretary of State', 28 February 1949 and CO 583/277/30658/46, 'Creasey to Gater', 11 July 1946.
56. PRO: CO 323/1522/21, 'Minute by Sir. J. Shuckburgh to C. Parkinson', 2 November 1937.
57. See PRO: CO 323/1522/21, 'Sir C. Parkinson to Sir D. Cameron', undated, July 1937; and 'Sir D. Cameron to Sir C. Parkinson', 31 July 1937.
58. A. Spackman, 'Official Attitudes and Official Violence: The Ruimveldt Massacre, Guyana, 1924', *Social and Economic Studies*, vol. 22, no. 3, p. 318.
59. PRO: CO 111/726/60036/35, 'Governor British Guiana to Secretary of State for the Colonies', 17 October 1935; and 'Governor Northcote to Rt. Hon. J.H. Thomas', 7 December 1935.
60. PRO: CO 111/752/60270/38, Part 1, 'Jackson to Beckett', 3 November 1938; and CO 111/770/60270/1940, 'Governor of British Guiana to Secretary of State for the Colonies', 5 February 1940.
61. Cited in Kilkenny (1986) p. 18.
62. IOR: M-5-47, 'E.O. Hubbard, Foreign Office to D.J. Monteith', Burma Office', 9 January 1941.
63. NARA: RG 59 848N.00/11-448, 'E. Talbot Smith, American Consul, Accra to Secretary of State', 4 November 1948.

Chapter 5

1. B. Berry, 'The Concept of Race in Sociology Textbooks', *Social Forces*, vol. 18, no. 3, 1940, p. 412.
2. T.G. Standing, 'The Possibility of a Distinctive Culture Contribution from the American Negro', *Social Forces*, vol. 17, no. 1, 1938, pp. 105 and 106.
3. Jackson (1990) p. 99.
4. Bogardus (1928) pp. 41, 48 and 49. There were important exceptions to this naturalistic representation of prejudice. See, for example, one of the early attempts at sociologically situating racism in G. Spiller, 'Science and Race Prejudice', *Sociological Review*, vol. 5, no. 4, October 1922.
5. H. Wyndham, 'The Colour Bar in South Africa', in the *Spectator*, 29 August 1931, p. 263.
6. Lord Lugard (1965) pp. 81–2.

7. Lord Lugard (1965), pp. 80–2 and 429.

8. Buell (1965) vol. 2, p. 80.

9. See 'Introduction' by Sir A.C. Lyall in Chirol (1910) pp. xiii and xv.

10. Everett Stonequist's discussion of the Marginal Man explicitly refers to Maurice Barres' *Les Deracines.* See Stonequist (1961; originally published 1937).

11. Hetherington (1978) pp. 117 and 84.

12. W.O. Brown, 'Race Consciousness', p. 574.

13. G.B. Johnson, 'A Sociological Interpretation', p. 444.

14. See H.A. Miller 'Discussion' on J. Dowd 'Race Segregation in a World of Democracy', *American Sociological Society,* vol. 14, 1919, p. 204.

15. See, for example, the interwar correspondence deposited in the *Archives of the International Africa Institute,* London School of Economics.

16. These comments are based on an inspection of social science reading lists of Cambridge University and the London School of Economics.

17. See Donald Levine, 'Introduction' to Simmel (1971).

18. Stonequist (1961) p. vii.

19. See M. Ginsberg, 'The Problem of Colour in Relation to the Idea of Equality', *Journal of Philosophical Studies,* vol. 1, no. 2, April 1926, p. 222; and Ginsberg (1964) p. 139.

20. Crocker (1949) p. 91.

21. Locke and Stern (1942).

22. B. Malinowski, 'The Pan-African Problem of Culture Contact', *American Journal of Sociology,* vol. 48, 1942–43, p. 651; and Malinowski (1938) p. 60. Articles were originally written in the late 1930s.

23. Malinowski (1938), p. 68.

24. For a representation of Kenyatta as the 'individual who becomes the victim of aspirations he cannot achieve and hopes he cannot satisfy', see J.E. Goldthorpe, 'Educated Africans: Some Conceptual and Terminological Problems', in Southall (1961).

25. See Mair (1936) p. 284; and M. Fortes, 'An Anthropologist's Point of View', in Hinden (1944) p. 225.

26. Wilson (1968) p. 14 (originally published in 1941).

27. See ibid., p. 12; and Monica Hunter, 'Contact Between European and Native in South Africa', in Malinowski (1938), p. 24.

28. Westermann (1939) p. 333.

29. See correspondence in IMC/CBMS Archives, *Africa: Northern Rhodesia,* Box 1212.

30. Ibid.

31. YDA: The Joint IMC/Conference of British Missionary Societiy – Africa and India, 'Notes on a Conference of Secretaries of the British Mission Boards Conducting Work in Northern Rhodesia and Adjacent Territory', Edinburgh House, London, 7 November 1930.

32. SARI: B 93.1.3 'Report on Africa Tour'. Merle Davis and T.J. Jones, 13 January 1931.

33. Merle Davis (1931) p. 359.

34. IMC/CBMS Archives, Central Africa, Box 1211 'Report of the General Missionary Conference of Northern Rhodesia. Held in Broken Hill, July 18th–21st, 1931'.
35. Reuter (1918) p. 364.
36. An interesting account of Park's ambivalence toward the marginal man is well explored in Wacker (1983).
37. R.E. Park, 'Human Migration and the Marginal Man', *American Journal of Sociology*, vol. 33, 1928, p. 881.
38. Ibid., p. 893.
39. H.D. Lamson, 'The Eurasian in Shanghai', *American Journal of Sociology*, vol. 41, 1935–36, p. 647; and N.J. Spykman, 'The Social Background of Asiatic Nationalism', *American Journal of Sociology*, vol. 32, 1926–27, p. 406.
40. L. Hedin, 'The Anglo-Indian Community', *AJS*, vol. 40, no. 2, September 1934.
41. P.F. Cressey, 'The Anglo-Indians: A Disorganized Marginal Group', *Social Forces*, vol. 14, no. 2, December 1935, p. 266.
42. See K.L. Little, 'The Psychological Background of White–Coloured Contacts in Britain', *Sociological Review*, vol. 35, no. 1, 1943, pp. 21–2.
43. Stonequist (1961) p. 50.
44. Ibid., p. 59.
45. Ibid., pp. 148, 150 and 151.
46. Said (1985) p. 249.
47. See Füredi (1994a) for an elaboration of the argument.
48. Mencke (1976) p. ix.
49. L. Wirth and H. Goldhamer, 'The Hybrid and the Problem of Miscegenation', in Klineberg (1944) p. 336.
50. B. Malinowski, 'Race and Labour', the *Listener*, 16 July 1930, p. vii.
51. CCA: Box 136. J. Merle Davis, 'J. Merle Davis to Dr. F.P. Keppel', 9 October 1941.
52. Cited in Wirth and Goldhamer, in Klineberg (1944) p. 337.
53. PSF: Box 27, folder 2, 'A. Phelps Stokes to Professor Liston Pope', 10 January 1946.
54. L.C. Copeland, 'The Negro as a Contrast Conception', in Thompson (1939) pp. 158, 160, 169, and 172.
55. Lugard (1965) p. 589.
56. Zambia National Archives (ZNA): SEC 2/11/2/1135, 'Report on Madagscar Tour. 4th January to 4th February, 1943 by H. Franklin'.
57. NARA: RG226, Entry 108, Box 107, 'Subject: Return of Native Soldiers – Source: Z, 12 December 1943'.
58. See Capt. A.G. Dickson, 'An Experiment in Mass Education, Report on the Nyasaland and Northern Rhodesia tour of the Mobile Propaganda Unit', enclosed in 'Dickson to Lord Lugard'. 8 March 1943 in Box 36, Papers of the IAI.
59. See PRO: CO 875/8/8, 'Mobile Propaganda Safari in Uganda', Enclosure to 'H.C.G. Gurney to G.F. Seal', 17 May 1943.
60. NARA: RG 59 848N.401/10-1945, 'T.A. Hickok, American Consul,

Accara to Secretary of State', 18 October 1945 and PRO: WO 269/1, 'HQ, E. Af. Command, Nairobi circular to officers', 11 July 1946'.
61. *The Times,* 21 August 1947.
62. PRO: WO 269/2, 'Appendix A "Notes of Possible Causes and Types of Unrest"', by HQ E. Af CMND, 9 November 1946.
63. Grundlingh (1987) p. 541.
64. Military Information Bureau, Pretoria (MIB), NMC: NAS 3/36/4, BOX 28. 'Colonel E.T. Stubbs to General Len Beyers', 15 March 1943.
65. MIB: DNEAS Group 2 vol. 20, NEAS General, 'Stubbs to Beyers', 11 May 1943.
66. See NARA: RG 59 848T. OO/8-B4G, 'J.L. Touchette to Department of State', 8 August 1946 and PRO: CO 847/35/6 no. 2, 'Native administration policy: notes for further discussion' by A.B. Cohen, 3 April 1946.
67. ZNA: SEC 1/1766, vol. 3, 'Notes on Nothern Rhodesian Askari' by Major N.O. Earl-Span, November 1944.
68. ZNA: SEC 1/1766, vol. 3, 'H. McDowell, 'Some Psychological Aspects of Resettlement', 11 November 1942.
69. See Füredi (1994) chapter 2 for a discussion of these developments.
70. CBMS, Africa Committee, Race Relations, Box 261, 'Report on Investigation into Condition of the Coloured Population in a Stepney Area by Phyllis Young, March 1944'.
71. CBMS: Africa Committee, Box 260, 'Rev. H.M. Grace to CMS, Hull', 12 August 1944.

Chapter 6

1. Williams (1989) p. 178; Barkan (1992).
2. PRO: CO 875/5/21, 'Report on the State of Public Opinion in Bermuda made by the Terminal Censorship', enclosure to 'Governor, Bermuda to Secretary of State for the Colonies', 8 September 1942.
3. PRO: INF 1/560, 'Information Officer, Jamaica to H.V. Usill, MOI', 12 January 1941; and H. Johnson, 'The Anglo-American Caribbean Commission and the Extension of American Influence in the British Caribbean, 1942–1945', *Journal of Commonwealth and Comparative Politics,* 1985, 184.
4. IOR: LM/WS/1/567, 'Cipher Telegram: War Office to Commander in Chief, India', 13 March 1944 and NARA: RG 59 844.00/3-945, 'Social and Political Forces in Dependent Areas of the Caribbean', p. 247.
5. CBMS: Box 260 Africa Committee. Race Relations, 'Canon H.M. Grace to secretaries of Missionary Societies', 9 December 1942; and 'A. Cross, Mindolo to Miss B.D. Gibson', 9 April 1940.
6. CBMS, Africa Committee, Race Relations, Box 260, 'Miss Kathleen Stephenson to Home Education Secretary, CMS, Hull', 1 June 1944.
7. Myrdal (1962) p. 1004.
8. See *Survey Graphic Magazine,* March 1936.

9. CBMS: Africa Committee Race Relations, Box 261, 'U.S. Negro Troops'.
10. PRO: CO 968/78/13, 'Minute by Mr. Bigg', 24 August 1942.
11. Cited in C. Thorne, 'Racial Aspects of the Far Eastern War of 1941–1945', *Proceedings of the British Council*, vol. 80, 1980, p. 330.
12. Thorne (1978) p. 7; Lauren (1988) p. 136; and Iriye (1981) p. 50.
13. MIB: Chief of the General Staff, Group 2, Box. no. 1 G2/1/9/1 vol. 1, 'Col. E. Stubbs to Adjutant General', 26 June 1941.
14. Dalfiume (1969) p. 58.
15. See 'Something's Happened to the Negro', *New Republic*, 8 February 1943, p. 175; 'Jim Crow in the Army', *New Republic*, 13 May 1944, p. 339; and 'Black and White', *New Statesman*, 4 August 1944, p. 74.
16. John Butler Library, IPR Collection, Box 468, 'Security in the Pacific and the Far East: A Memorandum on Certain American Immediate Post War Responsibilities', Papers of D. Tyler, 1942 Conference at Mont Tremblant.
17. Johnson (1943) p. 142.
18. NARA: RG 226, Entry 108, Box 193, Folder N212, 'From G. Stone to OSS', 10 943. Enclosure 'Conversation with Dr. George Sacks and Mrs Sacks, members of the SACP'.
19. Eden and Maze are cited in Thorne (1985) pp. 30 and 27.
20. Cited in Thorne (1978) p. 8.
21. Tugwell, cited in H. Johnson 'The Anglo-American Caribbean Commission and the Extension of American Influence in the British Caribbean 1942–43', *Journal of Commonwealth and Comparative Politics*, 1985, p. 188; and NARA: RG208, Entry E-76, Box 239, 'Capt. F. Auberjonois, to J. Allen, Chief PWS, Morocco', 25 January 1943.
22. See Thorne (1985) p. 18 and PRO: CO 968/5/9 'Minute by T.K. Lloyd', 12 March 1942.
23. CA: SwinII, No. 515 'Swinton to Cranborne', 17 July 1942.
24. IOR: M/3/955, 'Copy of letter from Frank A.A. Reynolds, DSP, Lashio, Burma, attached to Police Force in the Northern Shan States-Burma', 29 May 1942.
25. See Dilks (1971) p. 433.
26. PRO: CO 968/92/2, 'Telegram. Secretary of State for the Colonies to Resident Minister, Accra', 29 September 1943.
27. See Palmer (1986).
28. NARA: RG 226, Entry 106, Box 4, 'OSS Rand A Branch, Africa Section, Psychological Warfare Weekly Roundup, no. 23, August 23–30, 1943'.
29. See PRO: CO 968/92/2 , 'Minute by A.H. Poynton', 20 December 1943; and Palmer (1986) p. 5.
30. PSF: Box 37, Folder 5, 'Draft, The Atlantic Charter and Africa From an American Standpoint', Study by the 'Committee on Africa and Peace Aims' Chairman A. Phelps Stokes, May 1942, Box 37, Folder 2, 'Remarks on the Memorandum by the Committee on African Peace Aims by B. Malinowski', undated , circa April 1942; and 'Criticism of

the Proposed report by the Committee on Africa and Peace Aims', W.E.B. Du Bois, 28 April 1942.
31. Cited in Grundy (1983) p. 70.
32. Cited in Crozier (1985) p. 104.
33. S.C. Menefee, 'Japan's Psychological War', *Social Forces*, vol. 21, no. 4, 1943, p. 428.
34. H.C. Brearley, 'The Negro's New Belligerency', *Phyloni*, vol. 5, no. 4, 1944, pp. 339–41.
35. NARA: RG 208 Entry 374, Box 430, 'Psychiatry Amongst African Troops, by Capt. W. Bembovitz', undated, circa February 1943.
36. PRO: INF1/560, 'F.A. Stockdale, Office of the Comptroller, Barbados to H. Beckett, Colonial Office', 15 July 1943.
37. Myrdal (1962) p. 1018.
38. PRO: CO 875/7/1/12, 'Public Opinion in Northern Rhodesia', enclosure to 'Governor, Lusaka to Secretary of State', 28 July 1942.
39. PRO: CO 323/1663, 'Minute by A. Dawe, 13 December 1939.
40. Cited in Füredi (1994a) p. 34.
41. R. Firth, 'Social Problems and Research in British West Africa', *Africa*, vol. 17, no. 2, 1947, p. 82.
42. Cited in Plummer (1996) p. 86.
43. Cited in C.R. Koppes and G.D. Black, 'Blacks, Loyalty, and Motion-Picture Propaganda in World War II', *Journal of American History*, vol. 73, 1986, p. 385.
44. NARA: RG 208, Entry E-76, Box 234 'The Negroes' Role in the War: A Study of White and Coloured Opinion' by Survey Division of OWI, 3 July 1943.
45. Ibid., p. 386.
46. Kearney (1991) p. 180.
47. Ibid., p. 181.
48. K.B. Clark, 'Morale of the Negro on the Home Front: World Wars I and II', *The Journal of Negro Education*, vol. 12, Summer 1943, pp. 426, 427.
49. Plummer (1996) p. 87.
50. See Kellogg (1971) pp. 216–17.
51. Southern (1987) p. 81. Also see Goldfield (1990) p. 41.
52. Jackson (1990) p. 240.
53. Storry (1979) p. 13.
54. Kearney (1991) p. xvi.
55. Thorne (1980) p. 377.
56. See Lauren (1988); and Iriye (1981).
57. A copy of this document can be found in PRO: FO 371/35949, F5780. The discussion on whether or not a statement on race equality should be issued is located in PRO: FO 371/27889.
58. Cited in Lauren (1988) p. 141.
59. Southern (1987) p. 49.
60. Goldfield (1990) p. 37.
61. Buck (1942) p. 29.

62. For a discussion of this crisis, see Füredi (1994a) chapter 2.
63. IOR: M-4-2610, 'Despatch no. 11 from the Standing Committee on UK representation in India', 8 July 1947.
64. PRO: INF 1/560, 'Plan of Propaganda for Jamaica', 3 August 1942, paper no. 199.
65. PRO: CO 875/11/1, 'Note by Edmett', 30 December 1941; and FO 371/46324, 'Cecil Day to J.C. Sterndale Bennett', 17 February 1945.
66. See the discussion in PRO: CO 875/5/6.
67. PRO: CO 875/5/6, 'Memorandum circulated to all African colonies', 13 November 1941.
68. PRO: INF 1/559, 'OPC Plan of Propaganda to British West Africa', Paper No. 514, 1 July 1944.
69. IOR: M-4-2656, 'Long Term Publicity for Burma' by T.L. Hughes, 12 July 1944.
70. See IOR: M-5-47, 'Extract from the Defence Bureau Intelligence Summary', 31 December 1938, 'E.O. Hubbard, Foreign Office to D.J. Monteith, Burma Office', 9 January 1941; and M-4-2656, 'Long-term publicity for Burma by T.L. Highes', 12 July 1944.
71. IOR: M-3-861, 'L.H. Foulds, Foreign Office to W.T. Annan, Burma Office', 2 January 1944, enclosure, 'Psychological Warfare in Burma – Joint Intelligence Committee's weekly summary, no. 45, 17 November 1943'.
72. IOR: M-5-84, 'T. Hughes, Governor of Burma's Camp, Simli, to Sir J. Walton', 23 July 1943.
73. NARA: RG 208, Entry 370, Box 375, 'Background for the Basic Plan for Burma', OWI-Bureau of Overseas Intelligence, 13 September 1943.
74. NARA: RG 208, Entry 370, Box 31, 'Research Memorandum', from: Psychology Division to: John M. Potter, 6 April 1942.
75. Buck (1942) pp. 22, 29.
76. NARA: RG 208, Entry E-76, Box 239 'F. Auberjonois, PWS Rabat to J. Allen, Chief PWS, Morocco', 25 January 1943.
77. NARA: RG 208, Entry 370, Box 31 'Psychology Division to J.M. Potter', 6 April 1942.
78. S.C. Menefee,'Japan's Psychological War', *Social Forces*, vol. 21, no. 4, 1943, p. 428.
79. Koppes and Black, 'Black Loyalty', p. 390.
80. PRO: INF 1/560, 'F.A. Stockdale to H. Beckett', 15 July 1943; and OPC, 'Plan for Propaganda to the West Indies'; Paper No. 472, 18 January 1944.
81. PRO: INF 1/560, 'OPC. Plan for Propaganda Jamaica', 21 September 1942.
82. See PRO: INF 1/560, 'Governor Jardine to Oliver Stanley', 29 March 1943; 'OPC. Plan of Propaganda to the British West Indies. General Policy Plan. Paper 316', 12 January 1943; and 'A.R. Thomas, Colonial Office to H.V. Usill, MOI', 25 October 1943.
83. IOR: L/I/1/902, 'E.M. Jenkins, Dominion Office to C.E. Sayers, MOI', 19 March 1944.

84. Tinker (1974) p. 43.
85. NARA: RG 59, 846c.00/71, 'G.A. Armstrong to Secretary of State', 19 March 1942.
86. IOR: M-S-862, 'J.C. Walton (Burma Office) to A.H. Seymour, Burma Mission, Washington', 20 April 1942; and 'A.H. Seymour to E.O. Binns, Secretary to the Governor of Burma', 14 April 1942.
87. The British delegation to the 1945 San Francisco meeting of the United Nations reported that pragmatic considerations influenced its acceptance of the provision of racial equality. See PRO: FO 371/46324, 'World Organisation, Racial Equality and Domestic Jurisdiction', 8 June 1945.
88. PRO: FO 371/40716, 'Telegram from Sir A. Cadogan to the Foreign Office', 29 September 1944.
89. Ibid.
90. See the interesting discussion in Lauren (1988) pp. 142–59.
91. This point is clearly argued in C. Anderson, 'Afro-Americans, the United Nations, and the Struggle for Human Rights, 1944–47', *Diplomatic History*, vol. 20, no. 4, Fall 1996.

Chapter 7

1. See Laurens (1988) chapters 5 and 6.
2. Cited in *News Chronicle*; 7 May 1949.
3. See Myrdal (1962) p. 1018. Also see, John Lafarge 'How the Churches Suffer', in Maciver (1949) p. 81; and Robert K. Merton, 'Discrimination and the American Creed', in Maciver (1949) p. 114.
4. Dollard (1957) p. xii.
5. Little (1948) pxi.
6. Laurens (1988) p. 189.
7. Ibid., p. 190.
8. Heald and Kaplan (1977) p. 317.
9. Burk (1984) p. 24.
10. M. Dudziak, 'Desegregation as a Cold War Imperative', *Stanford Law Review*, vol. 41, 1988, pp. 63–5. Justice Department brief cited p. 65.
11. T. Parsons, 'Introduction: Why "Freedom Now", not Yesterday?', p. xx; and K.B. Clark, 'Introduction: The Dilemna of Power', in Parsons and Clark (1966) p. xiv.
12. M.L. Krenn, '"Unfinished Business": Segregation and U.S. Diplomacy at the 1958 World's Fair', *Diplomatic History*, vol. 20, no. 4, 1996, p. 591.
13. Dudziak, 'Desegregation as a Cold War Imperative', pp. 111–12.
14. Baldwin (1964) pp. 117–18.
15. Soward (1950) p. 21 and *The Times*; 24 June 1956.
16. PRO: INF 12/303, 'COI: Far East Publicity Committee – Minutes', 13 March 1950.
17. PRO: CO 859/129/1, 'Circular to Governors' by A. Creech Jones, 8 January 1947. See Governor Philip Mitchell's justification of discrimi-

natory practices in Kenya in PRO: CO 859/129/1, 'P. Mitchell to A. Creech Jones', 28 February 1949.

18. See PRO: FO 053/1860, 'P.H.G. Wright. Brief for the Minister of State, On Racial Disturbances', 5 September 1958.

19. See Noer (1985) pp. 34–5; and C. Anderson, 'African Americans, the United Nations and the Struggle for Human Rights, 1944–47', *Diplomatic History*, vol. 20, no. 4, Fall 1996.

20. PRO: PREM 11/3665, 'Bob Menzies to H. Macmillan', 15 January 1962.

21. See Noer (1985) p. 27.

22. NARA: RG59 841E.411, 'P.N. Jester to Department of State', 21 January 1954.

23. See NARA: RG59 844.00//1-1845, 'W.H. Christensen to Department of State', 18 January 1945; and RG59 848N.00/11-448, 'E. Talbot Smith to Secretary of State', 4 November 1948.

24. Burns (1959) p. 5.

25. PRO: PREM8/143, 'Sir H. Rance to Lord Pethick-Lawrence', 16 September 1946.

26. C. Belshaw, 'Native Politics in the Solomon Islands', *Pacific Affairs*, vol. 20, no. 3, 1947, p. 192.

27. See NARA: 844.00/ 6-2145, 'D.L. Gamon to Department of State', 21 June 1945. Rabia is cited in Kilkenny (1986) p. 18.

28. See the discussion in NARA: 844C.00/3-2848.

29. See Crocker (1949) p. 49. PRO: CO 583/277/30658/46, 'Creasey to Gater', 12 July 1946, CO875/7/9, 'Report on the Activities of the Information Office, Quarter Ending September 1949', D.C. Fletcher; and CO 537/5807, 'R.J. Viles to J.K. Thompson', 27 April 1950.

30. See PRO: CO 537/3816, 'Governor John Shaw to Arthur Creech Jones', 16 August 1948, CO 537/6412, 'Political Report for the Six-Month Period ending the 30th of June 1950' and 'Political Report for the Month of July, 1950' and RHL: MSS Brit. Emp. 428-431, Ingham Papers, Box 5, File 5, 'Communist organisational work and information activities in Jamaica and prospects for combating them' by W.H. Ingham, undated, circa September 1953. Ingham's comments on African nationalism can be found in the same file in an undated 1953 speech on the Mau Mau.

31. Payne (1984) p. 14.

32. See the discussion in PRO: FO 371/116975.

33. PRO: FO 371/116985, 'Impressions of the Bandung Conference by W.R. Crocker', 8 June 1955.

34. See *Christian Science Monitor*, 23 January 1955; and *Newsweek*, 1 January 1955.

35. Melady (1966) p. 52.

36. Lind (1955) 'Introduction', p. ix.

37. Sukarno and Senghor are cited in Lauren (1988) pp. 210 and 213.

38. Cited in Füredi (1994) p. 122.

39. S. Hertzberg 'Saving Asia for Democracy', in *Commentary*, April 1950, p. 331.

40. F.B. Sayre, 'The Question of Independence', *Foreign Affairs*, vol. 30, no. 4, July 1952, p. 564.
41. PRO: CO936/217/4/5, 'The Problem of Nationalism in the Colonies' by W.H. Ingrams, July 1952.
42. Crocker (1956) p. 13.
43. See 'Preface', *International Science Bulletin*, vol. 2, no. 4, 1956, p. 458.
44. See NARA: RG59 844C.00/3-2848, 'W.P. Hudson, American Consul, Antigua to Secretary of State', 28 March 1948; and RG59 511-45K5/4-251, 'H. Bloom, American Consul, Accra to Department of State', 2 April 1951.
45. V. Purcell, 'Race Relations', *International Affairs*, April 1950, p. 252.
46. M. Perham, 'The British Problem in Africa', *Foreign Affairs*, vol. 29, no. 4, July 1951, p. 637.
47. H.V. Hodson, 'Race Relations in the Commonwealth', *International Affairs*, vol. 26, April 1950, p. 305.
48. St Clair Drake (1954) p. 83.
49. See W.J. Kolarz, 'Race Relations in the Soviet Union', in Lind (1955).
50. Crocker (1956) p. 5.
51. See P. Meyer, 'Stalin Follows in Hitler's Footsteps', *Commentary*, vol. 15, January 1953, p. 18. See also H. Seton Watson, 'The Colonial System of the USSR – Soviet Communism and the Backward Peoples', *Commentary*, vol. 15, May 1953.
52. PRO: FO 371/6701, 'G.H. Bolsover, British Embassy to Heathcote-Smith', 31 March 1947.
53. C. Dreher, 'Racism and America's World Position', *Commentary*, 1947, p. 169.
54. E. Heimann, 'The West and the East', *Social Research* , vol. 16, no. 1, March 1949, p. 61. Also see M.F. Asley Montagu, 'The Nature of Race Relations', *Social Forces*, vol. 25, no. 3, March 1947, p. 388.
55. See V. Harlow, 'Our Challenge to Communism from the Political View', *Corona*, August 1951.
56. PRO: CO 537/5138, 'Confidential Report on the Findings and Recommendations of the Informal Group Investigating the Political Significance of Colonial Students in the UK under the Chairmanship of Sir C. Jeffries', 11 April 1948; and 'A.B. Cohen to C. Jeffries', 21 April 1948.
57. See the report by the Research Department of the FO, 'The Political Scene in Africa', November 1958 in PRO: CO 936/570.
58. See the discussion in Cummings (1990) pp. 690–7.
59. PRO: CAB 129/71, C. (54) 37, October 1954, 'Commonwealth Membership. Memorandum by Secretary of State for Commonwealth Relations (Lord Swinton)'.
60. PRO: CO 1027/23, 'Arden-Clarke to Lyttelton', 6 June 1953.
61. PRO: FO 953/320, 'Information Work in the Far East, by John Pilcher', 12 March 1948.
62. PRO: FO 953/1244, 'Guidance on Publicity Towards South East Asia', 17 March 1952. Minute by R.H. Marett, 8 July 1952.

63. See Füredi (1994a) pp. 73–5.
64. PRO: CCO 507/1/1, 'Memorandum to Sir David Maxwell Fyfe, Home Office', 20 April 1954.
65. PRO: CO 1027/23, 'Governor Arden Clark to Secretary of State for the Colonies', 16 June 1953.
66. See PRO:FO O953/1200, 'Minutes of the Sixth Meeting of United States and British Information in Malaya', 29 January 1951.
67. PRO: CO 859/165/1, 'Minute by G. Foggon', 9 May 1950, and 'Minute by A. Cohen', 25 August 1950.
68. PRO: CO 1027/31, 'H. Foot to P. Rogers', 27 August 1953; and 'L.J. Simpson, Information Services Department, FO to C Barnes, Overseas Press Office, COI', 4 November 1953.
69. NARA: RG 59 844C.00/3-2848, 'W.P. Hudson, American Consul, Antigua to Secretary of State', 28 March 1948.
70. NARA: RG 59 841E.411, P.N. Jester to Department of State', 2 January 1954.
71. PRO: FO 953/1200, 'Minutes of the Eighth Meeting of United States and British Information Officers in Malaya', 31 August 1951. For a discussion on the availability of a black labour attaché in West Africa, see NARA: RG50 870.062/4-2051, 'Office Memorandum Meeting with Harold D. Snell', 30 April 1951.
72. See Laurens (1988) p. 191; and PRO: FO 371/67600, 'British Embassy, Nanking to UN Department, FO', 18 March 1947.

Chapter 8

1. Krenn, 'Unfinished Business', p. 592.
2. See PRO: CO 859/2479, 'Note on Cases of Alleged Colour Discrimination', circa May 1953; and *Daily Herald*, 11 December 1953.
3. See PRO: FO 371/67601, 'Draft paper to be submitted to Sub-Commission on Protection of Discrimination and protection of Minorities' by Elizabeth Monroe, 25 March 1947. Minute by Mr Heathcote-Smith, 23 March 1947.
4. Burns (1948) p. 150.
5. H.V. Hodson, 'Race Relations in the Commonwealth', *International Affairs*, vol. 26, July 1950, p. 307.
6. NARA: RG226, Entry 103, Box 194, File N426-450, 'Report on Press', 20 October 1943. Hoernle (1945) provides an argument for the salience of cultural difference.
7. Malik (1996) p. 170.
8. One important exception was the French anthropologist Claude Lévi-Strauss. Malik has argued that Lévi-Strauss regarded the 'struggle against all forms of discrimination' as 'detrimental' to cultural diversity. See Malik (1996) p. 169.
9. Cited in Dudziak, 'Desegregation as a Cold War Imperative', p. 86.
10. Laurens (1988) p. 171.

11. Burns (1948) p. 33.
12. Crocker (1956) p. 13.
13. Royal Anthropological Institute of Great Britain (1936) p. 18.
14. See 'Correspondence', C.G. Spencer, in the *Spectator*, 28 February 1931.
15. Mason (1954) p. 34.
16. G. Berreman, 'Caste in India and the United States', *Sociological Review*, vol. 66, no. 2, p. 127.
17. Hugh Tinker, 'Race, Nationalism and Communalism in Asia', in Mason (1960) p. 133.
18. Cohn (1966) p. 140.
19. Bodleian Library (Oxford), Conservative Research Department (CRD), CRD 2/34/17, 'Memorandum from G.F. Sayers to Sir Michael Fraser', 1 January 1964.
20. A. Metraux, 'UNESCO and the Racial Problem', *International Social Science Bulletin*, vol. 2, no. 3, Autumn 1950, p. 386.
21. M. Beloff, 'Race Relations and the Colonial Question', *Confluence*, vol. 2, no. 2, 1953, p. 52.
22. Kohn (1966) p. 140.
23. Melady (1966) pp. 22–3.
24. See, for example, Little (1952).
25. See Daniel Bell's article 'Ethnicity and Social Change' (1975) in Bell (1980).
26. See Jackson (1990) p. 276.
27. See Pettigrew (1980) p. xxviii.
28. Stanfield (1993) p. xviii.
29. M. Banton, '1960: A Turning Point in the Study of Race Relations', *Daedalus*, vol. 13, 1974, p. 35.

Chapter 9

1. Copeland, in Thompson (1939) p. 152.
2. St. Clair Drake (1954) p. 3.
3. Crocker (1956) p. 8.
4. Le Melleand Shepherd, in Barclay, Kumar and Simms (1976) p. 381.
5. PRO: CO 859/165/1, 'Minute by Sir Charles Jeffries', 4 September 1950.
6. PRO: DO 35/2593, 'Sir P.A.P. Waterfield to Sir P. Liesching', 29 January 1951.
7. Snyder (1962) p. 105.
8. Plummer (1996) p. 313.
9. Fanon (1970) p. 46.
10. Ibid., p. 47.
11. Bell (1980) pp. 150 and 206.
12. See *Sunday Times*, 31 July 1994.

Bibliography

Archives and Private Papers

Britain

India Office Library (IOR) – Waterloo, London.
International Africa Institute (IAI) – London School of Economics, London.
International Missionary Council (IMC/CBMS) – School of Oriental and African Studies, London.
Public Record Office (PRO) – Kew Gardens, London.
Rhodes House Library (RHL) – Oxford.

South Africa

Military Information Bureau (MIB) – Pretoria.
South African Institute of Race Relations (SAIRR) – Johannesburg.

United States

Carnegie Corporation Archives (CCA) – Columbia University, New York.
Institute of Pacific Relations Archives (IPR) – Columbia University, New York.
Phelps–Stokes Fund (PSF) – Schomburg Center for Research in Black Culture, New York
National Archives (NARA), Washington DC.
Rockefeller Archive Center (RAC) – Pocantico Hills, NY.
Yale Divinity Archive (YDA) Yale University, New Haven.
Yale University Library (YUL) – Yale University, New Haven.

Unpublished Theses

Drake, St Clair. (1954) Value Systems, Social Structure and Race Relations in the British Isles (PhD Thesis: University of Chicago).
Kearney, R. (1991) Afro-Americans and Japanese 1905–1945 (PhD Thesis: Kent State University).
Kellog, P.J. (1971) Northern Liberals and Black America: A History of White Attitudes, 1936–1952 (PhD Thesis: Northwestern University).

Unpublished Papers and Reports

Kilkenny, R.W. (1986) 'And so they've captured Demerara'. A Preliminary Investigation of US–Guiana Relations During the Second World War, paper given for 18th Conference of Caribbean Historians, Nassau, Bahamas, April 1986.

Palmer, A. (1986) Black American Soldiers in Trinidad 1942–43, paper given for 18th Conference of Caribbean Historians, Nassau, Bahamas, April 1986.

Payne, H.W.L (1984) The Original PPP in Office – 133 Days to Freedom, paper given for the 16th Conference of Caribbean Historians, Cave Hill, Barbados.

Walton, S. (1997) Introduction to Lord Hailey of Pagnell and Shapur (Oxford).

Published Works

Adorno, T.W. (1969) *The Authoritarian Personality* (New York: Harper Brothers).

Bagehot, W. (1872) *Physics and Politics* (London: J. King and Co.).

Baker, R.S. (1922) *Woodrow Wilson and World Settlement, vol. 2* (New York: Doubleday, Page and Co.).

Baldwin, J. (1964) *The Fire Next Time* (New York: Doubleday).

Banton, M. (1987) *Racial Theories* (Cambridge: Cambridge University Press).

Barclay, W., Kumar, K. and Simms, R.P. (eds) (1976) *Racial Conflict, Discrimination and Power* (New York: AMS Press).

Barkan, E. (1992) *The Retreat of Scientific Racism. Changing concepts of race in Britain and the United States between the world wars* (Cambridge: Cambridge University Press).

Barnes, L. (1935) *The Duty of Empire* (London: Victor Gollanz.).

Bearce, D. (1961) *British Attitudes Towards India 1784–1858* (London: Oxford University Press).

Beer, G.L. (1923) *African Questions at the Paris Peace Conference* (New York: Macmillan Co.).

Bell, D. (1980) *Sociological Journeys: Essays 1960–1980* (London: Heinemann).

Blacker, C.P. (1952) *Eugenics: Galton and After* (London: Gerald Duckworth and Co.).

Bogardus, E. (1928) *Immigration and Race Attitudes* (Boston: D.C. Heath and Co.).

Bourne, K. and Cameron Watt, D. (eds) (1991) *British Documents on Foreign Affairs. Part 2, Series 1. The Paris Peace Conference of 1919. Vol. 12. The Far East* (London: University Publications of America).

Buck, P.S. (1942) *American Unity and Asia* (New York: John Day Company).

Buell, R.L. (1965) *The Native Problem in Africa, vols. 1 and 2* (London: Frank Cass).

Bull, H. and Watson, A. (eds) (1984) *The Expansion of International Society* (Oxford: Clarendon Press).

Burk, R.F. (1984) *The Eisenhower Administration and Black Civil Rights* (Knoxville: University of Tennesee Press).

Burns, Sir A. (1948) *Colour Prejudice: with particular reference to the relationship between Whites and Negroes* (London: Allen and Unwin).

Carnegie Commission (1932) *The Poor White Problem in South Africa. Report of the Carnegie Commission* (Pro Ecclesia – Drukkery: Stellenbosch).

Carr-Saunders, A.M. (1936) *World Population: Past Growth and Present Trends* (London: Oxford University Press).

Chirol, V. (1910) *Indian Unrest* (London: Macmillan).

Coupland, Sir R. (1935) *The Empire in These Days* (London: Macmillan).

Crocker, W.R. (1931) *The Japanese Population Problem. The Coming Crisis* (London: George Allen and Unwin).

—— (1949) *Self-Government for the Colonies* (London: Macmillan).

—— (1956) *The Racial Factor in International Relations* (Canberra: The Australian National University).

Crozier, A.J. (1988) *Appeasement and Germany's Last Bid for Colonies* (London: Macmillan).

Cumings, B. (1990) *The Origins of the Korean War*, vol. 2 (Princeton: Princeton University Press).

Dalfiume, R.M. (1969) *Desegregation of the US Armed Forces: Fighting on two Fronts, 1939–53* (Columbia, Missouri: University of Missouri Press).

De Conde, A. (1992) *Ethnicity, Race, and American Foreign Policy* (Boston: Northeastern University Press).

Dilks, D. (1971) *The Diaries of Sir Alexander Cadogan –1945* (London: Cassell).

Dollard, J. (1957) *Caste and Class in a Southern Town* (Garden City, NY: Doubleday).

Donaldson, J. (1928) *International Economic Relations* (New York: Longmans, Green and Co.).

Donaldson, P.J. (1990) *Nature Against US: The United States and the World Population Crisis 1965–1980* (Chapel Hill: University of North Carolina Press).

Dover, C. (1939) *Know This of Race* (London: Secker and Warburg).

—— (1937) *Half-Caste* (London: Secker and Warburg).

Dower, J.W. (1986) *War Without Mercy: Race and Power in the Pacific War* (New York: Pantheon Books).

Dryhurst, N.F. (ed.) (1919) *Nationalities and Subject Races: Report of a Conference Held in Caxton Hall, Westminster, June 28–30, 1916* (London: P.S. King and Son).

Dubow, S. (1989) *Racial Segregation and the Origins of Apartheid in South Africa, 1913–1936* (Basingstoke: Macmillan).

Dutt, R.P. (1936) *World Politics: 1918–1936* (New York: International Publishers).

Elliot, W.Y. (1932) *The New British Empire* (New York: McGaw Hill).

Embree, A.T. (1963) *1857 in India* (Boston: D.C. Heath and Co.).

Emerson, R. (1960) *From Empire to Nation* (Cambridge, Mass.: Harvard University Press).

Fanon, F. (1970) *Toward the African Revolution* (Harmondsworth: Penguin).

Freeden, M. (1986) *The New Liberalism: An Ideology of Social Reform* (Oxford: Clarendon Press).

Fryer, P. (1984) *Staying Power; The History of Black People in Britain* (London: Pluto Press).

Füredi, F. (1992) *Mythical Past, Elusive Future; History and Society in an Anxious Age* (London: Pluto Press).

—— (1994) *Colonial Wars and the Politics of Third World Nationalism* (London: I.B. Tauris).

—— (1994a) *The New Ideology of Imperialism: Renewing the Moral Imperative* (London: Pluto Press).

—— (1997) *Ambivalent Westernisers – The Missionary Encounter with Traditional Societies* (Cambridge: NAMP).

Ginsberg, M. (1964) *The Psychology of Society* (London: Macmillan).

Goldfield, D.R. (1990) *Black, White and Southern Race Relations and Southern Culture, 1940 to the Present* (Baton Rouge: Louisiana State University Press).

Gong, G.W. (1984) *The Standard of 'Civilization' in International Society* (Oxford: Clarendon Press).

Gossett, T.H. (1971) *Race: The History of an Idea in America* (Dallas: Southern Methodist Press).

Gregory, J.W. (1931) *Race as a Political Factor* (London: Walls and Co.).

Griswold, A.W. (1966) *The Far Eastern Policy of the United States* (New Haven: Yale University Press).

Grundlingh, A. (1987) *Fighting Their Own War: South African Blacks and the First World War* (Johannesburg: Raven Press).

Grundy, K.W. (1983) *Soldiers Without Politics: Blacks in the South African Armed Forces* (Berkeley: University of California Press).

Hailey, L. (1956) *An African Survey* (London: Oxford University Press).

Heald, M. and Kaplan, L.S. (1977) *Culture and Diplomacy: The American Experience* (Westport: Greenwood Press).

Henderson, W.O. (1962) *Studies in German Colonial History* (London: Frank Cass).

Hetherington, P. (1978) *British Paternalism in Africa, 1920–1940* (London: Frank Cass).

Himmelfarb, G. (1985) *The Idea of Poverty* (London: Faber and Faber).

Himmelfarb, M. and Baras, V. (eds) (1978) *Zero Population Growth For Whom? Differential fertility and minority group survival* (Westport: Greenwood Press).

Hinden, R. (ed.) (1944) *Fabian Colonial Essays* (London: Oxford University Press).

Hitchens, C. (1990) *Blood, Class and Nostalgia: Anglo-American Ironies* (London: Chatto and Windus).

Hofstadter, R. (1955) *Social Darwinism in American Thought* (Boston: Beacon Press).

Hogben, L. (1939) *Dangerous Thoughts* (London: George Allen and Unwin).

Horne, G. (1986) *Black and Red: W.E.B. Du Bois and the Afro-American Response to the Cold War, 1944–1963* (Albany: State University of New York Press).

Hunt, M.H. (1983) *Ideology and US Foreign Policy* (New Haven: Yale University Press).

Huntington, E. (1924) *The Character of Races* (New York: Scribner).

Huxley, J. (1947) *UNESCO: Its Purpose and its Philosophy* (Washington, DC: Public Affairs Press).

Institute of Pacific Relations (1925) *History, Organization, Proceedings, Discussions and Addresses* (Honolulu: IPR).

International Missionary Council (1928) *The Christian Mission in the Light of Race Conflict. Report of the Jerusalem meeting of the International Missionary Council, March 24th–April 1928*, vol. 4 (London: Oxford University Press).

—— (1928a) *The Christian Mission in Relation to Industrial Problems*, vol. 5 (London: Oxford University Press).

Iriye, A. (1981) *Power and Culture; The Japanese–American War 1941–1945* (Cambridge, Mass.: Harvard University Press).

Jackson, W.A. (1990) *Gunnar Myrdal and America's Conscience. Social Engineering and Racial Liberalism 1938–87* (Durham: University of North Carolina Press).

Jencks, C. (1992) *Rethinking Social Policy: Race, Poverty and the Underclass* (Cambridge, Mass.: Harvard University Press).

Johnson, C.S. (1943) *To Stem This Tide. A Survey of Racial Tension Areas in the United States* (Boston: The Pilgrim Press).

Johnston, H. (1920) *The Backward Peoples and Our Relations With Them* (Oxford University Press: London).

Jones, G. (1980) *Social Darwinism and English Thought: The interaction between biological and social theory* (Brighton: Harvester Press).

—— (1988) *Science, Politics and the Cold War* (London: Routledge).

Kenyatta, J. (1938) *Facing Mount Kenya* (London: Macmillan).

Kirk, D. (1942) *The Fertility of the Negro* (Princeton: Office of Population Research).

Klineberg, O. (ed.) (1944) *Characteristics of the American Negro* (New York: Harper).

Kneebone, J.T. (1985) *Southern Liberal Journalists and the Issue of Race, 1920–1944* (Chapel Hill: University of North Carolina Press).

Kohn, H. (1966) *Political Ideologies of the Twentieth Century* (New York: Harper and Row).

Kuklick, H. (1991) *The Savage Within: The Social History of British Anthropology* (Cambridge: Cambridge University Press).

Lagemann, E.C. (1992) *The Politics of Knowledge: The Carnegie Corporation, Philanthrophy and Public Policy* (Chicago: Chicago University Press).

Langer, W.L. (1951) *The Diplomacy of Imperialism* (Alfred A. Knopf: New York).

Lansing, R. (1921) *The Peace Negotiator* (New Haven: Yale University Press).

Lauren, P.G. (1988) *Power and Prejudice: The Politics and Diplomacy of Racial Discrimination* (Boulder, Col.: Westview Press).

Lind, A.W. (1955) *Race Relations in World Perspective: Papers read at the Conference on Race Relations in World Perspective, Honolulu, 1954* (Honolulu: University of Hawai Press).

Little, K. (1946) *The Relation of White People and Coloured People in Great Britain* (South Malvern: Le Play House Press).

—— (1952) *Race and Society* (Paris: UNESCO).

Little, K.L. (1948) *Negroes in Britain* (London: Kegan Paul, Trench, Trubner).

—— (1948) *Negroes in Britain: A Study of Racial Relations in English Society* (London: Kegan Paul, Trench, Trubner).

Locke, A. and Stern, B.J. (eds) (1942) *When People Meet: A Study in Race and Culture Contacts* (New York: Progressive Education Association).

Lugard, Lord F. (1965) *The Dual Mandate in British Tropical Africa* (London: Frank Cass).

Lukács, G. (1980) *The Destruction of Reason* (London: Merlin Press).

Maciver, R.M. (ed.) (1949) *Discrimination and National Welfare* (Port Washington, NY: Kennikat Press).

Macmillan, W.M. (1949) *Africa Emergent* (Harmondsworth: Penguin).

Madden, F. and Fieldhouse, D.K. (eds) (1982) *Oxford and the Idea of Commonwealth* (London: Croom Helm).

Mair, L.P. (1936) *Native Policies in Africa* (London: Penguin Books).

Malik, K. (1996) *The Meaning of Race: Race, History, and Culture in Western Society* (Basingstoke: Macmillan).

Malinowski, B. (1938) *Methods of Study of Culture Contact in Africa* (Oxford: Oxford University Press).

—— (1945) *The Dynamics of Culture Change: An Inquiry into Race Relations in Africa* (New Haven: Yale University Press).

Mason, P. (1954) *An Essay on Racial Tension* (London: Oxford University Press).

—— (ed.) (1960) *Man, Race and Darwin* (London: Oxford University Press).

Masterman, C.F.G. (1960) *The Condition of England* (London: Methuen).

Masuoka, J. and Valien, P. (eds) *Race Relations. Problems and Theory. Essays in Honor of Robert E. Park* (Chapel Hill: University of North Carolina Press).

Matthews, B. (1924, 1930) *The Clash of Colour* (New York: Doran).

Matthews, F.H. (1977) *Quest for an American Sociology: Robert E. Park and the Chicago School* (Montreal: McGill-Queen's University Press).

Melady, T.P. (1966) *The Revolution of Color* (New York: Hawthorne Books).

Mencke, J.G. (1976) *Mullattoes and Race Mixture: American Attitudes and Images, 1865–1918* (Boston: UMI Research Press).

Merle Davis, J. (1933) *Modern Industry in Africa* (Oxford: Oxford University Press).

Meyer, F.S. (ed.) (1965) *The African Nettle* (New York: The John Day Company).

Miles, R. (1993) *Racism after 'Race Relations'* (London: Routledge).

Miller, H.A. (1924) *Races, Nations and Classes, The Psychology of Domination and Freedom* (Philadelphia: J.B. Lippincott Company).

Money, L.C. (1925) *The Peril of the White* (London: W. Collins and Sons).

Myrdal, G. (1962) *An American Dilemma: the Negro Problem and Modern Democracy* (New York: Harper and Row).

—— (1968) *Asia Drama, vol. 3* (London: Allen Lane).

Nicolson, H. (1933) *Peacemaking 1919* (Constable: London).

Noer, T.J. (1985) *Black Liberation: the US and White Rule in Africa, 1948–68* (Columbia: University of Missouri Press).

Nye, R.A. (1975) *The Origins of Crowd Psychology and the Crisis of Mass Democracy in the Third Republic* (London: Sage).

O'Reilly, K. (1989) *'Racial Matters': The FBI's Secret File on Black America* (New York: The Free Press).

Oldham, J.H. (1924) *Christianity and the Race Problem* (London: Student Christian Movement).

Orwell, G. (1950) *Shooting an Elephant and Other Essays* (London: Secker and Warburg).

Park, R.E. (1950) *Race and Culture* (Glencoe: Free Press).

—— and Burgess, E.W. (1926) *Introduction to the Science of Sociology* (Chicago: The University of Chicago Press).

Parsons, T. and Clark, K.B. (eds) (1966) *The Negro American* (Boston: Beacon Press).

Persons, S. (1987) *Ethnic Studies at Chicago 1905–45* (Chicago: University of Illinois Press).

Pettigrew, T.F. (ed.) (1986) *The Sociology of Race Relations. Reflection and Reform* (New York: Free Press).

Pfaff, W. (1993) *The Wrath of Nations* (New York: Simon and Schuster).

Plummer, B.G. (1996) *Rising Wind: Black Americans and US Foreign Affairs, 1935–1960* (Chapel Hill: University of North Carolina Press).

Puttnam Weale, B.L. (1910) *The Conflict of Colour* (London: Times).

Reuter, E.B. (1927) *The American Race Problem* (Boston: Scribner).

Rich, P. (1984) *White Power and the Liberal Conscience* (Manchester: Manchester University Press).

—— (1986) *Race and Empire in British Politics* (Cambridge: Cambridge University Press).

—— (1993) *Hope and Despair: English Speaking Intellectuals and South African Politics 1896–1976* (London: British Academic Press).

Roberts, A.D. (ed.) (1986) *The Cambridge History of Africa, vol. 7, 1905–1940* (Cambridge: Cambridge University Press).

Robinson, C.J. (1987) *Black Movements in America* (New York: New York).
Robinson, R.E. and Gallagher, J.A. (1983) *Africa and the Victorians* (London: Macmillan).
Royal Anthropological Institute and the Institute of Sociology (1936) *Race and Culture* (London: RAI).
Said, E.W. (1985) *Orientalism* (London: Penguin Books).
Schapera, I. (ed.) (1934) *Western Civilization and the Natives of South Africa* (London: George Routledge and Sons Ltd.).
Schrieke, B. (1936) *Alien Americans* (Chicago: Chicago University Press).
Sewell, J.P. *UNESCO and World Politics: Engaging in International Relations* (Princeton: Princeton University Press).
Shepherd, G.W. (1970) *The Study of Race in American Foreign Policy and International Relations* (University of Denver: Denver).
Sherwood, M. (1984) *Many Struggles: West Indian Workers and Service Personnel in Britain - 1939-45* (London: Karia Press).
Simmel, G. (1971) *Georg Simmel on Individuality and Social Forms* (Chicago. University of Chicago Press).
Snyder, L. (1939) *Race; A History of Modern Ethnic Theories* (New York: Longmans, Green and Co.).
—— (1962) 'New Introduction' to *Race: A History of Modern Ethnic Theories* (New York: Harper and Row).
Southall, A.W. (ed.) (1961) *Social Change in Modern Africa* (London: IAI).
Southern, D.W. (1987) *Gunnar Myrdal and Black–White Relations: The Use and Abuse of an American Dilemna, 1944–64* (Baton Rouge: Louisiana State University Press).
Soward, F.H. (1950) *The Adaptable Commonwealth* (London: Oxford University Press).
Spengler, O. (1938) *The Decline of the West* (London: George Allen and Unwin Ltd.).
Spiller, G. (1911) *Inter-Racial Problems - Communicated to the First Universal Races Congress, held at the University of London, 26–29 July 1911* (London: P.S. King and Son).
Stanfield, J.H. (ed.) (1993) *A History of Race Relations* (Newbury Park: Sage).
Staniland, M. (1991) *American Intellectuals and African Nationalists, 1905–1970* (New Haven: Yale University Press).
Stanley, B. (1990) *The Bible and the Flag* (Leicester: Appolos).
Stepan, N. (1982) *The Idea of Race in Science: Great Britain 1800–1960* (London: Macmillan).
Stocking, G.W. (1972) *Race, Culture and Evolution, Essays in the History of Anthropology* (New York: The Free Press).
Stoddard, L. (1920) *The Rising Tide of Color Against White World Supremacy* (New York: Scribner's).
Stoecker, H. (1986) *German Imperialism in Africa* (London: C. Hurst and Company).
Stonequist, E.V. (1961) *The Marginal Man: A Study in Personality and Culture* (New York: Russell and Russell).

Teitelbaum, M.S. and Winter, J.M. (1985) *The Fear of Population Decline* (Orlando: Academic Press).

The Year Book of World Affairs, 1970 (1970) (London: Stevens and Sons).

Thompson, E.T. (ed.) (1939) *Race Relations and the Race Problem* (Durham: Duke University Press).

Thompson, W.S. (1939) *Danger Spots in World Population* (New York: Alfred A. North).

—— (1946) *Population and Peace in the Pacific* (Chicago: Chicago University Press).

Thorne, C. (1978) *Allies of a Kind, The United States, Britain and the war against Japan, 1941–1945* (London: Hamish Hamilton).

—— (1985) *The Issue of War: States, Societies and the Far Eastern Conflict of 1941–1945* (London: Hamish Hamilton).

—— (1989) *Border Crossings. Studies in International History* (Oxford: Basil Blackwell).

Thurlow, R. (1987) *Fascism in Britain* (Oxford: Oxford University Press).

Tinker, H. (1977) *Race Conflict and the International Order* (London: Macmillan).

Toynbee, A. (1948) *Civilization on Trial* (London: Oxford University Press)

Turner, C.H. (ed.) (1923) *Public Opinion and World Peace* (Washington DC: ILCA).

Wacker, R.F. (1983) *Ethnicity, Pluralism, and Race: Race Relations Theory in America Before Myrdal* (Westport: Greenwood Press).

Webb, S. (1907) *The Decline of the Birth Rate* (London: Fabian Society).

Westermann, D. (1939) *The African Today and Tomorrow* (London: Oxford University Press).

Willcocks, J. (1904) *From Kabul to Kumasi* (London: Grant Richards).

—— (1904a) *From Kabul to Kumasi – Twenty Four Years of Soldiering and Sport* (London: John Murray).

Williams, V.J. (1989) *From a Caste to a Minority: Changing Attitudes of American Sociologists toward Afro-Americans, 1891–1945* (Westport: Greenwood Press).

Willoughby, W.C. (1923) *Race Problem in the New Africa* (Oxford: Clarendon Press).

Wilson, G. (1968) *Economics of Detribalization in Northern Rhodesia, Part 2* (Manchester: Manchester University Press).

Wright, F.C. (ed.) (1939) *Population and Peace: A Survey of International Opinion on Claims for Relief from Population Pressure* (Paris: League of Nations).

Index

Index compiled by
Sue Carlton